THE UGANDAN FINANCIAL SYSTEM
Scrutiny of the Institutions, Markets, Assets, Agents & Intermediation.

MUGERWA Paul

MBA (Investment Management)

Lecturer: Financial Economics, Risk Mgt &

Investment Researcher

School of Business and Computing

Bugema University, Uganda

CEO, Asante Capital Hub Ltd

Financial services, Tax & Business Consultancy

Kampala, Uganda

E-mail: tatagracia2007@gmail.com / asantecap@gmail.com

Glimpses into the Global Financial Systems & Perspective.

THE UGANDAN FINANCIAL SYSTEM: Scrutiny of the Institutions, Markets, Assets, Agents, and Intermediation

ISBN: 978-9970-9067-4-1

Investment Editor: Mutimba Patrick, CFA, MBA, FAIA

Production Editor: Kerosi Josephat Bosire, PhD- Finance

Sole Contributor: Mugerwa Paul, P.O Box 36750 Kampala;

+256 782640448

Language Editor: Lukwago Moses, PhD

Layout Design: Wakabi Joe

Cover page Design: Ssenono Emmanuel (Corporate Impression Agency)

Publisher: EPS Publishers Limited

Content Fields: Financial economics; Investments; Financial Markets; Monetary Studies; Personal, Corporate & Public Finance.

DETAILED TABLE OF CONTENT

The book provides a strong foundation to understanding not only the Ugandan financial system but how most financial systems from the least developed to the very well-developed financial markets work. With the growth in global interconnectedness and post global financial crisis, it is imperative that all us not just those who are literate in matters of finance but also those in other professions understand how a typical financial system works.

The book address first the structure of the financial system from its basic form and goes on to elaborate on its functioning. It further gives good treatment to various available financial assets available for investment and how these work. I find the book quite useful for students of finance, banking and practitioners. However the book is also written in a manner useful for any non-finance person keen on understanding how financial markets work and what investment assets are available for consideration.

Obatsa Barack, CFA – East Africa Portfolio manager: African Alliance Kenya Investment Bank

This is a brilliant and fascinating book- Paul's range of research is both impressive and inspiring, and his conclusions are provocative. He has put together complex data relating to Uganda Financial System, presented it is in a simple and logical way making the book a delight to read. It should be required reading for anyone serving in the government, working in an NGO or company, trying to build a career- or simply trying to navigate in this increasingly complex financial world'.

Mayienda Reuben, Director Finance: World Vision Uganda

Great insight and invaluable contribution.

Open up a national daily and all you see are news about the economy and the pillars that support its quest or lack of it. Many readers are left with more questions than answer on how the financial sector works. I have had the privilege to read this book by Mugerwa Paul and every chapter responds to a need as well as provide an answer.

This is a fresh look into the financial system at the period when the East African common market is at the hands of the weavers and architectures. Anybody interested in knowledge of the financial system, preparing for the professional examinations and player in the financial sector must read this book. For policy makers, they will find this piece of work an easy read, insightful and informative. Well done Paul as I wait for your next book

Kerosi Josephat Bosire, *PhD Finance - DVC-Academics: University of Kigali*

This Book is a work in progress on opening up the mind of that inquisitive reader into the complexities of financial intermediation in Uganda & EAC. Given that the search for knowledge is a continuous persistent effort; I will it by echoing the words of Calvin Coolidge (23rd U.S President), "Nothing in the world can take the place of persistence. Talent will not; nothing is more common than unsuccessful people with talent. Genius will not; unrewarded genius is almost a proverb. Education will not; the world is full of educated derelicts. Persistence and determination alone are omnipotent". Mugerwa's master-piece depicts this reality in his analysis.

Kiyingi Allan, *Tax Professional at KPMG – Uganda; and formerly Senior Tax Auditor at URA.*

Managing a non-bank financial institution, this book can help me to comprehend Uganda's financial sector better and will go a long way to improve our resource mobilization efforts given that we do not take deposits from the public.

Abaasa Albert, *Country Operating Officer – Platinum Credit Uganda*

Let me take this opportunity to thank the author of this book which is very well balanced to provide knowledge between the academia and the business community in the field of finance. The content is very well blended and provided current data which any user will find very helpful.

Nabulya Jesca *- Financial Economist & Lecturer: Bugema University*

This book is quite informative and richly packed with valuable analysis on both the Ugandan and EAC financial systems. It is apt for use by students at various higher educational levels, financial and non-finance managers, and investors not pursuing any academic career due to its hands-on approach to financial information.

Bahati Samuel *- Finance Dep't: Inter-University Council for East Africa.*

I have personally read through this book but one thing is real: anyone who needs financial literacy or investment guidance a "Ugandan perspective" this book is a must read. Thanks Paul, you have shown so much love for your country by writing such knowledgeable literature.

Ssendawula Enock *– Economist & Deputy Director: Springfield High School*

How much do you really know about finance? When Ugandans are tested on their financial literacy, the results are appalling. Personal finance is now a very important part of everyone's knowledge. For the people that want to learn the basics of investing and how things work in our financial markets, consider this a good starting point.

The content is a good introduction to the way markets and investing work. I don't think you can get a better unbiased approach. Whether as a student or one who graduated years ago, this book is a really good overview of the dynamics of the investment world in a frontier market like Uganda and beyond. By teaching yourself and those around you about money, you help them discover the relationships between earning, spending and saving: thus, understand the value of money. Financial literacy can begin at any stage: as a university student or as one who has been employed for many years, or as one still looking for employment, there's something for everyone to learn.

Semakula A. E. Brian – *Financial Manager: Mercantile Bank*

In a volatile economy like Uganda, knowing how a financial system works is of a paramount importance. I therefore appeal to all Ugandans especially my colleagues in down town Kampala (Kikuubo) to read this book so that you equip yourselves with the right knowledge for the right financial decisions in as far as investing and money management are concerned.

Mukwaya Joseph – *Importer, trader & CEO: God is Able Enterprises*

After painstakingly going through this manuscript, written by an erudite scholar, I found out that the book covers most important areas in finance and financial studies. It rigorously traces the genesis of financial market and their instruments.

References were made using Ugandan economy and Africa in general. The book will not only be useful to diploma students and undergraduate students but will also be of great benefit to the graduate students and other related field who wants to improve or widen their scope. It is a well structured and seasoned set of collection of academic knowledge and can prepare students for their academic pursuit and excellence. I therefore strongly recommend it for reading and other research references that it might be needed for.

Osinusi, Kunle Bankole - *N.C.E (Maths/Econs); B.sc (Economics); M.Sc (Economics) U.I; PhD (Economics) Cand. (KIU).*

Since the financial crisis, financial practitioners have been keenly aware of the need to combine successfully practical and theoretical knowledge. Financial market is an area where competing theories of asset pricing and empirical observations that can undermine confidence in our theoretical beliefs. Knowledge is evolving, even though some of the most intractable challenges and market failures appear to repeat themselves with alarming regularity from Europe to China to U.S issues of market bubbles, banking system failure and some at times market anxiety sentiment.

This book is designed to meet the needs of students as well as practitioners in financial markets who wish to gain a clear understanding of the linkages in the financial system with the focus of bringing together theory and practical applications. The book puts into context the different components of the financial system and will help those who wish to understand their connectivity.

KABOYO M. Stephen –*Former Director, Bank of Uganda (Financial Markets Dep't); CEO – Alpha Capital Partners (Sovereign Assets Management)*

Acknowledgements

The challenge in thanking all the people who have assisted in the research and also review of this book is that I run the risk of publishing another book (separate on its own) due to the endless list of individuals and organizations that have really been of help; since it has a lot of fieldwork in a host of organizations. Certainly, errors are not the responsibility of these excellent people who have helped us but of Mugerwa Paul. I'm greatly thankful to all those who assisted me in this endeavor; and I have tried to respond to what William Safire once said in reference to writers like me,

"Write what you see, because what history needs more of is first-person testimony."

And so among the many, there are: the resourceful Mr. Mayanja Ali, Mr. Wakabi Joe, and Mr. Ssenono Emmanuel, in the lay-out, concept and cover page designing ; content and conceptual advisors Dr. Bosire Josephat, Mr. Mutimba Patrick, Mr. Byarugaba Richard and Dr.Mutaasa Kafeero; but also Elizabeth Onyas (administrative assistant to Mr. Byarugaba – MD of NSSF Uganda), she passionately linked me to the MD. I'm greatly indebted to my gorgeous wife Rebecca Nakisozi Mugerwa; Muko William Ssekandi; and my lovely parents Mr & Mrs. Paul & Ritah Ssali who gave all the support I needed from my tender age up to now in my career as a financial economist.

Frankly, I was fortunate to have the following Reviewers of this book, whose advice was so invaluable:

Public Finance Experts

Mulema Stephen, CFA – Director Financial Markets: Bank of Uganda.

Kaboyo Stephen – Former Director Financial Markets (10 years): Bank of Uganda.

Byarugaba Richard – Managing Director: National Social Security Fund Uganda.

Private Sector & Corporate Finance

Kyewalabye John-Marie – Project Coordinator - CEDP Private Sector Foundation-Uganda.

Kakumba Robert, PhD-Cand. – Former Business Manager: Nkumba University

Ssemakula Bryn – Financial Manager: Mercantile Bank Uganda

Ssimwogerere Katende – Finance Dep't: State House of Uganda

Ssekandi William – Senior Accountant/Bursar: Gayaza High School

Abaasa Albert – Country Operating Officer: Platinum Credit Uganda

Kasaato Gerald Paul - Head of Investments : NSSF (UG)

Kizito Denis – Senior Actuary: UAP Insurance

Birungi Margaret Katagira – ENHAS...............................

Allan Kiyingi – Tax Professional: KPMG – Uganda; and formerly Senior Tax Auditor at URA

Ssendawula Enock – Economist & Deputy Director: Springfield High School.

Personal Finance Experts

Mugerwa William – Director & Consultant: Asante Capital Hub; & the Business Tutor.

Kabuye Rosette, Phd – Director: Peniel Beach Hotel.

Not-for-Profit Organisations

Mayienda Reuben – Finance Director: World Vision Uganda

Bahati Samuel – Finance Dep't: Inter-University Council of East Africa.

Business & Entrepreneurs' Community

Mutaasa Kafeero (Honorary Doctorate), Business & Real Property Mogul in Uganda.

Mukwaya Joseph – Director: God is Able Enterprises.

Academia, Research & Technical Education

Kerosi Josephat Bosire, Phd Finance & Mgt – DVC-Academics: University of Kigali.

Aik Jane - CEO/ED & Training Manager: Uganda Institute of Banking & Financial Services.

Nakayiwa Florence, PhD Econ. – Director Planning, Dev't & Investments: Makerere University.

Kibirango Moses, PhD-Cand. – Dean, School of Business: Bugema University.

Basemera Sandra – Economist & Senior Researcher: IPSOS Uganda

Kunle Bankole Osinusi, PhD-Cand. Economist & Lecturer: National Open Univ. of Nigeria.

Nyangenya Jeff, PhD-Cand. Finance & Consultant

Nabulya Jesca – Lecturer Financial economics: Bugema University.

International Finance Environment

Zirimwabagabo Vincent – Auditor: General Conference of the SDA Church (World).

Kibirige Moses – Financial Inclusion : World Bank Group.

Mutimba Patrick, CFA, FAIA, MBA - Director of Financial Sector Management Programme: Macroeconomic & Financial Management Institute of Eastern & Southern Africa (MEFMI).

Obatsa Barack, CFA – East Africa Portfolio manager: African Alliance Kenya Investment Bank.

Lugolobi Robert - Tax Justice & Campaign Advisor: Action Aid Zambia.

Editorial Team

Dr. Lukwago   (Phd Linguistics – Makerere University)

Mr. Mutimba Patrick, CFA, FAIA, MBA

Dedication

This publication is dedicated to:

My lovely children- Namuli Gracia Ritah and Katumba Gentil Reuben

My dear brothers- Steven, Solomon, Andrew, Paul, Blasious, Theodore, Hymas, Emma.

My gorgeous sisters- Tracy, Vicky, Sanyu, Winfrey, Ruth, Zoe.

Foreword

Financial economists and investment gurus progressively affirm that the soundness of a country's financial system significantly affects not only personal finance, corporate finance, and public finance; but also investment decisions, and the management of financial institutions. It also has a profound impact on the domestic macroeconomics and global competitiveness of an economy in international economics. A major downside, however, to fully exploiting the benefits of a financial system by all players has been the appalling levels of financial literacy in the country that are so evident across the board (including some top players in the financial sector).

With Mugerwa Paul's "The Ugandan Financial System: Scrutiny of Institutions, Markets, Assets, Players, and Intermediation", we finally have a comprehensive financial system text that is a wonderful blend of the financial economics and investments theory mingled with practical application of the nitty-gritty of a financial system. This is simplified for the consumption of any prospective investor; practicing managers; policy-makers in the financial sector; students preparing for: professional exams in finance and business courses. I'm greatly honoured to introduce this ground-breaking publication, since I have personally been inspired while studying this book authored by a scholar and practitioner in the investment world.

The book's orientation is neither overly sophisticated nor watered down, but rather a mix of insight and dogmatism that creates an inherent flexibility for the structuring and simplified comprehension of finance and investments. The author begins with an evaluation from the barter system to the contemporary monetary economies; then goes ahead to various types of financial systems that are determined by economic ideologies such capitalism and Islamic beliefs of interest-free financing. He looks in detail at financial institutions, financial markets (both domestic & foreign), financial assets (domestic & global), financial players (agents), and finally the financial intermediation; all this well furnished with the most up-to-date information both on Uganda and the East African Community financial systems.

Financial education and investments basics are a huge requirement for everyone in this modern financial world. Therefore, it is essential to instil these concepts in any rational citizen as early as humanly possible and in a mode that most learners can appreciate.

This text achieves this goal in such an appealing and inviting way that readers will actually enjoy their journey toward an understanding of the investment dynamics and those of the financial system.

BYARUGABA Richard
Managing Director, NSSF- Uganda

Preface

Why Study "The Ugandan Financial System: Scrutiny of the Institutions, Markets, Assets, Agents & Intermediation"?

Glance

It is the 9 PM (21hr) business news on your favourite TV station; you have just heard that the Uganda shilling is drastically depreciating against regional and international currencies by 31.5% to reach an all-time-low, and Bloomberg's consensus predicts further drop above the UGX 3,800 for a Dollar by the end of the 2015; other financial markets like bond markets and equity markets are also apparently struggling; coupled to numerous bank closures. Could this imply that the economy is being relegated to a failed financial system, and that investors should opt for off-shore investments besides other sound regional economies where to prudently invest??

Will the financial system improve in the future so that it is rational to invest in a new building or purchase a Stanbic Bank share? Is it logical for Asante Capital Hub Ltd to raise funds by issuing stocks or bonds, or instead go to the bank like Centenary bank for a loan? For the importing folks, should one be concerned that imports will become quite expensive given the challenges in the domestic and global economy?

This publication is aimed at answering such questions by scrutinizing how the following constituencies/ players of the financial system operate: financial institutions (such as banking, non-banking, collective investment vehicles, Central banking, etc); financial markets (such as money, bonds, stocks, foreign exchange, and mortgage markets; and the Uganda Commodities' exchange); financial assets (such as securities (stocks and bonds), derivative contracts, and currencies); financial agents (such as the household, corporate/business, and government sectors); and financial intermediation (intermediaries, intermediation, and dis-intermediation).

As a matter of fact, a financial system of a country doesn't only affect one's daily life but involves in-flows and out-flows of funds and transactions in the league of trillions of shillings and other currencies throughout the economy. This, by default, affects business operations, social and individual welfare, the macroeconomics of Uganda and even that of other financial systems beginning with the EAC region to others. Besides, what happens to the financial system is of great concern to politicians, and can even have a major impact on elections as has been evidenced in many economies world over.

Thus, the *Ugandan Financial System* publication has potential to reward you with an appreciative conception of many exciting issues in the gigantic areas of financial economics/ investments, such as: personal finance, corporate finance, not-for-profit organizational resource mobilization, and public finance.

This book grew from my teaching experience of finance, investment and economics courses at Bugema University and other tertiary institutions; but also from the finance and business consultancy I've been doing at Asante Capital Hub Ltd and other organizations; coupled with my involvement as an investor in the EAC financial markets; and above all my empirical research I've done which entails personal interviews with the technicians of the EAC financial systems such as portfolio managers, CFOs, CEOs, directors and economists in the public sector, private sector, academia, and business community.

PART 1

Introduction

FINANCE IN A FINANCIAL SYSTEM

Chapter 1

EVOLUTION FROM THE BARTER TO CONTEMPORARY MONETARY ECONOMIES

To better appreciate the imperativeness of money in a financial system, it is logical to imagine a society without any financial services. How on earth would folks go about their daily business in the absence of either money or financial intermediaries, and this can be exhibited in a two sector model in a given society: the household and the business sectors. The business sector produces goods & services, through the exploitation of resources such as labour, land among others resources which are owned by the household sector. Then the household sector is in turn given goods & services produced by the business sector in exchange of their resources. In this barter system of economy (simple economy), there is neither government nor foreign trade sectors, not even money as a medium of exchange. Therefore, the household sector is left with two options upon receipt of the goods & services:

- Consumption; commodities provided from the place of work can either be consumed/ enjoyed directly now or be exchanged with other households so as to widen the variety of consumption

- Investment; a portion of current consumption can be fore gone so as to create resources for asset-building, hence producing higher levels of consumption in the future when the household also enters the business sector and produces more resources.

The obvious challenge with this system that was faced by our ancestors was spending a lot of time and resources in search for other households interested in exchanging their commodities. This definitely necessitated a mechanism that would facilitate transactions and render them more efficient by converting commodities into something small, portable, standardized, and generally acceptable.

Monetary Economy

The introduction of money in the financial system facilitated the transaction and exchange of, for example labour and dodge the inconvenience of carrying tins of beans or pieces of meat to the market to exchange them for medical or teaching services. Before the money facility, many items have been used as means of exchange, in quest for simplification of transactions, ranging from commodity money to the contemporary electronic money. The production of cotton in Uganda is largely responsible for the initial monetization of the country's economy, which were all influenced by the goals of the British (colonial masters) basically for production of raw materials for export to home industries.

It has been recognized that the evolution of money has so far gone through seven important stages depending on the progress of human civilization at different times and places. These include:

i)   Commodity money: where various types of commodities have been used as money depending on the level of civilization and means of livelihood of a given society such as pastoral, agricultural, hunting, fishing, among other societies. Stones, axes, shells, grains, tobacco, animal skins (both domestic & wild), spears, bows & arrows, but due their defects as a medium of exchange, societies went ahead to look for better alternatives as money.

ii)   Metallic money: with the discovery of precious metals and their being valuable due to improvement in civilization and trading activities amongst communities, metallic money was introduced. Silver, copper, gold, tin were initially used as money in its raw form, but later coins of predetermined weight were used as a medium of exchange. On the contrary, due to their shortcomings as a form of money such as unreliable supply, lack of portability and other merchants would actually melt it to earn more money selling it; these forced societies to look for other convenient alternatives of money.

iii)   Paper money: this development came as a result of goldsmiths who kept strong safes to store their gold since they were believed to be honest merchants, where people would keep their gold for safe custody. In return, goldsmiths would give them a receipt promising to avail the gold on demand. These receipts from the goldsmiths were given to sellers of commodities by buyers since they represent value that was in store/ custody of the goldsmiths. Later, this system was used by central banks, whereby they would issue paper money that is backed by gold reserves which would regulate the supply of paper money. However, this type of money was affected by changes in supply and prices of such metals as gold and silver, and such as system would not be responsive to changes in level of economic activities in a given society.

iv)   Credit Money: this evolution of money in modern financial world was characterized by the use of cheques as money; since it performs the same function as bank notes in the transfer of money and obligations from one entity to another. Of course, a cheque is not real money but a written order since it expires with a single transaction, and it has a specified sum. On the contrary, due to safety and convenience in the contemporary financial system, large transactions are made through cheques nowadays, leaving bank notes to small transactions.

v)   Near Money: this stage has been characterized as the use of close substitutes for money that are highly liquid assets; at this stage, money has become intangible. Financial assets such as insurance policies, unit trust funds' certificates, bills of exchange, saving certificates, debentures, treasury bills and notes, bonds, share certificates, etc; where ownership is now transferable merely by book entry.

vi)   Electronic Money (e-money): this is one of the most recent stages in the evolution of money whereby money as actually become not only intangible but invisible through payment and transaction systems such as mobile money, Electronic Funds Transfer (EFT), Real Time Gross Settlement (RTGS), plastic money (credit cards), etc. This has enabled the monetary authority to streamline and monitor funds/ money transfer within the financial system. It has brought a lot of safety, convenience but also the integration of many households who were initially in the informal financial systems closer to the formal financial system.

vii)   Crypto Currencies: these are also called virtual currencies, and Bit-coin is apparently the newest form of such currency with a uniquely designed and decentralized platform. These currencies provide a way to transfer digital property from one internet user to another; which transfer of assets has potential to be used in buying and selling financial assets like stocks and bonds. In the future, this could prompt investors to consider investing in assets denominated in a virtual currency as part of their overall investment strategy. This is evidenced by the fact that of all the bit-coins minted in 2009 – 2010, more than 60% remain unspent and some took more than a year to be spent: implying that some investors may already be using bit-coins as an alternative investment. The bit-coin system has potential to interrupt the existing payment systems though its development has addressed outstanding issues that were characterized with other stages of money such as: market risk, counterparty risk, transaction risk, operational risk, privacy risk, and regulatory risk. Since its inauguration in 2009, it has facilitated more than 60 million transactions between 109 million accounts; and currently, there are 14 million minted bit-coins worth USD 3.5 Billion

Monetization of the financial system has ushered in investments, which has trained households to put aside some resources currently so as to produce a return in the future. This has seen many people, basically in modern economies, significantly reducing on their current consumption in a bid to put resources into capital formation (asset-building) such as building industries, purchase of machines, buying financial assets (like stocks, bonds, insurance policies, pension funds, etc). And this is done by majorly the household sector but also the business sector. Economies need people who are ready to sacrifice current consumption in anticipation for fruits that come with investments; they should be willing to defer present consumption and put their resources at risk within the productive business sector upon a promise for attractive returns, with the use of risk management systems. In contemporary sophisticated financial systems, households (real owners of assets) invest their aggregate resources in the business sector which acts as stewards for resources of the household sector for more value/ net-worth creation on the part of the households. This state-of-affairs has ushered in the philosophy of economies of collective strategies, whereby households now pool their resources through a variety of investment vehicles (shall be discussed later) for better risk management and value creation. This has consequently led to the development of the financial markets to assist the flow of funds from the households to the business sector; and thus create more value to the household, the business and the government sectors through, among others the multiplier effects. It is actually this reason that the author decided to make an analysis of the financial system, not only of Uganda but also glimpses of financial systems of the Sub-Saharan Africa since there are lots of commonalities amongst them: financial institutions, financial markets, financial assets, financial agents, and financial intermediation.

Chapter 2

THE FORMAL & INFORMAL FINANCIAL SYSTEMS

Financial System

This is a system of rules and practices which coordinates & regulates the monetary & economic affairs of a country. It is an interaction of policy makers, a monetary system, financial institutions, financial markets, financial agents & intermediation so as to accelerate the flow of financial capital from savings to investment. It also entails the legal, political and institutional frameworks that govern them.

A financial system refers to a system which enables the transfer of money between investors and borrowers. It could be defined at an international, regional or organization level. The term "system" in "Financial System" indicates a group of complex and closely linked institutions, agents, procedures, markets, transactions, claims and liabilities within an economy.

i) Formal Capitalistic Financial System

Uganda's financial system can be broadly classified into the formal financial system and the informal financial system. The formal financial system is one that is well regulated and domiciled under the Ministry of Finance Planning and Economic Development (MoFPED); Bank of Uganda (B.O.U); the Capital Markets Authority (CMA); Uganda Retirement Benefits Regulatory Authority (URBRA); Insurance Regulatory Authority- Uganda (IRA-U); money, capital and foreign exchange markets; insurance companies; brokerage firms; deposit money banks; development finance institutions; fund managers; and other regulatory & self-regulatory bodies in Uganda. The following are among the statistical data that characterized the Ugandan financial system:

Financial System Information	Nature	Amount & No. of Users	Period
Mobile money transactions	Financial inclusion	a) UGX 2.5 Billion monthly transactions. b) 19.5 registered mobile money customers.	2nd Quarter of 2015.
Banking & Forex branches.	Financial deepening	a) 504 branches. b) 719 ATMs c) 226 forex bureau	June 2013.
Credit Reference Bureau Liberalization: CompuScan CRB Ltd exclusivity period as sole provider of credit reference services expired on 30th Sept. 2012	Financial integrity & Credit history	At least, there are 2 players in the credit reference services.	June 2015
B.O.U foreign exchange reserves growth.	Financial system protection.	Reserve portfolio valued at USD 2.9 Billion: internally managed is USD 1,864 M in short-term financial assets. And USD 1,036 M externally managed by reputable international asset managers.	June 2015
Double licensing of fund managers for pension & long-term assets.	Regulatory.	7 fund managers were licensed by both CMA & URBRA.	December 2013

Source : Researcher & BOU Data

ii) Informal Financial System

On the other hand, the informal financial system is one that is not regulated and there is a weak relationship/ integration with the formal financial system. This includes the following:

- Individual money lenders such as neighbours, relatives, traders, landlords, and store owners

- Groups of persons operating as funds or associations, and functioning under a system of their own rules, and brand themselves as fixed funds, associations, saving/ investment club, SACCOs, financial cooperatives, microfinance institutions, Rotational Savings & Credit Associations (ROSCAs), Community-Based Organisations (CBOs).

- Partnership firms consisting of local brokers and non-bank financial intermediaries such as finance companies.

This financial information on Uganda's financial system clearly indicate deliberate steps taken by the government to achieve both the domestic and global targets in line with financial inclusion and deepening compared to many Sub-Saharan African economies that are faring very poorly in many dimensions. However, there is still a long way for Uganda to attain a position of developed financial system given the appalling statistics as shown above just to compare with her counterpart, Kenya.

iii) Other Financial Systems: Islamic Financial System

This financial system is premised on the principles the Quran and Islam that have a sense of cooperation- helping one another and aiming at eliminating exploitation so as to establish a just society through the elimination of "Riba" or interest in all its forms in the financial system. Islamic banking/ finance may be viewed as a form of ethical investing/ lending in an interest-free banking environment. Besides, other ethical restrictions include prohibition on alcohol, gambling, and the consumption of pork: such funds would never knowingly invest in companies involved in such business.

This financial system offers a balance between extreme capitalism and communism by helping households the freedom to produce and create wealth under an environment guided by Divine principles of goodness and piety, and human trusteeship of resources. In capitalistic systems, competition for resources and markets breeds wastage and consequently uncontrolled greed but in Islamic financial system, the idea of man representing God on earth gives business people a feeling of co-operation with other for the good of society as a whole leading to prudent and conservative management of God given resources. This system forbids the use of its finances for misleading, dishonourable, immoral and other purposes harmful to society.

Malaysia is the sole example of Islamic country with a complete Islamic financial system such as: Islamic markets (capital, money and equity markets); Islamic financial institutions (central banking, other banking structures).

Fundamentals of Islamic Banking

- It is premised on the principle of trusteeship keeping in mind that all earthly resources belong to God who has made humans trustees for them. Humans are therefore accountable to God for the use of these resources; this is in direct contrast to extreme capitalism and communism.

- It is based on caring for others contrary to self-interest that is engrained in human nature; implying that individual happiness and collective interests go hand in hand. It maintains that the wealth and integrity of a society can only increase when the haves give part of their wealth to the have-nots basically to please God

- Productive efforts as a means of serving God: productive enterprise is looked upon as a means of serving God, and wealth should be spent in the cause of God.

- It strongly advocates for the protection of consumers against the exploitations of the traders and manufacturers.

- It advocates for treating wealth as a means and not an end: this is because economic welfare is viewed as a means to peace, freedom from hunger and fear of others.

- It strongly supports the proper functioning of the market since it prohibits dishonesty, fraud, deception, coercive practices, hoarding, speculations and collusion among producers and traders against consumers' interests as is common with monopoly and oligopoly in capitalistic economies.

Chapter 3

HISTORY/EVOLUTION OF FINANCE AS A DISCIPLINE

In the wake of the 20th century, finance, though closely linked with economics, emerged as a separate field from economics; some financial economists actually define finance as the applied economics due to its usage of economic tools of analysis. The major focus of this study reflected the developments of finance, such as, the building of giant Industrial Corporation by Rockfeller, Carnegie, Du Pont, among others. These ushered in the usage of financial instruments that were so key in major investment decisions like mergers and acquisitions.

With the development and implementation of antitrust laws, corporate consolidations became less prominent, and alternative patterns of growth were emphasized. Attention shifted to financial assets like stocks and bonds and other securities used for raising capital; and the role of the wholesale banks or intermediaries in security offerings also received much interest. No doubt, the great bull market of the 1920s in the Western economies contributed to the emphasis in raising capital using modern avenues.

On the contrary, the shock of depression in 1930s ushered in an era of conservatism, and attention shifted to such topics as preservation of capital, maintenance of liquidity, re-organization of financially distressed corporations, and the bankruptcy process. Governments of many frontier-market economies assumed a much larger role in regulating business through the establishment of Securities and Financial services Acts which would later serve to monitor the corporate performance of companies but also to protect the investors' interests.

The 1940s and 1950s offered new knowledge in the study and practice of corporate finance. However, in the mid-50s a major shift in finance took place: from a descriptive approach to a more analytical and decision-oriented approach. Up to that time, the study procedures of finance had been descriptive or definitional in nature; and the orientation had been from the viewpoint of a third party or an outsider.

The first area of study to generate the newfound enthusiasm for decision-related analysis was capital budgeting; where the financial manager was presented with analytical techniques (capital rationing techniques) for allocating resources among the various assets of the firm. The enthusiasm spread to other decision making areas of the firm such as cash and inventory management, capital structure formulation, and dividend policy. The emphasis shifted from that of the outside looking into that of the financial manager forced to make tough routine decisions affecting the performance of the firm.

Finance originated from economics and accounting: economists use a supply-and –demand framework to explain how prices and quantities of commodities are determined in a free enterprise economy. On the contrary, accountants provide the record-keeping mechanism for showing ownership of financial instruments used in the flow of financial resources between savers and borrowers; and they also record revenues, expenses, and profitability of firms that produce and exchange commodities.

i) Finance as a Discipline

The field of finance is quite broad in perspective; and simply defined, finance is a body of facts, principles and theories dealing with the raising and managing of money by individuals, businesses and governments. It covers essential areas of financial planning and financial institutions as well as managerial finances by the above three financial agents of the financial system. Melicher & Norton (2003) define finance as the study of how individuals, institutions, governments, and businesses acquire, spend, and manage financial resources

It is technically separated into three sub-categories: personal finance, corporate finance and public finance. All these categories are concerned with activities such as pursuing sound investments, obtaining low-cost credit, attracting funds for liabilities, and for banking. Yet each has its own specific considerations: for example, individuals need to plan for retirement expenses, which mean investing enough money during their working years and ensuring that their asset allocation fits their long-term plans. On the other hand, a large firm may have to decide whether to raise additional funds through a bond issue or stock offering or sale of its assets. Merchant banks may advise the firm on such considerations and help them market the securities. On the contrary, public finance, in addition to managing funds for its day-to-day operations, a government body has larger social responsibilities whose goals include attaining an equitable distribution of income for its citizens and enacting policies that foster macroeconomic stability.

ii) Role of finance to individuals (Personal finance)

Surprisingly, households are the main players (financial agents) in any given financial system but not government agencies, large corporations and institutions. They provide up to 80% of savings flows in our financial system and economy in any given year. This is because, of the three main sources of savings: personal savings, business savings (retained earnings), and government savings, personal savings far outweigh the other two sources combined as a source of saving.

Simply put, all financial institutions obtain their funds (that they use to invest and loan out) basically from households' checking and savings accounts; certificates of deposits; pension funds; insurance funds; unit trust funds. All these are from avenues such as: savings from working people; policy-holders premium payments for life, health, property and liability insurance; sale of shares by unit trust funds for future financial goals by households.

The individual's financial problem is how to maximize his or her welfare by appropriately using the available resources: how one divides his income between consumption and investment by making rational choices between consumption expenditure and investment expenditure; how one chooses from among available investment opportunities; and how one raises money to provide for increased consumption or investment. Therefore, personal finance is the study of how households prepare for financial emergencies, unforeseen loss of income, protect against premature death and loss of property, and accumulate wealth over time.

The role of finance to an individual/ household depends on, among others: the overall net-worth of an individual, his long-term financial goals, his level of financial literacy, his financial blue-print, and the level of financial system depth in the country.

But basically, personal financial management would help a household:

- To make informed economic & financial choices that will lead to better financial health & success.

- Better informed to make decisions that affect the economy & the financial system.

In a simplified way, good personal financial management would help a household in the following financial areas of one's life:

- Financial capacity: Personal finance is concerned with understanding the individual resources available by examining one's net worth and household cash flows. From this analysis, one can determine to what degree and within which time period personal goals can be accomplished.

- Adequate protection: Personal financial management includes the analysis of how to protect one's household from unforeseen risks such as: liability, property, death, disability, health and long term care. Some of these risks may be self-insurable, while others would require the purchase of an insurance policy. Since insurance also enjoys some tax benefits, utilizing insurance products may be a critical piece of the overall investment planning.

- Tax planning: typically income tax is the single largest expense to households; and managing taxes is not a question of if you will pay taxes, but when and how much. Uganda's tax system uses a progressive tax: as one's income grows, a higher marginal rate of tax must be paid. So, understanding how to take advantage of the myriad tax incentives when planning one's personal finances can make a significant impact in saving you money in the long-term.

- Investment and Asset-building: planning how to accumulate enough resources for large purchases and life events is so critical in life. Major reasons to build asset base include, purchasing a house or car, starting a business, paying for education expenses, and saving for retirement. Achieving these goals requires forecasting costs and systematic financial planning so as to achieve one's financial goals. A major risk to the household in asset-building is macroeconomic disequilibrium like inflation which can be hedged through prudent portfolio management (asset allocation: stocks, bonds, money market instruments, real estate and real property investments). The allocation should also take into consideration the personal risk profile of every investor, since risk attitudes vary from person to person.

- Retirement planning is the process of understanding how much it is likely to costs to maintain a reasonable lifestyle at retirement and coming up with a plan to distribute assets to meet any income shortfall. Methods for retirement plan include taking advantage of government allowed structures to manage tax liability including: individual structures, or employer sponsored retirement plans.

- Estate planning involves planning for the disposition of one's assets after death to one's heirs; family; friends; or charitable groups.

iii) Role of finance to businesses (Corporate finance)

Like households, business also faces the problem of allocating resources and raising money; and management must determine which investment to make and how to finance those investments so as to maximise the wealth of its owners. But just like all the other financial agents, corporate finance also encompasses the study and role of financial markets, financial assets, financial agents, financial institutions, financial intermediation; and the activities of government, with emphasis on those aspects relating to financial decision-making processes of companies.

The role of finance in an organisation depend on, among others: the size of the company, long-term objectives of the firm, level of development of the domestic financial system, and the firm's interactions with the global financial system.

Basically, the major finance-related roles in a firm include:

- Financing and Investment: This includes supervising firm's cash and other liquid assets, raising additional functions when needed, and investing funds in viable projects.

- Accounting and Control: This include maintaining financial records, controlling financial activities, identifying deviations from planned and efficient performance and managing payroll, tax matters, inventories, fixed assets, and computer operations.

- Forecasting and Long-term Planning: This involves forecasting revenues and costs, technological changes, capital market conditions, funds needed for investment, demand for the firm's product, and using forecast and historical data to plan future operations.

- Pricing: This entails determining the impact of pricing policies on profitability by making good use of price elasticity analyses.

- Other functions: This includes credit and collections, risk management & insurance, and incentive planning (dividend policies).

iv) Role of finance to government (Public finance)

The public sector is considered a powerful engine of economic development and an important instrument of self-reliance. The main contribution of public finance to the country's economy is as follows:

- Employment: Public finance has been instrumental in creating thousands of jobs to tackle the unemployment problem in the country. Public sector accounts for about two-thirds of the total employment in the organized industrial sector in Uganda; this has contributed a lot towards the improvement of working and living conditions of workers by serving as a model employer.

- Social Justice & equity: it contributes towards the achievement of constitutional objectives like reducing the concentration of economic resources in private hands, in curbing monopolies, in accelerating public control over the national economy and in bringing about a income equality in the economy.

- Development of agriculture: public finance plays an important role in the field of agriculture in the way of financing agricultural inputs as a subsidy to its citizens such as fertilizers, pesticides, insecticides and mechanical implements used in agriculture. Through various research institutes public finance augments agricultural productivity by introducing new high-yielding variety of seeds preventing crop disease and innovating new agricultural practices

- Foreign Exchange Earnings: Public finance has a great role in improving the balance of payments position of the county; public enterprises save valuable foreign exchange through export promotion like the AGOA deal.

- Development of the private sector: In order to encourage the development of small scale and medium-sized industries in the country, public finance aids in facilitating the growth of the private sector through linking it to development partners like the World Bank, and also acquiring grants and loans to subsidize the production of the private sector.

- Community Development: public expenditure has seen the development of townships to provide all the civic amenities to their employees and citizens. This has witnessed the construction of roads and other infrastructural facilities to link these townships to other parts of the country; this has been very helpful in improving community life.

- Balanced regional development: public finance uses the policy of dispersal of industries which aims at removing regional disparities .In some countries; there is a major problem of regional economic disparities whereby certain areas are heavily concentrated with industries actives yet others are backward areas which may go with without even any industry. Thus, through the extension of public expenditure, the government deliberately removes such regional bottlenecks.

v) Career Options in the field of Finance

The world of finance offers a wide array of career opportunities to prospective students who would wish to develop professionally in the gigantic field of finance; these range from the broad sub fields of: financial management; depository financial institutions; contractual savings firms; financial services firms; among others. Thus, training in finance serves as a stepping-stone to a number of the top corporate positions world-over and many students approaching the field of finance for the first time might wonder what career opportunities exist.

Career at a Glance

Finance Job/Position	Job/Career Description
Cash management analyst	This involves monitoring and managing the firm's daily cash flows.
Tax analyst/ expert	This is about preparing financial statements for tax purposes.
Insurance broker	This entails selling insurance to individuals and businesses, but also participating in the process of claims.
Mortgage analyst	This comprises analyzing real estate loan applications and assisting in arranging of mortgage financing.
Financial analyst	This involves evaluating financial performance and preparing financial plans
Stock broker	This entails assisting clients in purchasing financial securities and building investment wealth.
Capital expenditure analyst	This comprises estimating cash flows and evaluating asset investment opportunities (capital budgeting).
Cost analyst	This involves the comparison of actual operations against budgeted operations.
Research analyst	This entails analyzing the investment potential of real property and securities for institutional investors.
Loan analyst	It involves evaluating consumer and commercial loans applications.
Bank teller	This involves assisting customers with their daily checking and banking transactions.
Security analyst	This engrosses analysing and making recommendations on the investment potential of specific securities
Financial planner	This entails analyzing individual client insurance needs and investment plans to meet one's financial goals.
Investment research analyst	This engrosses conducting research on investment opportunities for a corporate treasury.
Investment banking analyst	It entails conducting financial analysis and valuation of new securities that are being issued. He is also in charge of creating securities
Portfolio Manager	It entails a process of combining securities in a portfolio tailored to the investor's preferences and needs, monitoring that portfolio, and evaluating its performance.
Risk/ insurance Manager	

Source : Researcher's Data

Chapter 4

OVERVIEW OF THE FINANCIAL SYSTEM

OVERVIEW OF THE UGANDAN FINANCIAL SYSTEM

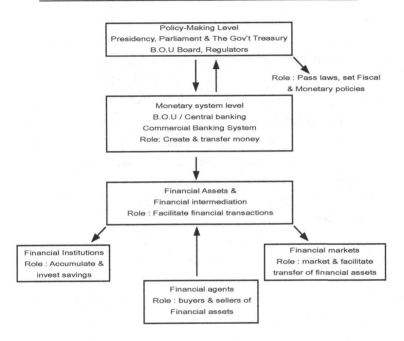

i) Preview & interconnectivity amongst constituents of a financial system

To better understand the operations of the financial system; and the interconnectivity amongst all its constituents, allow me use this hypothetical illustration:

Gracia Company wants to establish an efficient inexpensive Information Technology product in the form of an investment platform that links small income earners basically from the rural areas of Uganda with financial services such as:

investments in financial markets and commodities exchanges; but also financial advisory in real time. But the company does not have funds to actualise this brilliant and ground-breaking invention. On the other hand, Becky has some good savings she amassed through both inheritance and also her work life, which is lying under-utilised some in her ceiling and others on her bank account. If only Gracia Company and Becky could be linked so that Becky could avail the finances required for the establishment of this investment product that will create a lot of value for Gracia Company, Becky, rural dwellers, corporate bodies, and the economy at large; all financial agents will be better off. This could be actualised through the working of the financial system: Gracia Company (**manufacturer** with deficit financing) would be advised (**financial intermediation**) by Asante Capital Hub (**financial institution**) a financial services firm on how it can access funds through issuing shares, bonds and other instruments (**financial assets**) so that Becky (household/ net saver/ **financial agent**) with surplus funds on her bank account (**financial institution**), can transfer some of her money through either buying equity or debt instruments from Gracia Company via the securities exchange (**financial markets**) which are regulated by the State (**government**) so as to protect the investors' interests..

Likewise, when a local government needs to construct a bridge, a road, a school, an airport, etc; it will definitely require more funds than the collections from local property taxes and other financial hand-outs. Therefore, a good financial system is so crucial to our economic health (individually and socially) that is why it is critically important to scrutinise the whole structure and operation of our financial system so as to appreciate its contribution to the economy.

Simply put, a financial system should make possible the creation of productive capital so as to meet the demands of the economy. And productive capital formation takes place whenever resources are used to produces commodities, buildings, machinery or other capital goods that are essential in the production of both consumer goods.

NB: Globally, the above constituents of the financial system are efficiently connected and work to facilitate the flow of financial resources from points of surplus to points of deficit yet with productive uses of such resources, basically in developed economies. Contrarily, Uganda's situation is one of constituents that either deliberately dis-intermediate the financial flows or due to high financial illiteracy that many financial agents are not informed of opportunities within the financial system so they choose to keep their funds in pillows, ceilings, pots and some in bank accounts (household) yet for the corporates, they keep excess funds in highly illiquid and less profitable real assets.

ii) Functions of a financial system

A major role of the financial system is to mobilise and allocate domestic savings: by operating as an efficient conduit (link) for the allocation of resources from net savers (people with surplus incomes) to net investors (organisations with deficit financing).

- It serves to monitor the corporate performance of investments in financial markets and institutions: by exerting corporate controls on underperforming firms in an economy.

- It provides efficient payment and settlement systems across geographical regions and industries: this ensures quick and safe movement of funds so as to create value for households, businesses, and governments.

- It serves to optimise the allocation of risk-bearing and reduction: by limiting, pooling, and trading risks involved in saving & allocating credit. This aims at containing risks within acceptable limits.

- The financial system helps to disseminate price-related information which is critically valuable in both economic and financial decision-making among financial agents.

- It offers portfolio adjustment facilities done by financial markets and intermediaries like banks and unit trust funds including: services of providing a quick, cheap and reliable way of buying and selling a wide variety of financial assets.

- The financial system serves to lower transaction costs that are incurred in the trading of financial assets: research has established that frontier market economies are characterised by high intermittent transaction costs which adversely affect the development of financial markets and financial system depth.

- It promotes the process of financial deepening and broadening such as: increasing of financial assets as a percentage of GDP (equity, bond, insurance assets).

- It serves to determine the return that equates aggregate savings and borrowing which renders the whole economy a good investment environment.

iii) Characteristics of a good financial system

A good financial system allows entities to achieve their purposes; in particular facilitates financial markets to be complete and efficient, where:

- Investors can save for the future at fair rates of return determined by the Market.

- Creditworthy borrowers can obtain finance.

- Hedgers can manage their risks.

- Traders can obtain the currencies, commodities, and other assets they need for their operations.

If markets can perform these functions at low transaction costs, then they are said to be operationally efficient. If asset prices reflect all the information associated with fundamental value in a timely fashion, then the financial system is informationally efficient, with prices reflecting fundamental values. Besides, in informationally efficient markets, capital is allocated to its most productive use, due to allocational efficiency.

Informational efficiency is brought about by traders who bid prices up and down in response to new information that changes estimates of securities' fundamental values. If markets are operationally efficient, asset prices will have more informational efficiency since low transaction costs encourage trading based on new information.

Below are the Critical areas necessary for designing
(and features of) a good financial system:

- A well-functioning financial system should have a strong legal and regulatory environment that protects the rights and interests of investors so as to attract and facilitate more investments.

- It should have a stable currency (money): large fluctuations and depreciations in value of money leads to financial crises and hinders the growth of the economy.

- A good financial system ought to have established sound public finances and public debt management such as: setting and controlling public expenditure priorities; and raising adequate revenues to fund the national budget.

- It should have an efficient central banking institution that supervises and regulates the operations of the banking system in the country.

- It should maintain a sound banking system with both domestic and international banking operations: since these are the core financial intermediaries in all economies.

- This financial system should have efficient information systems with proper disclosure practices and networking of information systems.

- It should have well-functioning securities markets which promote economic growth by mobilising and deploying funds into productive uses; lowering cost of capital for firms; enhancing liquidity; and attracting foreign investments.

iv) Financial System & Economic Growth

"An efficient & safe payment system provides an enabling environment for economic growth and financial system soundness."

Financial systems tend to evolve around a banking sector seeking to achieve economies of scale in order to offset the costs of collecting and processing information designed to reduce uncertainty thereby facilitating a more efficient allocation of financial resources. Efficient financial systems help countries to grow, partly by widening access to external finance and channeling resources to the sectors that need those most. A well-developed financial system also can help an economy cope better with exogenous shocks such as terms of trade volatility and move them away from natural resource based development. In a well functioning economy, banks tend to act as quality controllers for capital seeking successful projects, ensuring higher returns and accelerating output growth. However, a competitive banking system is required to ensure that banks are effective forces for financial intermediation channeling savings into investment fostering higher economic growth.

Mugume (2008) argues, in reference to the performance of Uganda's banking industry that a financial system's contribution to the economy depends upon the quantity and quality of its services and the efficiency with which it provides them.

The economic development of any country is dependent on its financial system: its banks, stock markets, insurance sector, pension funds and a central bank with authority or at least influence over currency and interest rates. In developed countries, these two sides of the economic coin work together to promote growth and foster macroeconomic stability. Therefore, a country like Uganda which is still in a developing stage and characterized by the lack of a strong & sound financial system normally works against the national economy which would otherwise contribute to economic development. For this reason, we need to explore the relationship between financial system and economic development. And below are some of the roles of the financial system in economic development of a country:

The Country's banking system: Banks are the cornerstone of a national financial system and their key services are to provide a safe haven for the earnings of individuals and finance to companies in need of capital for a variety of investment objectives. Without this source of available capital, businesses would be hard-pressed to continue growing and returning a profit to their stakeholders. By channeling savings into the business sector through loans and also offering loans to individuals for asset-building in form of cars and homes, banks boost overall economic growth and development.

The Economy's financial markets: Stock markets provide an opportunity for households to invest in companies; and by issuing shares, public companies pay off debt or raise capital for their operations. The bond market provides another means to raise money: when a household or an investment company buys a bond, it receives a steady stream of interest payments over a set period. The bond market is accessible to companies as well as governments, which also need a reliable stream of funds to operate. Without the bond market, a government could only raise money by levying taxes, an action that tends to dampen business activity and investment within the economy. Besides, the money markets; foreign exchange markets; mortgage markets; derivative markets all work together to provide liquidity within the financial system, manage investment risks, facilitate global transactions, and avail finance for huge capital investment to all financial agents which significantly contributes to economic development.

Management of financial crisis: Globally, confidence and trust in an economy's banking system are central to macroeconomic health: if banks cannot redeem savings accounts and savers begin to fear a loss of their money, a bank crisis results. This quickly drains cash from the bank and can eventually lead to a systemic failure (where a couple of banking institutions fail simultaneously). Bond and stock markets rise and fall with the demand for securities; when individuals fear risk or lose their trust in those capital markets, they sell their securities and cause the value of companies to fall. This, in turn, complicates businesses' capacity to raise money, either from banks or capital markets. Therefore, the regulators' capacity to foster financial system soundness (through prudent management of financial institutions and markets to shield the economy against financial crises) significantly correlates with the achievement of economic development.

Management of monetary policy instruments: Issuing currency and setting interest rates policy is the function of central banks, such as B.O.U, which are responsible for monetary policy. The central bank through their credit control measures loan out new money to the banks; by controlling this flow, B.O.U also keeps currency exchange rates steady, which is vital for foreign trade and new investment. A restrictive monetary policy (setting a higher interest rate) tends to support currency value, while lowering the rate encourages lending and investment but at the risk of currency devaluation and inflation. Reliable and consistent monetary policy fosters economic stability and growth. Hence, the prudent management of the monetary policy instruments through the interests rate and foreign currency rate regimes (which are a function of a well-functioning financial system) would facilitate the economy's development.

v) Reforms in the Financial System

Due to a host of financial system reforms, the level of monetisation in Uganda increased from 6% in 1993 to approx. 21% by 2014. Besides, the share of bank deposits to GDP has risen to approx. 11.5% currently; saving alternatives widened to nationals holding dollar accounts within Uganda, and also investing in global financial markets. Purpose of Financial Reforms:

- To strengthen the financial sector

- To encourage competition

- To increase domestic resource mobilisation

Hence, among the reforms, these are:

- Macroeconomic Stabilization: the government has been able to impose control over public expenditure so as to curb inflation. In the 1990s, government stopped borrowing from the banking system which saw the control of apparent high rates of monetary growth that had fuelled high inflation. Consequently, inflation has been firmly under control for the last 16 years averaging only 5.9% per annum since 1992/93.

- Exchange rate reforms: in the early 1990s, the management of exchange rate of the Uganda Shilling was liberalized especially in 1992 so as to render it be determined by market forces instead of being administratively fixed by the Bank of Uganda.

- Still in the same period, the State deregulated its interest rate regime and eliminated direct credit.

- Since then, the government has introduced market-based systems of monetary policy management that have served to foster macroeconomic stability and financial system soundness.

- In the 1990s, the State restructured its state-owned banks and strengthened the banking regulatory environment by ensuring: capital adequacy; satisfactory asset quality; and acceptable liquidity and management standards for commercial banks.

- The State has also undertaken Public expenditure reforms through budgetary reforms aimed at improving efficiency and effectiveness of government expenditure. This entails giving taxpayers better value for money from public services and prioritizing public expenditure on government's major objective of poverty eradication. This further saw the introduction of Integrated Financial Management System (IFMS) for public financial management across all Government departments; and also strengthening Budget Implementation and Reporting and Budget Transparency.

PART 2

FINANCIAL INSTITUTIONS

These are institutions which serve the purpose of channeling funds from lenders to borrowers; this is done through a complex system of hold money balance or borrowing from individuals, risk reduction through allowing specialist institutions to evaluate borrowers' credit worthiness so as to lend out at an established interest rate to those borrowers.

Over the last Century, the financial services industry has significantly evolved. Initially, the banking industry operated as a full-service industry with all financial services: commercial banking, investment banking, stock brokerage, insurance providers, etc. In the early 1930s, the economic and industrial collapse resulted in the separation of some of these activities. In the 1970s & 1980s, new relatively unregulated financial services industries sprung up such as: unit trust funds, brokerage funds, securitizers, etc; that separated financial services functions even further. In the wake of the 21st Century; regulatory barriers, technology, and financial innovation changes were such that a full set of financial services could again be offered by a single financial services holding company.

These institutions have been classified according to their nature of operation and the legal mandate, and these are: banking financial institutions; non-banking financial institutions; collective investment vehicles; the Central Bank; and other regulatory bodies of the financial system.

Chapter 5

BANKING FINANCIAL INSTITUTIONS

"A sound financial/banking sector will increase opportunities for access to credit for development."

The banking financial institutions comprise all the banks that operate within the financial system, and these include: commercial banks, credit banks, merchant banks, development banks, and others like MDIs that are allowed to mobilize deposits and loan out to the public. On the other hand, banking has also been categorized depending on the nature of the clientele and category of predominant transactions, such as: retail banking; wholesale banking; and international banking.

i) Historical Background of the Banking sector in Uganda

Uganda's banking sector has evolved from the first commercial bank established in 1906 – the National Bank of India (this later became the Grindlays Bank; and is the current Stanbic Bank) to the current 25 commercial banks, three credit institutions and four Microfinance Deposit-taking Institutions (MDIs). Despite the rapid growth in the semi-formal and informal financial system in the country, the formal financial system has also undergone several policy, structural, legal and regulatory reforms with various degrees of results.

This evolution, basically in the banking sector, has been characterized by bank closures, mergers and acquisitions for more than a century of banking experience in Uganda. Before independence in 1962, the banking sector was dominated mainly by foreign-owned commercial banks. In addition to the National Bank of India, the following banks began operation: Standard Bank in 1912; Bank of the Netherlands in 1954, which later merged with Grindlays Bank.

Later, the Uganda Credit and Savings Bank which became Uganda Commercial Bank (UCB) in 1969 following an Act of Parliament in 1965; and this was the first local commercial bank established in the country to cater for banking needs of indigenous Ugandans. Bank of Baroda had been established first in 1953, but regularized as a commercial bank in 1969 with the enactment of the Banking Act of 1969 (the first legal framework for regulation of the banking sector following the country's independence).

On the other hand, the country's central bank (Bank of Uganda) was established in 1966 under the Bank of Uganda Act 1966; and this was followed by the institution of the Uganda Development Bank under the UDB Decree of 1972. These two banks revolutionized banking in Uganda since the government-owned banks dominated the banking industry: UDB received all foreign loans and channelled them to the local companies for development; and UCB, with the biggest number of branches around 67 in number, handled the majority of the domestic customers. Then, the East African Development Bank which was established in 1967 would handle the East African Community (EAC) business and regional customers.

By 1970, Uganda had more than 290 commercial bank branches but this number reduced to 84 in the period between 1970s & 1980s following volatilities in political and economic atmosphere during that period; of which UCB owned a total of 50 branches. Privatization and divestiture of the public sector that was championed by IMF & World Bank significantly changed the banking landscape in Uganda as the dominance of state-owned banks between the 1960s and 1980s visibly decreased as several privately-owned banks were established in the 1990s. Bank of Uganda licensed over 10 private banks (mostly locally owned) between 1988 and 1999 to operate in the country.

A significant number of these banks were private local banks; and these included the Nile Bank Ltd, the Greenland Bank Ltd, the Cooperative Bank Ltd, the Gold Trust Bank Ltd, the Teefee Bank Ltd and Sembule Investment Bank, Equator Building Society, International Credit Bank, the TransAfrica Bank Ltd, Kigezi Bank of Commerce. Almost all of these banks and non-bank financial institutions have closed through merger, acquisition or outright closure. The implications of the bank closure or restructuring have been a reduction in branch network and limited access to financial services; though it has also occasioned a stronger and sound financial system that has resulted in improved confidence in the domestic economy.

ii) The Four Tiers in the Banking Sector

A tier is a French word which means to rank; it is a row or a layer in a series of similarly arranged objects. Tier is the core measure of a bank's financial strength from a regulator's point of view. It is composed of core capital, which consists primarily of common stock and disclosed reserves (or retained earnings), but may also include non-redeemable non-cumulative preferred stock. The Banking sector in Uganda is categorized into four Tiers as follows:

Tier 1-comprising of commercial banks E.g. Stanbic bank.

Tier 2-comprising of credit and finance companies E.g. Opportunity bank Uganda.

Tier 3-comprising of Microfinance Deposit-taking Institutions (MDIs).

Tier 4-all other financial intermediaries including SACCO's, Women groups, NGOs e.t.c

Tier I - Financial Institutions

This class includes commercial banks which are authorized to hold checking, savings and time deposit accounts for individuals and institutions in local as well as International currencies. Commercial banks are also authorized to buy and sell foreign exchange, issue letters of credit and make loans to depositors and non-depositors. Commercial Banks are regulated under the Financial Institutions Act 2 of 2004. They are supervised by the Bank of Uganda and are subject to prudential regulation by Ministry of Finance, Planning and Economic Development. The minimum paid in capital for commercial banks as per the Financial Institutions Act of 2004 is shillings 4 billion (almost US dollars 1.5 million) since January 2003.

Origin of Controlling Shareholders in Uganda's Banking Sector

The table below provides a synopsis of the origin of the parents of Uganda's 25 licensed Commercial banks as on 1st January 2015.

Locally or Govt controlled	Controlled by EAC Parent	Other African controlled	Foreign controlled
Centenary Rural Dev Bank	ABC Bank Uganda	Bank of Africa (Uganda)	Bank of Baroda (Uganda)
Crane Bank	Diamond Trust Bank	Cairo International Bank	Barclays Bank of Uganda
Housing Finance Bank	Equity Bank	Ecobank Uganda	Citibank Uganda
Finance Trust Bank	Imperial Bank Uganda	Guaranty Trust Bank	DFCU Bank
Tropical Bank	KCB Bank Uganda	Orient Bank	Standard Chartered Bank Bank of India (Uganda)
		Stanbic Bank Uganda	
		United Bank for Africa Commercial Bank of Africa NC Bank	

Source : Researcher & BOU Data

ASSET ALLOCATION AMONG COMMERCIAL BANKS AS OF DECEMBER 2014

Rank	Bank	Assets (USD) Millions	Market Share	Number of Branches
1	Stanbic Bank	1,300	19.0%	91
2	Standard Chartered Bank	965	15.8%	12
3	Crane Bank	575	9.1%	38
4	Centenary Bank	573	9.1%	62
5	Barclays Bank	496	8.2%	46
6	DFCU Bank	482	7.0%	45
7	Citibank Uganda	300	4.9%	01
8	Bank of Baroda	279	4.6%	14
9	Housing Finance Bank	220	3.5%	17
11	Bank of Africa	178	2.9%	33
12	Orient Bank	173	2.6%	20
12	Diamond Trust Bank	134	2.2%	20
13	Kenya Commercial Bank	131	2.1%	14
14	Equity Bank	123	2%	39
15	Imperial Bank Uganda	87	1.4%	05
16	Tropical Bank	84	1.4%	11
17	United Bank for Africa	60	1.0%	09
18	Ecobank	60	1.0%	11
19	Finance Trust Bank	44	0.7%	33
20	Guaranty Trust Bank	40	0.7%	07
21	Cairo International Bank	30	0.5%	05
22	NC Bank Uganda	25	0.5%	01
23	Bank of India (Uganda)	25	0.5%	01
24	Commercial Bank of Africa	19	0.3%	01

Source : BOU Data January 2015

It is estimated that asset allocation among 24 operational Ugandan commercial banks, at that time, broke down as follows:

Advantages of Commercial Banks.

- More locations: the most noticeable advantage of commercial banks is their retail store setup. Most are large, global companies, and they have hundreds of retail locations in major cities. This gives a household the ability to access his/her money and account from virtually any location.

- Discounts: commercial banks can provide low prices. They are like wholesale companies buying in bulk and selling at a discount. Most commercial banks will not charge fees to open or maintain checking and savings accounts, and their real estate loans are usually offered at low interest rates.

- Personal Services offered: commercial banks are setup to close thousands of deals every day. Because of this, personal service is sacrificed. One can talk to manager at a local bank, but commercial banks have centralized call centres to handle problems and disputes.

- More product offerings: commercial banks can offer more products and services to their customers. A commercial bank will offer everything a small local bank does, plus CDs, investment accounts, Commercial real estate loans and credit and debit cards.

- They are regulated institutions fulfilling the conditions of ownership, financial disclosure and capital adequacy that help ensure prudent management.

- Many have physical infrastructure including a large network of branches, from which to expand and reach out to a substantial number of microfinance clients.

- They have well established internal controls and administrative and accounting systems to keep track of a large number of transactions.

- Their ownership structures of private capital tend to encourage sound governance structures, cost-effectiveness and profitability, all of which lead to sustainability.

- Because they have their own sources of funds (deposits and equity capital) they do not have to depend on scarce and volatile donor resources.

- They offer loans, deposits and other financial products that are in principle, attractive to a microfinance client.

Tier II - Financial Institutions

This class includes Credit and Finance companies. They are not authorized to establish checking accounts or trade in foreign currency. They are authorized to take in customer deposits and to establish savings accounts. They are also authorized to make collateralized and non-collateralized loans to savings and non-saving clientele. These Credit institutions are also regulated by the Financial Institutions Act 2 of 2004. The minimum paid up capital required for credit institutions as per the Financial Institutions Act of 2004 is shillings 1 billion (equivalent to about US dollars 360,000) since January 2001.These are only three, namely:

- Opportunity Bank Uganda- A 100% subsidiary of Opportunity International.

- Post Bank Uganda

- Mercantile Credit Bank -A 100% subsidiary of General Machinery Limited

Advantages of Credit Institutions.

- Customers are owners: members of credit institutions have voting rights, thus, apart from receiving better services, members have a say in the operation of the credit institution.

- Credit institutions are non- profit: non- profit status means that more of the profits are shared with the owners/customers e.g owners/ customers of credit institutions receive dividend payments.

- There are fewer fees and higher saving rates: credit institutions typically offer free accounts with no minimum balance requirements and fees are absent.

- Interest rates on savings, certificate of deposits and some checking accounts often exceed those offered by financial banks.

- Interest charged for loans and Credits are often lower: some credit institutions are regulated such that the interest rate on loans and credit cards must not exceed a certain limit.

Tier III - Financial Institutions

This class includes microfinance institutions which are allowed to take in deposits from customers in the form of savings accounts. Members of this class of institutions are also known as Microfinance Deposit-taking Institutions or MDIs. MDIs are not authorized to offer checking accounts; and operate under Micro Finance Deposit Taking Institutions Act 5 of 2006. The minimum paid up capital required for MDIs as per the Micro Finance Deposit Taking Institutions Act of 2001 and Regulation 6 of Micro Finance Deposit Taking Institutions Act of 2003 is shillings 500 million (equivalent to about US dollars 180,000). These include:

- FINCA Uganda Limited

- Pride Microfinance Limited

- UGAFODE Microfinance Limited

Advantages of MDIs.

- MDIs provide financial services that allow poor people to save in times of prosperity and borrow or collect insurance when necessary allowing them to maintain a consistent level of consumption without selling off income producing assets.

- MDIs also provide an opportunity for expanding or pursuing new business opportunities that allow poor people to increase or diversify their sources of income.

- MDIs promote the development of traditional financial sector. By alleviating poverty, MDIs can deepen the market for poor traditional financial services.

- MDIs can also generate important non-economic benefits e.g access to financial services by women through MDIs enhance women's power and influence in the household, that is, their ability to make decisions over certain purchases.

Tier IV - Institutions

These institutions are not regulated by the Bank of Uganda. They are not authorized to take deposits from the public. However, they may offer collateralized or non-collateralized loans to the public. In 2008, it is estimated that there are over 1,000 such institutions in the country. There is no minimum paid up capital since the Bank of Uganda does not regulate these institutions. These include:

- All other Financial intermediaries such as: SACCOs, Women groups, NGOs, CBOs, ROSCAs, etc. These are regulated by three sets of institutional legislations.

- SACCOs are regulated by the Cooperative Societies Statute of 1991.

- NGOs are regulated by NGOs Registration Act of 2006.

- Companies are regulated by Companies Act of 2012.

Advantages of SACCOs and MFIs.

- Close to customers/members: SACCOs operate hand in hand with the members since the members are also responsible to its governance apart from being members.

- Easy access to internal funds: members of SACCOs and MFIs can easily access their financial accounts and records. Members can also access internal funds through borrowings.

- Low operating costs: interest rates on savings, certificates of deposits and some checking accounts often exceed those offered by banks.

- Member-based ownership: SACCOs operate in member based ownership, thus, members of a SACCO are the owners of that particular SACCO.

- Democratic & Participatory: every member of a SACCO has voting rights, thus, they influence its operation through democratic decision making using their rights.

Statistical Data on the Ugandan banking industry

Mobile money transactions – by June 2015, record has it that there were 19.5 million registered users of mobile money; and the 2nd Quarter 2015 transactions amounted to UGX 2.5 Billion in Uganda. The growth is attributed to the gap that still exists in financial inclusion with the number of citizens holding mobile money accounts far outstripping those with bank accounts which are on 6 million accounts.

Banking sector facilities and statistics – by end June 2013, there were 719 ATMs (automated tellers' machines); and 637 branches, of which: 78% are commercial bank branches, 16% are MDI branches, and 7% are Credit institutions' branches in Uganda. Banking assets amounted to UGX 15.5 Trillion (USD 6 billion); loans and deposits totalled to UGX 7.8 Trillion (USD 3 billion) and UGX 10.5 Trillion (USD 4 billion) respectively. Besides, 70% of the population aged 16 years and above are financially served though only 21% of the population is using banking services. As for the allocation of credit among sectors: building, mortgage, construction and real estate covered 24% of loans issued by banks; trade represented 21% of the total bank loans portfolio; manufacturing took 14% of the loans; personal and household loans accounted for 13%; and agriculture (the backbone of the Ugandan economy) took 7% of the total bank loans portfolio.

Among the banking institutions, 3 commercial banks were listed on the local stock exchange ie Stanbic Bank Uganda, DFCU, and Bank of Baroda Uganda. These three (3) banks had a combined market capitalisation of UGX 2 trillion (USD 805) which was 73% of the total market capitalisation of locally listed companies on the USE. This significantly highlights the importance of the financial sector to the Ugandan capital markets industry.

Foreign exchange bureaux totalled to 226 registered bureaux that were operating in Uganda.

Microfinance institutions in Uganda total to 47 institutions currently.

East African Community Financial systems Data:

	Uganda	Kenya	Rwanda	Tanzania	Burundi	Total EAC
Contribution of NSSF to GDP	6% Not liberalised	50% Liberalized	1% Not liberalized	20% Liberalized	0.24% Not liberalized	
Number of Microfinance Institutions	47	50	38	22	23	
% of Public Debt to GDP	35.4%	49.8%	29.4%	39.9%	14.2%	
Tax to GDP	11.7%	19.3%	13.6%	12.6%	14.1%	
Bond Securities to GDP	1.2%	N/A	N/A	N/A	N/A	
Insurance Penetration	0.8%	3.4%	2.2%	2.8%	1.3%	
Stock Market Capitalisation to GDP	30.7%	29.4%	N/A	4.7%	No Stock exchange.	

Data: World Bank estimates; Mix Market; Trading Economics.

Uganda's economy continues to perform below par thanks to persistent high lending rates, weak export performance and infrastructure gaps; thus rendering its 7% growth target vague since 2012. Lending rates have averaged more than 20 per cent over the past three years, amid high costs of funding experienced by banks. Though Bank of Uganda data indicates that the economy grew by 5% against a target of 5.8 % during 2014/15, down from 5.7 % against a target of 6.2 % in 2013/14; the World Bank now projects growth between 5% and 5.5 % during 2015/16 due to depressed investment flows attributed to uncertainty over election campaigns on the part of the investors. This, coupled to unrelenting suspense surrounding the US Federal Reserves' intentions of raising interest rates are potential to force B.O.U to adopt a 'wait and see' attitude before intervening in the forex market as a result of depleted stabilization resources. The country's large current account deficit caused by surging imports pegged to large infrastructure projects and depressed exports is expected to put further pressure on the shilling. Uganda's current account deficit increased from 7.9 % of GDP in 2013/14 to 8.8 % of GDP in 2014/15 while total export revenues fell by 2.8 % to $680 million at the end of June.

i)   Retail Banking

Commercial banking: entails the acceptance of deposits that can be withdrawn by cheques, and they perform a wide range of services that are quite unique from other financial institutions as discussed among the functions of banks (later in "vi").

Agricultural Banking: these are established mainly to provide the requisite finance for agricultural development projects and agribusiness initiatives such as: poultry, farming, fisheries, animal husbandry, forestry and timber production, but also for storage and marketing in this sector.

Industrial banking: these aim at encouraging the establishment and growth of medium and large-scale industries through the provision of medium and long-term finance for the private and public sector; provision of financial, technical and managerial assistance to indigenous enterprises.

Cooperative banking: these are responsible for promoting and giving assistance (financial, technical and managerial) to cooperative societies, companies and government agencies such as advice and preparation of feasibility studies.

ii) Wholesale Banking (investment/ merchant)

These banks were previously known as "merchant banks" because more than a century ago, they were bankers to merchants. Trade in the 19th Century was carried out using bills of exchange; so, these financial intermediaries would serve to facilitate the acceptance of trade bills of companies due their knowledge of the merchants since they were able to assess their credit risks and then facilitate trade transactions. In the early 1800s, most American securities were traded in Europe; and so most securities firms developed from merchants who operated a securities business as a sideline to their primary business. For example, the Morgans built their initial fortune with the railroads: in a bid to raise the money to finance railroad expansion, J. P. Morgan's father resided in London and sold Morgan railroad securities to European investors. Over time, the profitability of the securities businesses became evident and the securities industry expanded.

Due to modern development and sophistication of trade, the use of bills of exchange declined significantly, and so merchant banks found a lot more new things to do which later changed even their identity to "investment banks". In Uganda, such institutions include: African Alliance Ltd, Baroda Capital Markets Ltd, Crane Financial Services Ltd, Crested Stocks & Services Ltd, Dyer & Blair Ltd, Equity Stock Brokers Ltd, UAP Financial Services Ltd, SBG Securities Ltd, ICEA financial services Ltd; which now specialize in giving financial advisory to companies and in fund management. As financial advisers to companies, they: give advice on takeover and merger strategies and defenses; give advice on investment projects; advisory on the best way to raise capital; act as issuing houses; arrange underwriting of new issues; issue Eurobonds.

But also in the line of fund management, they: provide management for unit trusts and investment trust companies; manage pension funds and large private portfolios; organize the Eurobond market.

In money market operations, they: accept/guarantee bills of exchange; hold treasury bills and local authority bills; issue certificate of deposits; provide finance to companies; act as trustees especially in debenture issuing.

Since these firms are always in the market advising and doing analyses for various companies, they provide more than expertise to security issuers. They are bound to suffer with investors if it turns out that the securities they have underwritten were either faulty or exaggerated prices. Among the international wholesale/ investment banks are: Merrill Lynch, Goldman Sachs, etc.

iii) International Banking (Eurocurrency/Offshore banking)

This is a kind of foreign banking transactions that deals in Eurocurrency/Euro-deposits banking for transactions in a currency other than the Uganda Shillings (UGX) with both residents and non-residents of Uganda. A Euro-deposit is any currency deposited outside its country of origin such as UGX held in a Rwandan bank. There is a huge market in our financial systems for Eurocurrencies like Eurodollars, Euro-yen, etc; and the major part of international banking in the contemporary financial world is borrowing and lending in foreign currency. There are many foreign banks operating in Uganda whose main function is to provide services to nationals from other jurisdictions/ countries, for instance, for export and import transactions but also speculation in the foreign exchange markets.

Incidentally, the genesis of Eurocurrency banking was due to political factors way back in the 1950s during the Cold War between the U.S.A and the U.S.S.R; whereby USSR acquired dollars basically through the sale of its gold and other raw materials to the USA in a bid to purchase goods eg grains from Europe. The Soviets feared that the US might confiscate its dollars that were deposited in American banks if the Cold War heated up; so, Soviet dollars were placed in European banks which were outside of America's jurisdiction. Thus, it is believed that international banking and Euro-banks originated as the telex code of a Soviet-controlled Paris bank. Later, the Eurodollar system mushroomed in the 1960s as a result of new U.S restrictions on capital outflows and subsequent banking regulations. By and large, Eurocurrency banking grew as a percent of banks total stock of liabilities world over due to the following reasons:

- The growth of global trade: a drastic increase in international trade, coupled with the increasingly multinational nature of business activities basically financial services have sparked off such a growth in that sector.

- Government financial regulations and taxation: stringent financial regulations have for ages been the major stimulant to financial innovation and creation of alternatives, which saw many banks opt for the Eurocurrency market that has been loosely regulated yet highly profitable.

- Political factors: such as the USA – USSR relations significantly paved way for creation of such facilities in a bid to make business operations sustainable even in the face of political differences and hostility.

Eurocurrency banking has been criticized on the following grounds:

- Stimulant to global inflation: this unregulated business process has led to a production of vast pools of international liquidity that has potential to spark off global inflation because such volumes of money supply are not included in any measure of money supply eg M1, M2, etc. These Eurocurrency deposits are near-money instruments which may go unnoticed by many a Central banks and later influence an economy's price levels leading to macroeconomic disequilibrium (inflation).

- Eurocurrency system complicates the financial system's capacity to monitor and control money supplies by the monetary authorities, hence destabilizing the operation of the money multiplier in an economy.

iv) Development banking:

These institutions are set up to provide banking services that will help in the development of a particular sector or aspect of the economy. They are usually government-owned institutions that serve basically to enhance economic development rather than for profit motives; they bridge the gap in the provision of long-term finance for their clients. These include:

- East African Development Bank

- Uganda Development Bank

v) Functions / Role of Banks in Economic development / Financial deepening

Increasingly, scholars acknowledge that supportive policy for financial sector development is a key component of national development policy, and comparative analysis of the growth rates of different countries has produced convincing evidence that having a deeper financial system contributes to growth (Honohan and Beck, 2007). Countries with deep financial systems also seem to have a lower incidence of poverty than others at the same level of national income. At the firm level, growth also responds to access to credit and to the conditions that favor such access.

Financial systems tend to evolve around a banking sector seeking to achieve economies of scale in order to offset the costs of collecting and processing information designed to reduce uncertainty thereby facilitating a more efficient allocation of financial resources. The importance of a strong banking sector to a country's economic growth and development can't be over-emphasized. Efficient financial systems help countries to grow, partly by widening access to external finance and channeling resources to the sectors that need those most. A well-developed financial system also can help an economy cope better with exogenous shocks such as terms of trade volatility and move them away from natural resource based development. In this, banks tend to act as quality controllers for capital seeking successful projects, ensuring higher returns and accelerating output growth. However, a competitive banking system is required to ensure that banks are effective forces for financial intermediation channeling savings into investment fostering higher economic growth.

Banks are the predominant financial institutions in most developing countries and in Uganda comprise over 80 percent of the financial system's assets and loans. Banks are the primary mechanisms for the transmission of monetary policy and they play an important role in determining the supply of money in the economy. They also form the backbone of the payments system. Therefore, changes in the structure and performance of banks can have far-reaching implications for the whole economy but above all facilitating financial deepening in our under-developed financial system. The following are the functions/ roles of the banking sector in economic development and financial deepening:

- Banks offer a wide array of loans to financial agents in form of: personal, business, mortgage and agricultural loans. These may be short, medium and long-term loans for both consumption and investment expenditure.

- They avail finance through discounting bills of exchange and also giving loans against the bill which serves as security for the loan facility.

- They offer trustee facilities such as: acting in trust for money or property whose owners are either dead, incapacitated or minors.

- They provide tax planning and management facilities to the business community.

- Banks offer various accounts to their clients which serve as safe custody for depositors' savings, such as: savings, current, investment, fixed deposit, among other accounts.

- They facilitate payment and settlement systems which minimize risks of funds transfer, such as: cheques, standing orders, credit transfers, electronic transfer of money.

- They provide foreign exchange to business community that engages in foreign trade by intermediating between Central bank and the business community.

- Banks provide investment advice to business community in the way of risk management and investment appraising (new ventures).

- They offer a wide array of financial services such as: investment banking; lease financing; hire-purchase financing; guarantee services for their customers to acquire any kind of finance.

- Banks offer safe custody for valuable that are kept in banking strong-rooms, such as: gold, title deeds, bond certificates, wills, academic documents, among other valuables for their customers.

vi) Factors responsible for the growth of the Banking Sector

- Uganda has witnessed a relative stable political environment from 1986 when President Museveni took over power; this has been rather conducive to the development of the financial system. This can be evidenced by: the growth in GDP; development in financial institutions, markets and services; growth in foreign direct investments (FDI); among other economic variables and metrics.

- The growth in financial literacy among Ugandan; and the subsequent (though still slow) transition from short-termism to long-term perspective towards investment and business has served to boost the growth of banking sector in Uganda. Households and business sectors now view banking sector as safe for the custody of their funds and also as a means for asset-building through loans, among other financing facilities.

- Macroeconomic stability: Besides political stability, the country is also enjoying high levels of macroeconomic stability in the way of: reasonable inflation; relatively good interest rate and foreign exchange regimes; improved levels of employment; GDP growth rates; among other factors. These have led to higher confidence levels among foreign investors; and boosted the country's credit rating among foreign creditors.

- The strategic positioning of Uganda in the heart of East and Central Africa; coupled by its powerhouse in the field of regional peace-keeping that have facilitated trading relations within the region. This has served to attract financial institutions from the Anglophone, Francophone, Arab, among other worlds so as to connect to both East and Central African economies.

- Reduction in the levels of poverty: There has been significant and visible reduction in percentage of both rural and urban poor in Uganda, this has been due to: steady flow of income from agriculture; growth of both the service and tourism sectors that have employed many Ugandans.

- Favourable government policies that have stimulated small-scale industries; attracted foreign investments through tax incentives; and the establishment of the Microfinance Support Centre that has both streamlined micro-financing but also provided start-up financial resources to those in need.

vii) Financial Innovations & Inclusion (New developments in the banking industry)

"Financial innovation promotes financial inclusion and financial stability."

Globally, close to 2.5 billion people (half the world's adult population) lack one of the most basic amenities of modern life: a bank account. These folks are among the world's poorest, and are struggling to obtain the money they need to feed their families or start a business and create jobs, but their exclusion from the modern financial system represents a significant obstacle to the global effort to end extreme poverty and boost shared prosperity. Modern financial facilities like e-money accounts, debit and prepaid cards, mobile money conveniences and low-cost accounts are so instrumental in increasing financial access (deepening), reducing poverty, and empowering the poor in our struggling economies. This reality actually prompted the World Bank Group president Jim Yong Kim to call for universal access to finance by 2020 by all financial agents such as governments, the private sector, and other players to that effect.

Mugume, Apaa & Ojwiya (2009) inform that the Ugandan banking system has been subject to deep structural transformation since the early 1990s in large part due to financial sector reforms. By the late 1980s, the institutional fabric of the banking industry was severely damaged as a result of misguided financial policies and the effects of civil war and economic decline.

This therefore necessitated reforms to liberalize the financial sector and enhance its efficiency. As part of the banking sector reform measures, the government involvement in commercial banking was sharply reduced with the privatization of Uganda Commercial Bank (UCB) in 2001. Besides these, the following are some of the new developments (financial innovations) in the Ugandan banking industry:

Banks have developed new electronic banking solutions such as internet banking and Mobile banking eg Cente-mobile, etc. Prof. Tumusiime-Mutebile argues that mobile money transfers and banking services have had a transformative effect on access to financial services since their introduction in 2009 in Uganda.

B.O.U approved the introduction of custodial and trustee services by banks.

B.O.U approved more Mobile Money transfer business from MTN, UTL, Airtel, Orange Telecom, M-Cash and Ezee-Money.

The Interswitch banking facility which facilitates customers to access their funds and easily transact with other financial institutions even where they actually don't have accounts. Currently, there are 14 institutions on the Inter-switch platform, which include: Commercial Bank of Africa, DFCU, GT Bank, NC Bank, Post Bank, Centenary Bank, Finance Trust Bank, Imperial Bank Ltd, Orient Bank, United Bank of Africa, Cairo International Bank, FINCA, Opportunity Bank, and MTN Mobile Money.

MTN Lifecare: an insurance cover offered by MTN to its mobile subscribers for as low as UGX 24,500 a year for a benefit of UGX 5,000,000.

Mobile money withdrawal on banks' ATMs eg Centenary Bank Mobile Wallet. With growing sophistication, customers are shifting away from cash transactions to the greater security and convenience of electronic platforms. East Africa was the world pioneer of mobile money services such as Safaricom's M-Pesa and Zain's Zap. Currently firmly entrenched, the partnership between banks and the mobile service providers has broadened to actual bank accounts operated via mobile phone, e.g. MTN &Centenary bank, M-Kesho (Equity Bank/Safaricom) and Iko-Pesa (Equity Bank/Telkom Kenya).

Despite the significant growth of mobile money transactions (approx. 2.5 Billion for the 2nd Quarter of 2015 only), Bank of Uganda points out that the stock and value of mobile money deposits and transactions are still a small percentage of total deposits and transactions respectively in that they currently can't pose any systemic risk to the financial system. This is the reason as to why the Central bank has not introduced any special regulations for mobile money transfers and banking services to mitigate systemic risk.

Credit Reference Bureau: CompuScan CRB Limited's exclusivity period as sole provider of credit referencing services had expired on 30th September 2012. B.O.U signed an agreement with CompScan CRB to separate the Financial Card System from the CRB. This was followed by the drafting of Financial Institutions (Credit Reference Services) Regulations 2013 by MoFPED that would improve the CRB, FCS services and strengthen the supervisory process in a credit reference bureau competitive environment.

During the financial year 2014/2015, B.O.U licensed another credit reference bureau firm called Metropol Corporation (a Kenya-owned firm) following the liberalisation of CRB services. These services are becoming mandatory requirement during debt financing such as loan appraisal since they compile clients' credit histories drawn from banks, SACCOs, micro-finance, institutions, utilities providers and other financial service providers. This is done through aggregating financial information about companies and individuals; then providing lenders with a scientific mechanism to access credit worthiness of borrowers and facilitating risk management.

Improving Payments and Remittance Systems: the Bank of Uganda has taken some important steps to modernize the payment systems. The program aimed at achieving high quality, accessible, reliable, and affordable payment services, increasing confidence in the banking system, and reducing the dependency of the Ugandan economy on cash and checks. Under the project "financial inclusion in Rural Areas" with support from the UK who are providing up to £17 million over 5 years from 2012/13 to 2016/17. Statistics show that 1.78 million men and 2.4 million women, and the majority of small and medium businesses in Uganda do not have access to services that allow them to make the most of their financial resources.

Financing agriculture and small scale businesses: Under the project "Enhancing Farmers Access to Markets in East and West Africa" which is expected to last for at least for 5 years from 2014.The projects aims to improve the life of small scale farmers by increasing their access to local, regional, and international markets. The Ugandan banking system has also ensured development of small and medium sized enterprises in agriculture, industry and education sectors. B.O.U recently partnered with Agribusiness Initiative (aBi) Trust, whose primary objective is strengthening the competitiveness of Uganda's agricultural and agro-processing sector through improved performance of value chains.

Easy cross boarder payments: the East African Cross Boarder Payment System (EAPS) which is an initiative of the East African Central Banks became operational on 25 November 2013 in three countries namely; Kenya, Tanzania and Uganda. Rwanda and Burundi are expected to join at a later date when ready. EAPS is a multi-currency system in which payments are effected using any of the currencies of the EAC Partner States. It will make cross boarder payments easier and facilitate safe and efficient transfer of monetary value within the region; and in promoting regional trade and enhancing economic integration.

Easy access of banks in rural areas: the Ugandan banking system through, privately-owned banks have ensured that banks are brought closer to the people in the rural areas. Also under the same objectives of the project "financial inclusion in Rural Areas" with support from the UK who are providing up to £17 million over 5 years from 2012/13 to 2016/17.

On December 9th 2014 the many banks aimed at improving their IT platform in order to provide customized financial services in the areas of manufacturing, construction, transport and tourism. This is aimed at increasing tourism in Uganda and increased productivity through enriching the manufacturing system of Uganda.

By May 2015, 33% of Ugandan adults hold a mobile money account.

In the same period, Uganda ranked 4th in countries with the greatest financial inclusion efforts according to the 2015 Brookings Financial & Digital Inclusion Project (FDIP) report score card. This report evaluates access to and usage of affordable financial services across 21 countries with a four dimension assessment: country commitment, mobile capacity, regulatory environment, and adoption of basic traditional and digital financial services.

There were 3 commercial bank branches and 15 ATMs for every 1000 square kilometres and for every 100,000 adults in Uganda by May 2015.

28% of Ugandans above 15 years had an account at a bank or financial institution by April 2015 according to the World Bank Global Financial Inclusion.

Centenary Bank joined the Interswitch East Africa Network in 2015.

Chapter 6

NON-BANK FINANCIAL INSTITUTIONS

"Sufficient capital & liquidity levels in the financial system provide a buffer for financial institutions to absorb the adverse impacts of shocks."

i) Types of NBFI

Building Societies

These institutions channel private individuals' excess short-term money to households to borrow for the purchase of a house. Among their investments are: grant houses, mortgage purchases, and some personal loans; then surplus money is invested in treasury securities and local authority bonds, other banks using certificates of deposits.

The building industry in Uganda has drastically improved in the past decade due to good government policy that has favored the provision of adequate and decent shelter for all Ugandan (a range of policies such as political, economic and social). This industry has for years been championed by, Akright company, among other players in this sub-sector which have made projects such as Lubowa Housing estates.

These societies are rather crucial in the economy because: they avail mortgage loans to qualifying citizens to purchase houses and repay later; they sell housing and infrastructural bonds that individuals and organizations can invest their surplus funds; they also offer savings facilities which act as a custody for depositors' money.

Insurance Companies

These institutions protect financial agents against a variety of risk exposures that arise within the financial system by spreading losses of the unfortunate few over many policyholders through the collection of premiums. They perform financial intermediation since they mobilize /pool funds from the public which they use to compensate losses from their clients but the residue is invested in a wide variety of both real and financial assets of companies. They are so critical in: facilitating risk transfer; provision of long-term investment resources; development of financial markets; stimulate a savings culture; securities underwriting; among other functions they play.

National Social Security Fund

NSSF was established in 1985 by an Act of Parliament; its basic function is the provision of a more comprehensive and reliable social security system for Ugandan private sector employees since they were not covered in the public sector pension system. NSSF has customer centric, innovation, integrity, teamwork, and efficiency as its corporate values; and it has strived to prove to its investors that its strategic thinking coupled to its values are turned into realities for the betterment of each saver. It mobilizes funds through a statutory and compulsory contribution to the fund by the private sector employers and employee, which funds are used to provide pension benefits to contributors. NSSF invests these funds using its authority and capacity in investment management in a diversity of real and financial assets such as: real property, real estate, corporate and government debt instruments, listed equities and a few private equities in Uganda but also East African Community given its mandate regarding the permissible investment universe. Besides, almost all sectors of the economy are permissible: real estate development, energy, water, education, health, mortgage finance and SME development.

It has become the largest pension fund in East Africa, and a benchmark for the industry within and outside East African region. This has created a lot of value for NSSF's contributors since within the last decade; NSSF has been giving impressive annual interest rate to its saver such as 11.23% in June 2013; 11.50% in June 2014. NSSF had an asset base of approx. UGX 5 Trillion as of December 31st 2014; it had increased employer compliance from 52% in 2010 to 77% in 2014 (an average growth of 23% per year. The annual contribution more than doubled from UGX 295 Billion in 2010 to UGX 638 Billion in 2014; coupled with an increment in its monthly average benefits payout to more than UGX 10 Billion in the same period.

Besides, the fund has grown by over 150% over the last 5 years, becoming the largest financial institution in Uganda, and it had invested in a wide portfolio of asset classes: fixed income UGX 3.4 Trillion (81% of total portfolio); Equities UGX 432 Billion (10%); yet the fund is highly liquid. NSSF holds 40% of all government treasury bonds; 15% of all deposits in commercial banks; 80% of all equities listed on USE; yet 25% of its portfolio is invested in East African region due to domestic absorption incapacity and diversification strategy. Among its real estate include: Workers' House, Lubowa land, Pension Towers, and Temangalo land. Pension resources are often the only form of savings that many households have for their retirement; and they part of the employment income available to employees which are deferred until an employee has completed his/her work life. Besides, they contribute volumes of reliable investable resources to the financial sector before they are cashed out, which significantly boost long-term financing in our financial system.

Role of NSSF in boosting the financial system:

Provision of patient capital to firms and SMEs such as private equity with a view to exiting via the stock exchange.

Provision of long term finance to Government for infrastructure projects.

Supply the market with liquidity when no one has it at an acceptable premium depending on the risk.

Market making on listed securities. Examples include: Bonds, REITS, shares.

Offering housing solutions to address the housing deficit in Uganda. For example: mortgages, affordable housing...etc.

Underwriting listings on both stock markets and bond markets.

Savings and Credit Cooperatives (SACCOs)

These are most popular non-bank financial institutions, and they have significantly contributed to the development of the economy. Originally created to facilitate mortgage loans to their own members, they have now increasingly established their savings institutions, catering for small investors but also local and central governments in some cases. Many SACCOs actually pay good interest that is higher than what commercial banks and other investment avenues give to their savers' deposits. Some are actually allowed to issue large denominations of certificates of deposits that have boosted their resource mobilization capacities.

Discount Houses

These financial intermediaries originated in Britain (UK), and had never existed in other countries. They were so popular in the 19th Century when bills of exchange were frequently used, and their role was to discount bills of exchange, and act as a buffer (shock absorber) between the Bank of England and the clearing banks. They also acted as money market intermediaries by channeling banks' excess short-term funds to institutional borrowers such as: Central government, local authorities, companies, and banks.

Private Equity Investment

Unlike stocks and bonds that are sold to the public and are subject to oversight by the CMA, and whose dealings are managed by brokers and dealers in these publicly held securities; private equity investments are an alternative to public equity investing. With private equity investing, instead of raising capital by selling securities to the public, a limited partnership is formed that raises money from a small number of high net-worth investors; and within the wide universe of private equity sectors, such as: the venture capital funds and capital buyouts. In the real financial world, firms actively operate in both the above areas, and among the prominent players in the private equity industry are: Fanisi capital Ltd; Mara launch-pad Ltd; Assent Capital Ltd; and Genesis Kenya Ltd, etc

Venture capital firms provide the funds a start-up company needs to get established despite the absence of concrete financial soundness data and requisite cash flows that conventional sources of finance like commercial banks would require so as to fund and develop an innovator's brilliant business idea. This is normally called money supplied to young and start-up firms that can't sell stock to the public through investment bankers because the firms and their products are so new and have not yet proven that they can be successful. It is worth to noting that equity interests in these firms are very illiquid and the investment horizons are long-term, at least five years to a decade, which requires investors with a long-term perspective towards investing

Originally, true venture capitalism begun in the USA in the 1940s by the American Research and Development (ARD); though most venture capital funding during the 1950s and 1960s was for the development of real estate and oil fields. The late 1960s, witnessed a shift toward financing technology start-ups; and still high technology remains the dominant area for venture capitalism despite the fact that the source of venture capital funding has shifted from wealthy individuals to pension funds and corporations. Many a firms consequently have benefitted from venture capitalism, such as: Apple Computer, Starbucks, Netscape, Cisco Systems, Genentech, Staples, Microsoft, and Sun Microsystems.

The venture capital industry is still young in Uganda, compared to that of Kenya that even funded the first ever mobile money technology in the whole world under the M-pesa product; this has been so successful that many economies and telecommunication firms are replicating this product with their brands. Uganda has, among other, firms that are active in venture capitalism: Fanisi capital Ltd; Mara launch-pad Ltd; Assent Capital Ltd; and Genesis Kenya Ltd, etc.

Asset/fund Managers

These are intermediaries that are authorized/ mandated to manage pension resources of savers; and they are licensed by both the CMA and the URBRA given the nature of operations and the products they have. By the end of 2013, there were 9 (nine) licensed fund management companies in Uganda: NSSF-Uganda, Insurance Company of East Africa (ICEA), UAP Financial Services, Jubilee Insurance, Genesis Kenya Investments, African Alliance Uganda Ltd, Stanlib Uganda Ltd, Pine Bridge Investments, Pearl Capital Partners (PCP).

Chapter 7

COLLECTIVE INVESTMENT VEHICLES (C.I.V)

These are financial intermediaries that pool funds from individual investors (households) and invest them in a wide portfolio of securities/assets. Each investor has a claim to the portfolio established by the C.I.V in proportion to the amount invested; it is a mechanism for small holders to team up so as to enjoy economies of collective strategies, simply put, benefits of large scale investing. These are achieved through the following roles that C.I.Vs play: fund administration which is diversification of funds by investing in different assets; professional management thanks to their full time staff of security analysts and portfolio managers; and lower transaction costs due to large blocks of securities.

These investment vehicles are organized in such a way that investors either buy units or shares of ownership into these vehicles; and the value of each share/unit is called "Net Asset Value" (NAV). This equals assets minus liabilities expressed on a per share basis:

$$NAV = \frac{UGX\ 180\ Million - UGX\ 10\ Million}{10\ Million\ Shares} = UGX..... per\ Share$$

i) Types of Collective Investment Vehicles (CIVs)
Unit Trust Funds

These are pools of money invested in a portfolio that is fixed for the life of the fund; and its formation is done by a brokerage firm (Sponsor) which buys a portfolio of securities that are deposited into a trust. The sponsor then sells to the public units/shares in the trust referred to as "Redeemable trust certificates". All income and payment of principal from the portfolio are paid out by the funds trustees to the unit/share holders. Most unit trusts hold long-term fixed-income corporate and government securities, equities, real property in Uganda and EAC region, but also off-shore investments, and expire at their maturity; thus, there is little active management of such funds since the portfolio composition is fixed. Investors who wish to liquidate their units may sell them back to the trustees for the net asset value. Unit trust funds is the only collective investment vehicle that is operational in Uganda's investment industry at the time, though plans are underway also to introduce the real estate investment trusts so as both to boost the real estate industry but also enjoy the enormous benefits in the housing sector.

The UAP Financial services, one of the providers of unit trust funds revealed that its money market fund closed the first week of September 2015 with a daily yield of 12.27 % per annum (p.a) while the fund's benchmark (the 91 day T-bill) was priced with a net yield of 13. 43 % p.a on the yield curve. The UAP Umbrella fund had a daily yield of 14.44 % p.a while the UAP balanced fund closed with a bid price of UGX 1,288.46 representing a return of 12.39 % ytd (equivalent to an annualized net return of 17.33 %)

Commingled Funds

Commingled funds are partnerships of investors that pool their funds. The management firm that organizes the partnership, for example, a bank or insurance company, manages the funds for a fee. Typical partners in a commingled fund might be trusts or retirement benefit schemes with portfolios much larger than those of most individual investors, but still too small to warrant managing on a separate basis.

Commingled funds are similar in form to open-end unit trust funds. Instead of shares, though, the fund offers "units", which are bought and sold at net asset value. A financial intermediary may offer an array of different commingled funds, eg, a money market fund, a bond fund, and a common stock fund.

Investment Trusts

These are similar to unit trusts, but the difference is that investment trusts raise debt finance, which unit trusts do not do. They are also pooled investment vehicles which mobilize their resources through selling shares to institutions and individuals. They then channel investors' funds into a wide portfolio of long-term financial assets in Uganda and EAC region such as: equities, corporate and government debt securities, real property, and such off-shore investments.

There are two types of managed C.I.Vs: closed-ended funds and open-ended funds; of which the fund's board of directors/ trustees (that is elected by shareholders) hires an investment management company to manage the portfolio for an annual fee that doesn't exceed 1.5% of the assets/funds.

Real Estate Investment Trusts (REITs)

These are similar to a closed-end fund; and they invest in real estate or loans secured by real estate. Besides issuing shares, they raise capital by borrowing from banks and issuing bonds or mortgages. Most of them are highly leveraged, with a typical debt ratio of 70%.

There are two principal kinds of REITs: *Equity trusts* which invest in real estate directly, whereas *mortgage trusts* invest primarily in mortgage and construction loans. REITs generally are established by banks, insurance companies, or mortgage companies, which then serve as investment managers to earn a fee.

Endowment Funds

These are permanent assets such as money, securities, or properties that are invested to earn income that is used to support an organization's activities for a variety of reasons as per the organization. An endowment is a portfolio of assets donated to a nonprofit institution to aid in its support, and in their medieval origins, endowments consisted of farmland donated to churches, which would earn rental income from the land's tenant farmers. In modern times, endowment assets are held in financial instruments, which may include real estate investments too and in an invested portfolio, the modern endowment can realize capital appreciation as well as current income.

Endowments are legal entities that have been funded for the expressed purpose of *permanently* funding the endowment's institutional sponsor (i.e., beneficiary). The intent is to preserve asset principal value in perpetuity and to use the income generated for budgetary support of specific activities of institutions such as: universities, hospitals, museums, and charitable. An endowment fund, is created when Board of Trustee or University Council or Donor, specify that a gift is to be invested and only the income earned from the gift investment, may be spent for a specific purpose. The gift amount is referred to as the *principal* or *corpus.* It is held in a fund that is managed by the Finance Department or Development Department of the organization or delegated to a Fund Investment Management Company. Endowment fund administration is well represented in the Laws of Uganda from the Trusts Act of 1950s during the colonial times.

There are two types of endowment funds:

True Endowment Fund

True Endowment Fund is defined as a fund which the donor, stipulates that, the corpus must be held inviolate, in perpetuity and invested to generate income to be spent for a specific purpose. This type of endowment fund is strictly tied to the committed purpose as stipulated in some form of establishment agreement.

Quasi Endowment Fund

Quasi endowment funds, are funds designated by the governing Board of an institution or Board of Trustees for that purpose, are called Quasi Endowment funds. The funds are also invested for the purpose of generating income for a given purpose. Such funds are internally designated and allocated as endowment by the Board of Governors or Trustees or Council. But due to this nature of allocation, the governing Board may decide to spend the funds at any time. Sometimes donors may allow the corpus of their endowment fund to be spent. When this happens, it acquires the category of a quasi endowment fund. To spend the principal of a quasi endowment fund requires Board of Trustee approval or donor authorization in case of a quasi endowment fund.

Endowment Funds are not just theoretical financial concepts, but are practical instruments used all over the world to fund worthy causes in the social, economic and political spheres. Examples where endowment fund models are used include:

- Nobel Prize Awards
- Education funding e.g. Ford Foundation, Aga Khan Foundation

- University Administration: ex. Earth University in Costa Rica, Yale University, Makerere University, Uganda Christian University, Islamic University in Uganda
- Co-operative Colleges – UK, USA & Australia
- Conservation Trusts in Wildlife & Environmental sustainability eg Mugahinga
- Hospitals like Mengo Hospital

Objectives of Endowment funds:

The main objective of an Endowment fund is, to provide and guarantee greater financial sustainability and autonomy in all institutional programs.

Specific Objectives

- Sustainability: to enhance the ability to plan for the long-term and to meet the future needs of the institutions in particular: infrastructure development, research & publication, business development, community service, etc.
- Autonomy: to increase an institution's independence from funding trends outside its control.
- Leveraging: to be used by the institution as a basis for acquiring additional funding from various organizations in the field of the organization's operations.

Sources of Funding for Endowments

There are multiple places where organizations can turn in order to raise funds for an endowment. At the local level, there is potential for raising endowment funds from:

- Students & Alumni
- Private sector
- Wealthy individuals

- Government/ public sources

- General public

- Earned income

- Staff & Faculty

- University Council

- At the international level, endowment funding can come from:

- Bilateral/Multilateral overseas development assistance

- International Foundations in Australia, North America or Europe

- NGOs from Australia, North America, or Europe

- Multinational corporations

- Wealthy individuals

Hedge Funds

Like unit trust funds, hedge funds are vehicles that allow private investors to pool assets to be invested by a fund manager. Unlike unit trust funds, conversely, hedge funds are commonly structured as private partnerships and thus subject to only minimal regulations in economies where they operate (but not yet in Uganda). They typically are open only to wealthy or institutional investors. Many require investors to agree to initial *lock-ups*, that is, periods as long as several years in which investments cannot be withdrawn. These periods allow hedge funds to invest in illiquid assets without worrying about meeting demands for redemption of funds. Moreover, because hedge funds are only lightly regulated, their managers can pursue investment strategies involving, for example, heavy use of derivatives, short sales, and leverage; such strategies typically are not open to mutual fund managers.

Hedge funds by design are empowered to invest in a wide range of investments, with various funds focusing on derivatives, distressed firms, currency speculation, convertible bonds, emerging markets, merger arbitrage, and so on. Other funds may jump from one asset class to another as perceived investment opportunities shift.

i)   How funds are sold to the public

Most of these funds have an underwriter that has exclusive rights to distribute shares to investors. They are generally marketed to the public either directly by the fund underwriter or indirectly through brokers acting on behalf of the underwriters. This could be done through: mails; offices of the fund; over the phone; over the internet; on financial pages of local newspapers; through the sales force.

ii)   Role/ Benefits of CIVs in the Financial System

- Diversification of Risk: investors can secure a much wider diversification of risk, because these funds usually invest in different investments since studies have proved that the greater the diversification of a portfolio, the lower the risk in relation to the return

- Access to a variety of financial assets: by investing a small sum (either in a lump sum or on a regular saving basis), an investor through the CIVs can achieve a personal portfolio spread over a diversity of financial assets.

- Lower Transaction Costs: by investing in CIVs, investors incur lower costs than if they were to buy and sell a portfolio of individual securities directly. This is because transaction costs are generally inversely related to the size of the transaction, and investors benefit from the fund manager's ability to deal in larger quantities of shares at lower average dealing costs. Besides, fund managers can also allocate portfolios more efficiently than can individual investors.

- Professional Management: due to the complexity of analyzing information regarding individual securities, most individuals do not have the professional skills to manage their own investments. CIVs provide full time professional management in a direct and simple form and this is especially important where market information is not widely available.

- Investor Protection: CIVs have succeeded in developed markets due to an effective legal and regulatory framework. People need to have confidence that their money is protected from fraud, theft and other abuses. The CMA Act, the URBRA Act, the CIS Act, among other regulations provides the desired regulatory framework that will protect investors.

Chapter 8

CENTRAL BANKING

"Ensuring price and financial stability are critical objectives of modern Central Banks."

i) Background information about the Bank of Uganda

Glance

Central banks are the most important players in financial markets world over since they are the custodians of the financial system soundness, the monetary authorities charged with the management of the credit control mechanisms, commonly referred to as the *monetary policy*. Their actions significantly affect not only: interest rates structures, the availability of credit, the money supply, and their impact on financial markets and other macroeconomic fundamentals; but also personal finance, corporate finance and public finance. Given the fundamental role, it is only prudent for us as finance students and practitioners to understand the Bank of Uganda (the domestic Central Bank), its role as the custodian of the financial system, and its prudential management of the sovereign assets (basically the foreign exchange reserves) and its contribution not only to macroeconomic stability but to external-economy vulnerability management.

BANK OF UGANDA

It was established in 1966 after the abolition of the East Africa Currency Board, which used to serve as the monetary authority (defacto Central Bank) for the following countries: Uganda, Tanganyika, Ethiopia, Eriteria, Somaliland, Zanzibar, and Kenya. It was established in 1919 to ensure prompt and timely convertibility of E.A shilling into UK pound sterling, and vice versa at a fixed rate but later from 1962, it also acted as a clearing agent for commercial banks. This was abolished due to huge imbalances in the level of economic development of the member states, which rendered its work pretty difficult to treat them equally, but also from a public financial management perspective of each state, the challenge was compounded by the differences in natural resources endowment of these economies. This necessitated the establishment of a Central Bank in each member state so as to foster both economic stability and financial soundness of each country. Bank of Uganda was consequently set up by the Bank of Uganda Act 1966 which empowers it to foster macroeconomic stability and financial system soundness in Uganda.

B.O.U Annual Report (2013) informs that the Constitution of the Republic of Uganda 1995 grants Bank of Uganda the mandate as the central bank of Uganda; and the Bank of Uganda Act (Cap 51) vests the authority of the Bank in the Board of Directors who should conduct its affairs with prudence, and accountability by ensuring the Bank's compliance with the law and business ethics. Both the Bank's Board of Directors and the management wing are headed by the Governor (currently Prof. Emmanuel Tumusiime-Mutebile); and he is deputized by Dr. Louis Kasekende.

Its mission is "To foster price stability and a sound financial system"; and envisions "To be a centre of excellence in upholding macroeconomic stability". B.O.U holds as its core values "accountability, commitment, ethical behavior, excellence, transparency, and team work"; and its strategic themes/ pillars of excellence are "operational excellence, customer focus, strategic partnerships, and leadership".

ii) Functions as a Custodian & Controller of the Financial System *(Roles Played by B.O.U in Development of Uganda)*

The following roles are outlined by the Bank of Uganda Act of 1966, and they are aimed at ensuring the financial soundness of the economy through its macroeconomic policies, and at the same time operate on a commercial basis by offering services to commercial banks. Among others, these are:

- Currency Issuing & Management of Money supply; this is BOU's prime role, which actually requires the highest degree of efficiency and trust, since it has the monopoly of issuing currency to match the resources accumulated by various sectors in the economy since the variables are highly correlated for macroeconomic stability. The supply of money should neither be too much nor too little so as to promote economic growth. Money issued by BOU is termed as legal tender, both in form of notes and coins, and it is empowered to settle debts. On the contrary, BOU keeps some resources to back the Uganda shilling but also to justify any new currency issuing in case the need arises, and these include: gold; silver; Special Drawing Rights (SDRs); foreign exchange reserves in currencies eg U.S dollars, Euros, Pound Sterling, Canadian dollars. Besides the above, the fiduciary issue of currency is backed by factors such as: government expenditures; balance of payment position; credit and foreign exchange transactions.

- Banker to the Government: well as commercial banks are bankers to the general public, BOU is a banker to the government of Uganda in the following ways: transacts/ pays for the government; custodian/ receiver of government's finance in form of taxes &foreign aid; repayment of foreign loans; lender/ financier to government projects for short & long term basis.

- Advisor to the Government: this is in areas such as; economic policies, resource mobilisation (raising finance), management of private sector from financial management perspective (which project either the State or private sector should finance), management of inflation & value of the shilling.

- Manager of Public Debt: this is finance raised from citizens through the sale of government securities (treasury: bills, notes, and bonds) so as to finance different activities. BOU does this by: receiving the finance; advising on interest rates, and the conditions for the sale of those securities.

- Banker to Commercial banks: BOU does this role through roles such as: acting as a clearing house for receipts (inter-bank clearing facility); sole custodian of reserves & deposits from commercial banks' reserve ratio; short-term lending to commercial banks for liquidity problems; acts as arbitrator in disputes among commercial banks; authorised to sell or discount promissory notes & bills of exchange for commercial banks; financial controller/ inspection of commercial banks' activities.

- Creator of Financial Institutions: BOU is charged with the responsibility of establishing a wide range of financial services given the needs of the financial system. This entails the development of financial markets, basically capital markets for long-term financing towards economic development, but also the money markets and possibly the derivative markets for a sound financial system.

- Controller of Foreign exchange: this is the finance that an economy earns through the sale of goods and services to foreign economies, and it is in form of foreign currencies such as; Euros, Dollars, Pound sterling, Yen, Francs, Yuan, etc. The management of foreign exchange is aimed at fostering Balance of Payment (B.O.P) surplus ie favourable balance between inflows from abroad (receipts) and outflows abroad (payments); BOU will allow as little foreign exchange to leave the country so as to manage the macroeconomic stability of Uganda but also to hedge the economy against external vulnerability from the global financial system. Therefore, BOU is officially the sole seller of foreign currencies in Uganda and commercial banks can do this only with the approval of BOU, and Bureaux de Change are only transact on behalf of BOU that is why they are obliged to submit reports to BOU in a bid to compile statistics regarding the B.O.P position of the country but also the data is used in international trade decision-making process.

- Financial Manager to Commercial banks: banks are required by law to follow the guidance of BOU in their activities and operations, according to Financial Institutions Act & BOU Act. This could be in areas such as: investment areas for banks according to State's development plans; submission of periodic reports for statistics to judge the financial soundness of the economy; corporate financial planning; advice in the process of credit creation; advice on expansion of bank branches.

- Lender of the last resort: despite its role as the custodian and regulator of the financial system, BOU can also act as lender of the last resort in the following scenarios: under high inflationary situations that could occasion a banking crisis; when commercial banks fail to raise requisite capital for huge investments due to liquidity constraints.

iii) B.O.U & Financial Stability

"Ensuring financial stability is a collaborative effort of all regulators of the financial system: MoFPED, B.O.U, CMA, URBRA, URA, IRA-Ug, UCC (Uganda Communications Commission)."

Financial stability is the resilience of the financial system to unanticipated adverse shocks while enabling the continuing functioning of the financial system intermediation process. A stable financial system contributes to broader economic growth and rising living standards. The financial system performs one of the most important functions in the welfare of citizens by supporting the ability of households and firms to hold and transfer financial assets with confidence. B.O.U is committed to promoting the economic and financial welfare of Ugandans by actively overseeing a stable and sound financial system through the provision of critical services such as: liquidity & lender-of-last-resort facilities; overseeing key foreign and domestic clearing & settlement systems; conducting & publishing analyses and research; collaborating with various domestic & international policy-making bodies so as to develop policy.

iv) B.O.U's Prudential Management of the Foreign Exchange Reserves

"Effective communication of macro-prudential policy is essential in ensuring the resilience of the financial system."

B.O.U is guided by three cardinal objectives in sovereign assets (foreign reserves) management, which are chronologically followed in importance for macroeconomic vitality. These objectives are: safety of the funds (reserves); liquidity requirements of the financial system; and reasonable and consistent returns from investments, and these objectives influence, and are also influenced by both the investment philosophy of the economy and the development agenda of the country.

Objective 1: Safety of the assets (reserves)

B.O.U is the custodian not only of the sovereign assets (national wealth) but also of the Ugandan financial system, whose mission is to "foster price stability and a sound financial system" (B.O.U Annual Report, 2011). The fact that Uganda is among the struggling Frontier market economies, the only option it has is being a very conservative investor given the volatility of the economy and the relatively low volumes of current assets under management (foreign exchange reserves). B.O.U is guided by the old investment adage, "Better be sure but not sorry", as it manages the sovereign assets in volatile global financial markets.

Given both its custodial role and being a conservative investor, B.O.U's reserve portfolio is divided into two portions: the internally & externally managed portfolios. The internally managed portfolio is mainly invested on short term (0-1 year) money market instruments, which are aimed at boosting and managing the level of economic activities in the country through: employment creation, equitable distribution of national income, boosting the GDP. The investment horizon is rather short (0-1 year) due to low absorptive capacity but majorly safety of the assets since this time period is quite predictable, but also the investment is purely in fixed-income securities of high growth companies with sound governance systems within the country. As at June 30, 2013, the internally managed portfolio amounted to US$ 1,864 B; this is according to strategic benchmarks by B.O.U (B.O.U Annual Report, 2013).

Besides, externally managed portfolio was mainly invested in longer term (1-5 years) fixed income instruments, and it stood at US$ 1,036 B. This was prudently done with the help of internationally reputable fund managers because B.O.U doesn't have the infrastructure and capacity to do active investment management due to huge assets under management, and heavy time resources required in investment research. JP Morgan, Strategic Fixed Income, and Goldman Sachs, and others were allocated the external portfolio to be invested in very stable economies of the Great 7 (G-7) for external-economy risk management.

Due to prioritizing the safety of the assets, B.O.U's strategic asset allocation doesn't allow for investment in other asset classes regardless of their returns, and apparent safety and liquidity such as: listed equity; private equity; real property; real estate; debt instruments from both corporations and central banks (governments) which are not in the G-7 economic zone. This is because these are not safe and some are highly illiquid which would cost not only the sovereign assets but the soundness of the financial system, and facilitate its failure to eradicate extreme poverty and hunger. The safety requirement doesn't permit investments in East African Community economies due to high volatility in these economies. It also requires issuers to be of a certain credit quality, backed by asset liability structures as core determinants: if Uganda has a liability in dollars, the B.O.U will buy asset denominated in dollars (as a currency).

Finally, though the sovereign assets have grown to a tune of US$ 2.93 B as at end June 2013 representing 4.1 months of import cover, these assets under management are way below some of the smallest hedge funds in the U.S. Besides, B.O.U is very conservative due to fear of losing national wealth like the Colombian experience where Central bank tried to be an aggressive investor to the point of venturing in other asset classes like equity and more currencies but it lost 30% of its sovereign assets in 1990s; the governor and minister resigned, and they were later imprisoned.

Objective 2: Liquidity requirements of the financial system

B.O.U is the banker to the government of Uganda: due to both the short-term and long-term obligations of the State such as debt management, public expenditure, and investments which are recurrent and some long-term in nature; and needs permanent cash flows, liquidity management is key in sovereign asset management. B.O.U was managing an internal portfolio of US$ 1,864 B which it invests in highly liquid financial assets of financially sound firms with: good governance systems; capacity to contribute to GDP; and employment creation in the country. Besides, the externally managed portfolio is also invested in highly liquid fixed-income securities in the strongest and safest G-7 economies such as: USA, UK, Germany, France, Canada, Australia, and Japan; due to their solid and expertise in operations. This is done in treasury bills, bonds and deposits with governments such as USA and other G-7s; deposits in liquid funds with Multi-lateral institutions such as the World Bank, Bank of International Settlements, and others; corporate bonds from highly rated corporate issuers by international standards (AAA rating) such as General Motors, Ford, among others. Besides, investment is basically done in foreign sound currencies like US dollar, Great Britain Pound sterling, Euro, and recently added Canadian dollar since international assets tend to perform better than domestic assets when currency hedged.

As a liquidity management system, B.O.U manages sovereign assets in tranches such as: liquidity tranche for in-house highly liquid assets in instruments like treasury bills and bonds; emergency tranche for in-house government expenditures; and investment tranche through both in-house and external companies. B.O.U Annual Report (2011) informs that by end-June 2011, US$77.91 million held in the liquidity tranche was managed in the form of repurchase agreements, overnight deposits and current account balances; US$50 million was held in the emergency tranche in the form of deposits and Treasury bills of up to 3 months; and the investment tranche had US$1,174.96 million held in bank deposits, Treasury bills, the

World Bank Central Bank Facility (CBF), Equity at Afri-Exim Bank and US Treasury bonds under the Reserves Advisory and Management Programme (RAMP).

B.O.U further manages public debt by using simulation software (program) and the optimizer tool that guides in crucial public financial management variables such as: short-term obligations; imports requirements; intervention in foreign exchange markets; risk budget analysis for decisions on efficient portfolios. Given the macro-prudential liquidity management, Uganda has had a fairly stable economic growth averaging 6% per annum (a result of good macroeconomic policies); it was the 14th largest economy in Africa; per capita incomes at purchasing power stood at US$1400 by the end of 2011, and growing at an annual average of 4.2% over the last decade.

Objective 3: Reasonable and Consistent Returns

Despite the previous two objectives being of supreme importance, B.O.U is equally mandated to grow the sovereign assets but with reasonable and consistent returns (national wealth creation) vis-a-vis sound macroeconomic stability. In effect, though the sovereign asset preservation objective takes precedent and significantly affects the strategic asset allocation, reserves managers have found themselves seeking instruments with higher yields in an effort to enhance returns. This objective explains why B.O.U invests its assets in only: G-7 economies; highly-rated central and commercial banks' fixed-income instruments in those economies; fixed-income securities from AAA-rated corporate issuers. Besides, B.O.U uses international asset managers like JP Morgan which are highly experienced in global financial markets but it also gives them performance benchmarks, and advises on specific currencies as an asset class, and investments are basically in US and Euro denominated bonds.

By end-June 2013, Uganda's stock of foreign assets amounted to US$ 4,472.8 M, up from US$ 4,142.5 M at end June 2012; and reserve assets dominated the foreign assets contributing 65.5% of the total; total reserve position went up by 10.8% from US$ 2,643.8 M at end June 2012 to US$ 2,929.3 M at end June 2013. Besides, other investments in the form of currencies and deposits abroad accounted for 34.2% total assets, amounting to US$ 1,526 M at end June 2013; and during 2012/ 13, BOU's foreign exchange reserves, excluding valuation changes increased by about US$ 242.2 M, amounting to US$ 2.93 B as at end June 2013 representing 4.1 months of import cover (BOU Annual Report 2013; interviews). These financials are rather good indicators of prudent sovereign asset management by B.O.U's department of Financial Markets.

Levy-Yeyati (2008), in their study on the trade-off between cost of holding reserves and their potential benefits, argue that foreign reserves act as implicit collateral against borrowing: a high level of reserves lowers the risk premium associated with financial vulnerabilities of emerging and frontier market economies. This signifies that a relatively aggressive investment philosophy that has led to the current reasonable and consistent returns in sovereign assets responds to: dealing comprehensively with the debt problems of developing countries through national and international measures in order to make debt sustainable in the long-term.

Critical Analysis of B.O.U

It is the regulator of the financial and monetary system of the country, which is aimed at protecting the economy from both domestic and external shocks so as to achieve the national macroeconomic objectives.

It has a major resource mobilisation role which is aimed at availing financial and other forms of resource to the government to fund its annual budgets but also perspective plans in a bid to attain economic development.

The Central bank serves a critical role of lender of the last resort in the financial system for financial institutions basically banks so as to facilitate further capital formation and boost economic growth.

Bank of Uganda also plays an interventionist role in the financial system whereby, for matter of financial system soundness and macroeconomic stability, it intervene at time in the market forces that rule in the financial markets so as to influence and guide all financial players and intermediaries towards the government's desired economic objectives and outcomes. This is done the operations of the monetary policy instruments that affects most financial markets.

i) Limitations of BOU as Custodian of Financial System

As already explained, B.O.U, the custodian of the financial system works through fiscal and monetary policy instruments to foster prudent macroeconomic management and financial soundness in Uganda. On the contrary, these policy instruments have limitations, and among others these are:

- Large informal financial system whereby billions of money (large sums of money) are kept at home or hoarded by various people for various reasons eg fear of high taxation, negative attitude towards & ignorance about banking services, but not kept in banks.

- Lack of cooperation between commercial banks and BOU, whereby banks are not transparent enough to disclosure all their transactions which hinder BOU from controlling money supply.

- Some policy instruments like selective credit control which directs banks to specific areas where to give credit facilities like agriculture or Karamoja region may not be of interest to banks due to both high risks and low returns; hence, frustrating BOU's initiatives.

- Most banks don't get their credit/ finance from BOU, and as such increases in bank rates may not affect the rates charged commercial banks. Besides, some banks charge different rates from those approved by BOU, which frustrates all the initiatives by the Central bank.

- BOU has currently failed to synchronise/ streamline interest rates in financial markets: market rates don't change with Central bank rate (CBR). It is evident that the success of CBR depends on the extent to which other financial markets' rates change along with the CBR since the theory of bank rate policy presume that other rates of interest/ prices prevailing in financial markets change in the direction of the change in the bank rate. The failure of BOU to satisfy this critical condition has partly catalysed its ineffectiveness in credit control measures.

- BOU's custodianship role of Ugandan financial system is complicated by the existence of a big number of non-bank financial intermediaries which are not directly under the control of the monetary authority yet they do a lot of funds mobilisation and financing activities basically in the capital markets.

- Undeveloped financial markets: since money and capital markets in Uganda are rather undeveloped, with very few financial assets, and only traded by a few knowledgeable individuals renders BOU's initiatives of controlling the financial system fruitless.

- High liquidity preference by Ugandan: due to the alarming levels of financial illiteracy and also dubious dealings, majority of banks and individuals in Uganda enjoy keeping their money with themselves and so, they can't be influenced by BOU's monetary policies. They end up disorganising the commodities markets and consequently lead to macroeconomic disequilibria in Uganda.

- Uganda's banking sector is over-saturated by foreign banks since most of the high performing banks are foreign owned; this can render BOU's monetary policy ineffective by either selling foreign assets or drawing money from their head offices even when BOU has put in place a tight monetary policy.

- Besides, the success of BOU's monetary policy instruments like bank rate is greatly dependent not only on the elasticity of interest rates, but that of wages, costs and prices. This implies that when BOU changes its CBR; wages, costs and prices should automatically adjust themselves either to lower or higher levels depending on the CBR. On the contrary, given the inelastic (and of the CBR insensitive) wages and prices regardless of either inflationary or deflationary situations, the Central bank can't effectively act as the custodian of the Ugandan financial system.

Chapter 9

OTHER REGULATORS OF THE FINANCIAL SYSTEM

"A well-regulated financial sector builds confidence among citizens to freely use financial services."

i) Authorities (CMA; USE; URA; IRA; URBRA)

Capital Markets Authority

It is a semi autonomous body responsible for promoting, developing and regulating the capital markets industry in Uganda, with the overall objectives of investor protection and market efficiency. The capital markets industry in Uganda came into being in 1996 with the enactment of the Capital Markets Authority (CMA) Act Cap 84. The CMA Act established the Capital Markets Authority which paved the way for the formation of the Uganda Securities Exchange (USE) in 1997. At the end of December 2012, CMA had licensed 22 market players: 8 Broker/Dealers; 6 Fund managers; and 8 Investment Advisors.

Since inception, the capital markets in Uganda have witnessed the listing of 14 (equities) companies: 8 cross-listings from the Nairobi Securities Exchange; and 8 domestic listings. Besides, to date 9 corporate bonds valued at UGX 149 billion (US $ 64.04 million) have been issued and listed on the USE, of which four of these bonds have been redeemed. The government of Uganda also launched a government bond program in 2004 and currently 36 Government Bonds are listed at the USE.

USE had 40,000 investors; of which 8,920 investors had by December 2012 demobilized their certificates and opened Central Securities Depository (SCD) accounts.

CMA has a number of functions, these include;

- The development of all aspects of the capital markets with particular emphasis on the removal of impediments to, and the creation of incentives for longer term investments in productive enterprises.

- The creation, maintenance and regulation, through implementation of a system in which the market participants are self regulatory to the maximum practicable extent of a market in which securities can be issued and traded in an orderly, fair and efficient manner.

- The protection of investors' interests and investments.

- The operation of an investor compensation fund that would hedge against foul play arising from unprofessional conduct of the market players.

- In its role as a regulator, the CMA oversees the activities of the Uganda Securities Exchange (USE), licensed intermediaries such as broker/dealers and investment advisors. CMA also regulates the operation of Collective Investment Schemes.

- Regulating the business in stock exchanges and any other securities markets

- Registering and regulating the working of stock brokers, sub–brokers etc.

- Promoting and regulating self-regulatory organizations

- Prohibiting fraudulent and unfair trade practices

- Calling for information from, undertaking inspection, conducting inquiries and audits of the stock exchanges, intermediaries, self

– regulatory organizations, unit trust funds and other persons associated with the securities market.

CMA Vs USE

Capital Markets Authority (CMA) is the regulatory body that oversees the capital markets industry in Uganda, whereas the Uganda Securities Exchange (USE) is the actual market where capital markets products, namely, bonds, shares, are traded, and the USE is licensed and regulated by the CMA.

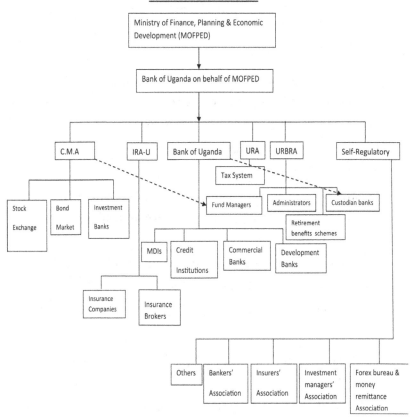

REGULATORY ENVIRONMENT
OF THE FINANCIAL SYSTEM

Capital Markets industry Products

There are various products available in the global capital markets industry depending on the level of development and the financial system depth in economies. On the contrary, Uganda's capital markets industry currently has three major products in which one can trade; shares; collective investment schemes; and government and corporate bonds.

Uganda Retirement Benefits Regulatory Authority (URBRA)

September 2011 saw the URBRA Act being accented to by His Excellency the President and thereafter published in the gazette; the URBRA Act intends;

- To establish an independent Authority to regulate the establishment, management and operations of the retirement benefits schemes in Uganda, in both the public and the private sector

- To supervise institutions which provide retirement benefits products and services

- To protect the interests of members and beneficiaries of retirement benefit schemes by promoting governance principles, transparency and accountability

- To establish a fund into which shall be paid all moneys for defraying the expenses of the Uganda Retirement Benefits Authority

- To promote the development of retirement benefits sector in Uganda

- To provide for the licensing of custodians, trustees, administrators and fund managers

- To provide for the appointment of inspectors and interim administrators

The Ministry of Finance has since commenced on the process of fully establishing the URBRA so as to render it fully operational by procuring offices for the authority and appointing full time staff to run this regulatory body. The authority has since then embarked on its task of licensing and publishing official players in that industry such as: custodians (banks), the retirement benefit schemes (RBS), fund administrators, fund managers, and trustees for the RBS.

Uganda Securities Exchange (USE)

The USE is the only Stock Exchange in Uganda since it officially commenced its operations in 1998; though information has it that there is yet another electronic stock exchange that will soon begin its operations within the fiscal year of 2015/2016.

The securities market scope covers a wide range of Market Players who include:

- Broker/dealers (must have a license to trade on the USE floor).

- Investment Advisors (also licensed by USE as either corporate or individuals to give advisory).

- Collective Investment Schemes (these pool the funds of their clients for investment purposes).

- Registrars.

- The Investing public.

The basic function of USE is to provide a platform for raising funds for investment in long-term assets. While this is extremely important as the engine through which the stock exchange is driven, there are other important functions of the USE which include:

- Mobilization of savings from the general public.

- Creation of liquidity not only on the stock market but also optimal liquidity in the financial system.

- Enhancement of the growth of related financial services sectors.

- Facilitation of equity financing as opposed to debt financing.

Insurance Regulatory Authority (IRAU)

The insurance industry saw a change in the name of the regulator from the Uganda

Insurance Commission (UIC) to now the "Insurance Regulatory Authority of Uganda" (IRAU).

This followed the gazette of the Insurance Amendment Act, which provided for this change mainly to help the public distinguish between an Insurance regulator and player since the public was confusing it to be one of the players in the insurance industry, which led to their failure to take their complaints to the regulator. The IRAU ensures effective administration, supervision, regulation and control of the Insurance industry in Uganda.

By April 2012, the Commission had licensed 22 insurance companies and 30 Insurance Brokers following their compliance with the requirements of the Act. The market was majorly dominated by non-life insurance services accounting for over 90% of the insurance business in Uganda. Although there are positive trends towards the development of the insurance industry at large, the insurance penetration is still low in Uganda compared to Kenya and Tanzania with less than 1% of GDP. Below is a list of insurance companies in Uganda regulated by the Insurance Regulatory Authority of Uganda as of January 2015:

Non-Life Insurance Companies

1. AIG Uganda Limited
2. Alliance Africa General Insurance Limited
3. Britam Insurance Uganda Limited
4. CIC General Insurance Uganda Limited
5. East African Underwriters Limited
6. GoldStar Life Assurance Company Limited
7. NIC General Insurance Company Limited
8. Statewide Insurance Company Limited
9. The Jubilee Insurance Company of Uganda
10. TransAfrica Assurance Limited
11. UAP Insurance Uganda Limited

Life Insurance Companies

1. GoldStar Life Assurance Company Limited
2. The Jubilee Life Insurance Company of Uganda
3. Liberty Life Assurance Company Limited
4. NIC Life Assurance Company Limited
5. Sanlam Life Insurance Company Limited
6. UAP Life Assurance Uganda Limited

Uganda Revenue Authority (URA)

This is a semi-autonomous body that is charged with administering/implementing the tax laws on behalf of the Minister of Finance after the tax bills have been passed by the Parliament and later assented by the President into laws/ Act. URA was established by an Act of Parliament in a bid to improve the tax administration in the country; it is under the Ministry of Finance (MoFPED) whereby it assesses and collects taxes from the public on the behalf of the Ministry. It is guided by the following legislations:

- Value Added Tax Act, Cap 349

- Income Tax Act, Cap 340

- Taxes and Duties Act, Cap 348

- Customs and Excise Act, Cap 335

- Stamps Act, Cap 342

- Customs Tarrif Act, Cap 337

- East Africa Community-Customs Management Act (EAC-CMA)

- Among others.

URA performs the following functions as an agency:

- It administers and gives effect to the laws or the specified provisions of the laws specified in the URA statutes through assessing and collecting tax revenues according to the laws.

- It advises the minister on revenue implications, tax administration and aspects of policy changes relating to all taxes referred to in the URA statutes.

- It performs other functions in relation to revenue as the minister may direct it.

ii)   Self-Regulatory Organisations- SROs/ professional bodies (Uganda Bankers' Association; Association of Investment managers; Uganda Insurers' Association; stock brokers; Uganda Forex Bureaux and Money Remittance Association ; capital market registrars; etc

PART 3

FINANCIAL MARKETS

These are markets in which funds are transferred from financial agents (households, businesses, and government) who have a surplus of available funds to financial agents who have a shortage of available funds.

A financial market is the place where financial assets (intangible asset whose value is derived from contractual claim such as bank deposits, bonds, and stocks) are created or transferred. These can be broadly categorized into: money markets, capital markets, derivative markets, foreign exchange markets, mortgage markets, and closely linked the commodities' exchange. The key functions are:

1. Assist in creation and allocation of credit and liquidity.

2. Serve as intermediaries for mobilization of savings.

3. Help achieve balanced economic growth.

4. Offer financial convenience.

Chapter 10

MONEY MARKETS

These are markets for short-term financial instruments that are close substitutes for money; they are highly liquid, easily marketable, and with little chance of loss (they are close to being money, hence the name "money market instruments). These markets (a network of markets that are grouped together for short-term finance) provide quick and reliable transfer of short-term debt instruments maturing in hours to not more than two years is used to finance the needs of customers, business, agriculture and governments. This is a market for short-term finances; funds to be used in business for a period ranging just hours to 2 or 3 years.

In the US and the West, money markets have been active since the early 1800s but have become much more important since 1970, when interest rates rose above historic levels, coupled with a regulated ceiling on the rate that banks could pay for deposits, resulted in a rapid outflow of funds from financial institutions in the late 1970s and early 1980s. This outflow in turn caused many banks and savings and loans to fail. The industry regained its health only after massive changes were made to bank regulations with regard to money market interest rates.

i) Types of money markets

Thus the money markets consist of the following sub-markets:

a) Call and Notice money market:

This is where money is traded for a period ranging from (just hours) one day to 14 days without collateral security.

b) Commercial bills market:

This is where bills of exchange, promissory notes, and invoices are traded, and /or discounted either with a broker or a bank.

c) Commercial paper market:

This is a market where highly rated companies raise short-term working capital requirements through the issuance of commercial papers for prospective buyers who could be individuals or corporate bodies.

d) Treasury bills market:

This is where the central government through the Secretary to the Treasury of Uganda issues short-term government securities which are traded by commercial banks and dealers so as to bail out the liquidity position of the government of Uganda. In the first week of September 2015, the BOU offered 91 day, 182 day and 364 day T-bills for a total of UGX 10 billion, 25 billion and 135 billion respectively. The 91 day and 182 day issues were oversubscribed while the 364 day issue was undersubscribed. The 91 day received bids worth 34 billion and BOU accepted bids worth 24 billion. The 182 day received bids worth 33 billion and BOU accepted bids worth 29 billion. The 364 day on the other hand received bids worth 114 billion and the BOU only accepted a total of 68 billion

e) Inter-bank Term market:

This type of money market is exclusively for commercial and cooperative banks which trade funds for a short period ranging from 14 days up to 90 days without collateral security. According to UAP Financial services, the interbank market (Uganda) was relatively liquid in the first week of September 2015, with the overnight rate remaining below 10% for most of the week. The o/n rate opened the week at 11.27% and hit a low of 6.76% on Wednesday and the 7 day rate averaged 16% over the week.

f) Certificate of Deposits (CD):

This is a market where commercial banks issue such instruments at a discount on face value to prospective buyers (investors); and the discount rate is determined by market environment.

Players in Money Markets

- This finance is issued/ sold by the following organizations: commercial banks; Government; Acceptance & discount houses; merchant banks; companies.

- The following are the buyers of such finance: individuals; companies; institutional investors; Government; financial institutions. Both these categories of players are discussed below:

- Ministry of Finance, Planning and Economic Development trades in this market through selling Uganda's Treasury securities so as to fund the national budget.

- B.O.U is a key player that buys and sells Uganda's Treasury bills, notes and bonds as its critical mechanism of monetary policy.

- Commercial banks also buy Treasury securities; but also sell certificates of deposit, plus short-term loans; they also offer households accounts that invest in money market securities

- Corporations engage in these markets through buying and selling a variety of short-term securities as a part of their cash management system.

- Investment firms such as brokerage companies transact on behalf of their clients in these money markets.

- Finance houses (companies) also engage in money markets through lending funds to their customers (households) for asset-building purposes.

- Insurance companies basically non-life insurance firms trade in such markets so as to maintain the liquidity needed to meet unexpected demands.

- Pension funds are also players who maintain funds in money markets instruments anticipating investment in other capital markets instruments like stock and bonds.

- Households are also participants through the purchase of money market unit trust funds.

- Money market unit trust funds engage in such markets by facilitating small investors to participate in money markets by aggregating their funds to invest in a wide array of money market assets.

Characteristics of such finance

- Securities traded in this market are highly negotiable; they can be easily bought and sold.

- This finance is usually not secured and as such it depends upon the goodwill of the issuer or buyer.

- This finance is short-term and basically used to solve liquidity problems of issuers.

- This finance is usually very expensive; essentially because it is unsecured.

- Trading in this market is not a perfect market situation since the demand for such finance far exceeds its supply, and then the Bank of Uganda intervenes in this market through its central bank rate (CBR), so as to influence the price or interest rates on such finance.

Chapter 11

CAPITAL MARKETS

Globally, capital markets have been so instrumental in fostering economic development not only in developed economies but also in emerging economies; and, the value of the volumes of traded securities (market capitalization) of the capital markets in boosting the GDP (as a percentage of GDP) in various economies cannot be underestimated. Ssejjaaka (2011) argues that emerging stock markets grew by over 430% overall and volumes increased from US $ 4b to US $ 4 trillion between 1980 and 2000 and it can be noted that investment opportunities in Sub-Saharan Africa have been expanding greatly with over 522 firms listing on stock exchanges by end of 2007. Kenya is one of the emerging economies in the Sub-Saharan Africa that is reaping big in the capital markets investments since it has more than 64 listed companies and 45 mutual funds, whose total market capitalization has a significant impact on the economy's GDP.

These are markets for long-term financing; funds that will be available in business for a period between 7 years to 25 years and above. These markets are not well developed in Uganda despite the government's initiative to stabilize the macroeconomic climate but due to major short-term perspective of Ugandans, coupled with low levels of financial literacy on their part that have seen a sluggish growth of such markets compared to the EAC giant economy, Kenya.

Capital markets have potential to provide well-functioning infrastructure such as electricity dams, reliable water supply, wide all-weather roads, airports and railways which are greater enablers of trade, investments and most importantly wealth creation. CMA-Uganda has undertaken a couple of measures to boost the domestic capital markets such as: nationwide education to increase the number of investors from the current 40,000 to 100,000 investors by 2025. Besides, the USE recently started a Growth Enterprise Market Segment (GEMS) to provide opportunities for well-governed SMEs with growth potential to acquire long-term financing from the capital markets. Figures indicate that at least UGX 874 Billions have been raised in the domestic capital markets since 1998 when the USE was opened and it is expected that another UGX 3 Trillion will be raised by 2020. So far, UGX 293 Billion have been raise in the bond market (corporate bonds); UGX 584Billion have been raised in equity markets (equities/shares); IPOs have raised UGX 290 Billion; rights issues have raised only UGX 45 Billion; and additional offers have raised UGX 249 Billion

On the contrary, the USE is among the frontier market economies whose performance is not so impressive as compared other markets such as Kenya's Nairobi Stock Exchange (NSE) that became operational in 1954 (so far 61 years old) with at least 64 listed companies on the NSE but the USE which is barely 18 years of existence with simply 8 local equities and 8 cross-listed firms many of which are significantly illiquid. Majority of investors on the USE are foreigners who understand the workings and potential benefits of the market; there are very few products on the market, and more than 50% of the listed firms are illiquid. Most shares available to the market are held by institutional investors who don't trade them eg NSSF alone has about 80% of the float yet it doesn't trade it. Besides, during the privatization move, a couple of firms had to be listed on the USE as a move to distribute the national wealth creation opportunities equally among citizens and institutions in Uganda as the success story has been for those listed firm on the exchange. Such firms that have not been listed yet they were government-owned include: Lake Victoria Hotel, Tororo Cement, Kinyara Sugar Works, Kakira Sugar Works, Uganda Telecom Ltd, among others, which would have created a lot of value for the investors, the government, the economy and the business sector as well. This implies that serious steps have to be taken by the government to liven up the USE's activities, among others these are:

- There is need to benchmark with the best capital markets in the world.

- Government should put up tax-free, high interest infrastructural bonds each year, after the country is still greatly deficient in real infrastructure.

- There is need to offer domestic investors inflation-adjusted bonds so as to absorb the monies/funds that are kept in pillows and under the mattresses (or pots and in house ceilings) but channel them into financing the real economy.

- The State should promote tax efficient alternatives during the process.

- There should strong stakeholder interactions that will serve to bridge the gaps/rifts amongst themselves.

- Governments should avail listed firms with tax reliefs for some period of time after listing on the USE.

- There is need to continually automate the exchange platform so as to increase accessibility even off web eg on phones.

The capital markets are further sub-divided into the stock (equity) market and the bond (debt) market.

i) The STOCK MARKETS (history of the USE)

A stock exchange is an association of stock-broking firms; which grew out of a trading carried on in London's coffee houses by business men in the 17th Century.

It brings together lenders and borrowers; and the main lenders are: pension funds; life insurance companies; individuals; investment trusts; unit trusts; general insurance companies.

Private individuals were once the most crucial group but now investors prefer to invest through institutional investor firms.

The market for stocks is undoubtedly the financial market that receives the most attention and scrutiny since great fortunes are made and lost as investors attempt to anticipate the market's ups and downs. The investment world has witnessed an unprecedented period of volatility over the last decade which has had significant effects of both personal finance and corporate finance but also on the financial system at large.

Primary market

This market provides opportunity to issuers of securities, Government as well as corporate, to raise resources to meet their requirements of investment and/or discharge some obligation. The issuers create and issue fresh securities in exchange of funds through public issues and/or as private placement. When equity shares are exclusively offered to the existing shareholders it is called *Rights Issue* and when it is issued to selected mature and sophisticated institutional investors as opposed to general public it is called *Private Placement Issues*. Issuers may issue the securities at face value, or at a discount/premium and these securities may take a variety of forms such as equity, debt or some hybrid instruments. The issuers may issue securities in domestic market and /or global financial markets.

This is the market for new long-term capital; securities are issued by the company directly to investors. The company receives the money and issues new security certificates to the investors. Primary issues are used by companies for the purpose of setting up new business or for expanding or modernizing the existing business; a case in point is UMEME Ltd which did an IPO so as to raise finances to invest in pre-paid electricity cards facility and to scale down on its debts. The primary market performs the crucial function of facilitating capital formation in the economy.

Methods of issuing securities in the primary market are:

-   Initial public offer

-   Right issue (existing company)

-   Preferential issue

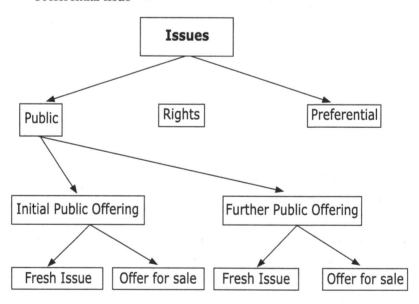

- Initial Public Offering (IPO) is when an unlisted company makes either a fresh issue of securities or an offer for sale of its existing securities or both for the first time to the public. This paves way for listing and trading of the issuer's securities.

- Rights issue is where a listed company proposes to issue fresh securities to its existing shareholders. These are normally offered in a particular ratio to the number of securities held prior to the issue suited for companies which would like to raise capital without diluting stake of its existing shareholders.

- Further Public Offer: is whereby an already listed company makes either a fresh issue of securities to the public or an offer for sale to the public.

- Preferential issue is an issue of shares or of convertible securities by listed companies to a select group of persons which is neither a rights issue nor a public issue. This is a faster way for a company to raise equity capital. The issuer company has to comply with the Companies Act and the requirements of the CMA.

Secondary Market

It is a market in which securities are traded after the initial/ primary offering gauged by the number of issues traded. In reality, majority of the trading is done in the secondary market, and it comprises of equity markets and the debt markets; whereby the over-the-counter market is the largest secondary market globally.

Functions of Securities Markets

Securities Markets is a place where buyers and sellers of securities can enter into transactions to purchase and sell shares, bonds, debentures etc.

- They perform an important role of enabling corporate bodies, entrepreneurs to raise resources for their companies and business ventures through public issues.

- There is transfer of resources from those having idle resources (investors) to others who have a need for them (business sector) is most efficiently achieved through the securities market.

- Securities markets provide channels for reallocation of savings to investments and entrepreneurship.

- Savings are linked to investments by a variety of intermediaries, through a range of financial products/securities.

Why should Securities Market be regulated?

- The absence of conditions of perfect competition in the securities market makes the role of the Regulator extremely important.

- The regulator ensures that the market participants behave in a desired manner so that securities market continues to be a major source of finance for corporate and government and the interest of investors are protected.

Who regulates the Securities Markets?

The responsibility for regulating the securities market is shared by

- Ministry of Finance, Planning and Economic Development (MoFPED),
- Bank of Uganda (B.O.U) and
- Capital Markets Authority (CMA).

The Uganda Securities Exchange

The Uganda Securities Exchange (USE) is the principal stock exchange of Uganda; founded in June 1997, the USE is operated under the jurisdiction of Uganda's Capital Markets Authority, which in turn reports to the Bank of Uganda (the national central bank) which also is under the Ministry of Finance, Planning and Economic Development. The exchange is governed by a Council whose membership includes: licensed brokers/dealers firms; investments advisors; a representative of the investors;

a representative of the issuers. There are 8 broker firms and 4 custodians; there are 16 listed firms with a total market capitalization of UGX 26,998 Billion (USD 9 Billion).

The USE's mission is: "To develop and manage the most efficient, transparent securities market that matches international standards and promotes a Partnership with the General Public, Foreign investors, Institutional investors, Employees, the Governments and other stakeholders in the development of Uganda's capital markets industry". And among the broker/dealers and investment advisors, there are:

- African Alliance (Ug) Ltd

- Baroda Capital Markets (Ug) Ltd

- Crane Financial Services (Ug) Ltd

- Crested Stocks & Services Ltd

- Dyer & Blair (Ug) Ltd

- Equity Stock Brokers (Ug) Ltd

- UAP Financial Services Ltd

- SBG Securities Ltd

It officially began trading in January 1998 with just one listing that was a bond issued by the East African Development Bank (EADB). By July 2014, the USE trading witnessed 16 listed local and East African companies' equities and had started the trading of fixed-income instruments. The exchange is open five days a week and normally trading activities begin from 8:30 AM to 12:00 AM, using an outcry traditional method of transacting. USE is a member of regional stock exchanges, such as: the East African Securities Exchanges Association (EASEA); and the African Stock Exchanges Association (ASEA). It operates in close association with the Dar es Salaam Stock Exchange (DSE) in Tanzania, the Rwanda Stock Exchange (RSE) and the Nairobi Stock Exchange (NSE) in Kenya; though plans are underway to integrate the four exchanges to form a single East African bourse.

In 2010, the Exchange adopted the Securities Central Depository (SCD) electronic trading system and other electronic modalities are being considered for the exchange. In this same year, Uganda Securities Exchange was the best performing stock exchange in Sub-Saharan Africa, with an ALSI (All-Shares Index) return of 74% between January and November 2010. The securities exchanges in Uganda is under the overall supervision of the regulatory authority, the Capital; Markets Authority (CMA) which provides a trading platform, where buyers and sellers can meet to transact in securities. This platform provided by USE is an automated one with effect from 20th July 2015 and there is no need for buyers and sellers to meet at a physical location to trade. They can trade through the computerized trading screens available with the USE trading members.

ALSI Index Graph

Source : USE Product Market / **ALSI** All Share Index / **LSI** Local Share Index

The trading on the USE from its establishment in 1998 used to take place through open outcry without use of information technology for immediate matching or recording of trades. Of course, this was time consuming and inefficient; and it imposed limits on trading volumes and efficiency. But in a bid to provide efficiency, liquidity and transparency, USE introduced an Automated Trading System (ATS) from the 20th July 2015 where a member can punch into the computer the quantities of a security and the price at which he would like to transact, and the transaction is executed as soon as a matching sale or buy order from a counter party is found. There is no capital gains tax; and among the roles of the USE, these are:

- Bringing companies and investors together through intermediation (shares, bonds and financial products) to both retail and institutional investors using the stock market infrastructure.

- Enabling issuers to raise new capital: IPOs; bonus and rights issues; and also private equity transactions.

- Facilitate the process of trading in securities by investors: using regulations such as listing and trading requirements, among other rules.

The following are some of the products that are traded/offered on the USE:

- Equity securities

- Fixed-income securities (debt instruments)

- Commercial Papers: these are money market securities issued by large firms to obtain funds for short-term debt obligations

- Unit trust funds.

ii) The BOND MARKET

A bond is a debt security; purchasing a bond is lending money to the corporation that has issued a bond. This corporation can be central or local governments, a municipality, a corporation, State agency or any other entity known as issuer. In return for the money, the issuer provides the buyer with a bond which is a promise to pay a specified rate of interest during the life of the bond and to repay the face value of the bond(the principal) when it matures (comes due).

Players in Bond Markets

- Central government: this issues long-term notes and bonds so as to finance the national budget.

- Local and Municipal governments: these issue long-term notes and bonds to fund capital projects like roads, schools, sanitation and health facilities.

- Corporations: these issue a variety of corporate bonds for numerous objectives such as growth.

- Households: these are the largest buyers of bond securities which are done through their deposits in financial institutions that are used to purchase bonds in capital markets.

Advantages of Investing in Bonds

- Bonds provide regular income and act as a cushion against the unpredictable ups n downs of the stock market. Bonds do not move in the same direction as stocks.

- Bonds income are predictable. One is able to know how much interest one is expecting to receive and how often they will receive it.

- The interest paid by short term bonds typically exceeds that paid by banks on saving accounts.

Disadvantages of Investing in Bonds

- Although bonds are less volatile than stocks, they are not immune to price fluctuations.

- When a company defaults on bonds, this may result into total loss of principal for the bond holder.

A couple of corporations in Uganda have issued bonds instruments to the public so as to raise funds for the achievement of their corporate objectives; and the following are among some of these firms and their bond issue details:

COMPANY	BOND SIZE	AMOUNT RAISED	PERIOD	BILL RATE	MATURITY	LISTING DATE
East African Development Bank	10 billion	10 billion	4 years	182 days+2.0%	Matured	January 1998
East African Development Bank	20 billion	20 billion	7 years	182 days	active	
Uganda Telecom	10.36 billion	10.36 billion	4 years	182 days	Matured	
MTN(Tranche 1)	5 billion	6.4 billion	10 years	182 days	redeemed	
MTN(Tranche 2)	2.5billion	2.5 billion	4 years	182	Matured	
MTN(Tranche 3)	2 billion	2 billion	4 years	182 days	Matured	2001
Standard Chartered Bank	23 billion	6.4 billion	10 years	182 days	Redeemed	May 2006
Housing Finance Bank	30 billion	35 billion	10 years	182 days	Matured	December 2005
Stanbic Bank	30 billion	30 billion	7 years	182 days	Redeemed	
African Development Bank(tranche 1)	12.5 billion	12.5 billion	10 years	182 days	Active	
African Development Bank(tranche 2)	12.5	12.5	10 years	182	active	
Kakira sugar works	75 billion	75 billion	4 years	182 days	active	

Data: Capital Markets Authority Database 2014

iii) How Securities are Issued and Traded

When firms need to raise capital they may choose to sell or *list* securities. These new issues of stocks, bonds, or other securities typically are marketed to the public by investment bankers in what is called the *primary market*. On the contrary, trading of already-issued securities among investors occurs in the *secondary markets* like the Uganda Securities Exchange (USE). It is imperative to note that trading in secondary markets does not affect the outstanding amount of securities; but ownership is simply transferred from one investor to another.

In the primary market, there are two types of issues of common stock:

Initial public offerings (IPO): these are stocks issued by a formerly private limited company that is going public, ie, selling shares to the public for the first time eg UMEME Ltd had its IPO in November 2013.

Seasoned equity offerings: these are offered by companies that already have floated equity eg, a sale by UMEME Ltd of new shares of stock in 2014 was a seasoned new issue.

However for bonds, there is a distinction between two types of primary market issues (public offering Vs private placement):

Public offering refers to an issue of bonds sold to the general investing public that can then be traded on the secondary market. Once the CMA has commented on the registration statement and a preliminary prospectus has been distributed to interested investors, the investment bankers organize road shows in which they travel around the country to publicize the imminent offering. These road shows serve to: generate interest among potential investors and provide information about the offering; provide information to the issuing firm and its underwriters about the price at which they will be able to market the securities. Shares of IPOs are allocated across investors in part based on the strength of each investor's expressed interest in the offering. IPOs commonly are underpriced compared to the price at which they could be marketed. Such under-pricing is reflected in price jumps that occur on the date when the shares are first traded in public security markets. The most dramatic case of under-pricing occurred in December 1999 when shares in VA Linux were sold in an IPO at $30 a share and closed on the first day of trading at $239.25, which was a 698% return for simply one day.

Private placement refers to an issue that usually is sold to one or a few institutional investors and is generally held to maturity. The fact that private placements are not made available to the general public, they generally will be less suited for very large offerings. Moreover, private placements do not trade in secondary markets like stock exchanges; which greatly reduces their liquidity and presumably reduces the prices that investors will pay for the issue

Public offerings of both stocks and bonds typically are marketed by investment bankers who in this role are called underwriters. More than one investment banker usually markets the securities; but a lead firm forms an underwriting syndicate of other investment bankers to share the responsibility for the stock issue. These financial services firms advise the issuing firm regarding the terms on which it should attempt to sell the securities, and a preliminary registration statement must be filed with the Capital Markets Authority (CMA), describing the issue and the prospects of the company. This preliminary prospectus is known as a *red herring* because it includes a statement printed in red, stating that the company is not attempting to sell the security before the registration is approved; and upon acceptance and approval by the CMA, it becomes the prospectus. At this point, the price at which the securities will be offered to the public is announced.

In a typical underwriting arrangement, the investment bankers purchase the securities from the issuing company and then resell them to the public. The issuing firm sells the securities to the underwriting syndicate for the public offering price less a spread that serves as compensation to the underwriters, a procedure called a firm commitment. In addition to the spread, the investment banker also may receive shares of common stock or other securities of the firm.

iv) Listing Rules on the Uganda Securities Exchange

There are three Market Segments:

- **Main Investment Market Segment (MIMS)**

    Main quotation market segment with stringent eligibility; listing and disclosure requirements

- **Alternative Investment Market Segment (AIMS)**

    Provides capital to small to medium size high growth companies that don't meet the eligibility of MIMS and is meant for institutional and high net worth investors

- **Fixed Income Securities Market Segment (FISMS)**

    Provides a separate market for government bonds, corporate bonds, commercial paper, preference shares, debenture stocks and any other fixed income instruments

Requirements for Listing on MIMS

- The issuer shall be a company limited by shares and incorporated under the companies Act (cap 85) as a public limited liability or if it is a foreign firm, it shall be registered under part X of the company Act.

- The issuer shall have a minimum authorized, issued and fully paid up share of 50000 currency points and net assets of 100000 currency points before the public offering of shares

- The issuer shall have published audited financial statements for a period of at least 5 years complying with International Accounting Standards for an accounting period ending on a date not more than six (6) months prior to proposed date of the offer

- The issuer shall have prepared financial statements for the latest accounting period on a going basis concern

- At the date of application, the issuer shall not be in breach of any of its loan covenants

- For the period of two years prior to the date of the application, no director of the issuer may be adjudged bankrupt, convicted of a felony; prohibited by court from acting as a director of a public issuer.

- The issuer shall have declared positive profits after tax attributable to shareholder in at least 3 years

- Allowing public shares offering, at least 20% of the shares shall be held by not less than 1000 shareholders

- Issuers shall comply with the detailed disclosure requirements

Requirements for AIMS

- Prior to submission of the application for the listing of an issuer on the AIMS a prospectus giving a summary of the nature of the issuer, its mode of operation, its business plan and its prospects shall be submitted to the exchange through a sponsoring broker.

- The issuer shall be a body corporate or registered as a public issuer ltd by shares under the companies Act Cap 85

- The issuer shall have minimum authorized, issued and fully paid capital of 10000 currency points and net assets of 20000 currency points before seeking listing

- At the date of application, the issuer shall not be breach of any of its loan covenants

- For the period of 2 years prior to the date of application, no director of the issuer may be adjudged bankrupt; convicted of a felony; prohibited by court from acting as director of a public issuer

- The immediate number of shareholders immediately following initial listing shall be 100

- The issuer shall have been in existence in the same line of business for a minimum of 2 years with good growth potential

- Issuer shall have produced audited financial statements for a period of not less than 2 years

- The accounts of the issuer shall not be older than 4 months before the date of listing and shall be audited.

- The issuer shall not have suitably qualified senior management with relevant experience for at least one year prior to the application for listing

- The issuer may not use the proceeds of a public issue to redeem any loans by the directors or the shareholders incurred prior to the listing

- At least one third of the issuer's board of directors shall consist of non-executive and independent directors.

- Issuers shall comply with the detailed disclosure requirements

Requirements for FISMS (other than government bonds)

- Issuer shall be a company, a government, a local government or any other body corporate.

- Issuer shall have net assets of 100,000 currency points before offering of the securities, if not so, the Issuer shall obtain a guarantee from a bank or other financial institution acceptable to the Committee.

- Issuer shall have published audited financial statements for three years complying with International Accounting Standards for an accounting period not exceeding six months before the proposed date of offer.

- Issuer shall have prepared financial statements for the latest accounting period on a going concern basis.

- At the date of the application, the Issuer shall not be in breach of any of its loan covenants.

- Issuer should have made profits in at least two of the last three years preceding the issue of the Commercial Paper or the Corporate Bond; and if not so, the Issuer should obtain a guarantee form a financial institution acceptable to the Committee.

- Issuer wishing to issue or list debt securities shall not be insolvent within the meaning of the Companies Act 85 and any amendments thereto.

- Total indebtedness of the Issuer, including the new issue of the Commercial Paper or Corporate Bond shall not exceed 400% of the Issuer's net worth (or a gearing of 4:1) as at the date of the latest balance sheet.

- The ratio of the funds generated from the operations to total debt for the three trading periods preceding the issue shall be maintained at a weighted average of 40% or more.

- The directors and senior management of an Issuer shall have collectively appropriate expertise and experience for the management of the business; and their details shall be disclosed in the issue information memorandum.

- Issuer shall ensure that each director is free of any conflict of interest as provided under these rules.

- If the Issuer is subject by law to the regulations of a regulatory authority, the Issuer shall obtain a letter of no objection from the relevant regulatory authority or such form of approval that the regulatory authority deem appropriate.

v) Rationale for going public/ listing on Stock exchanges

A listed company can raise permanent finance through issuing securities to the general public which can be invested in long-term ventures for company growth, such as: ordinary shares, convertible and irredeemable preference shares; and irredeemable debentures.

Such a firm is viewed as a credit-worth & established firm from the perspective of creditors, hence facilitating its obtaining finance on favourable terms since it can pay good and regular dividends, which are not a legal obligation.

These firms have access to cheaper finance that would significantly reduce on both the transaction costs and cost of capital; through the issuance of among other, rights issue.

Shareholders of a listed firm have access to ready secondary/ stock market for their shares, and through which they can gauge the value of their investments and also monitor their performance.

A quoted company has the opportunity to enjoy both national and global prestige, which will boost its goodwill & its ability to raise finance even globally.

It is only financially sound firms that the Uganda Securities' Exchange can approve for floatation/ listing, which serves as an assurance to potential shareholders that it is a viable investment.

Quoted firms will enjoy the privileges offered by the government to induce others to list on stock exchange such as tax allowances, and at times protection from competitors (Umeme Ltd).

These firms operate within specific ethical guidelines, which would help prevent such firms from engaging in unethical activities and practices during their operations.

A listed firm will be availed with information in form of feedback through the mechanism of share prices on the stock market infrastructure. This would reflect the public opinion regarding the corporate performance as embedded in changes in the share prices.

vi) Trading on Exchanges: USE; NSE; DSE; RSE (dealing procedures; participants; types of orders; market indexes; more details on EAC securities exchanges)

a) Structure and Players on the Uganda Securities Market

There are a number of professional participants of a securities market and these include; brokerages, broker-dealers, market makers, investment managers, speculators as well as those providing the infrastructure, such as clearing houses and securities depositories. A securities market is used in an economy to attract new capital, transfer real assets in financial assets, determine price which will balance demand and supply and provide a means to invest money both short and long term.

The current state of Uganda's financial markets can be described a Frontier market, which is at an early stage of development but with huge growth prospects.

Over the last two decades, financial sector reform has been implemented by, among other things, strengthening of the Central Bank, liberalization of the capital account, interest rates and the foreign exchange market; the reintroduction of treasury bills in 1990; privatization which has seen to the growth and development of the private sector in the country; the establishment of the Capital Markets Authority (to regulate the securities industry in the country) and the establishment of USE to facilitate a vibrant secondary market for issued securities. Through removal of restrictions on foreign participation in the sector has resulted into improved efficiency and innovativeness in the sector.

The market generally consists of:-

- The Regulator, Capital Markets Authority CMA (Uganda) which is an autonomous body that was set up following the enactment of the Capital Markets Authority Statute 1996 to Regulate, promote and develop Capital markets in the Country.

- The Market - Uganda Securities Exchange, which is the only Stock Exchange in the country. The USE is a Self Regulated Organization (SRO) meaning that it creates, amends and implements its own Rules and Regulations.

- The Market Players who include broker/dealers (have a license to trade on the USE floor), Investment Advisors, Collective Investment Schemes (who pool the funds of their clients for investment purposes), Registrars and the Investing public.

Companies listed on the Uganda Securities Exchange

1) Local listings

Company	Period when Listed	Issued Shares
Uganda Clays Ltd.	January 2000	900,000,000
British American Tobacco (BAT) Uganda Ltd	October 2000	49,080,000
Bank of Baroda (U) Ltd	November 2002	300,000,000,000
DFCU Ltd	October 2004	248,600,911
New Vision Printing and Publishing Co Ltd	December 2004	76,500,000
Stanbic Bank Uganda Ltd	January 2007	51,188,669,700
National Insurance Corporation	2010	403,880,000
UMEME Limited	November 2012	1,623,878,005

2) Cross-listings

Company	Primary Listing	Cross-listings	Issued Shares
East Africa Breweries Ltd	NSE	USE and DSE	790,774,356
Kenya Airways	NSE	USE and DSE	461,615,484
Uchumi Supermarkets	NSE	USE and RSE.	265,426,614
Centum Investment Co. Ltd	NSE	USE	604,947,013
Umeme Ltd	USE	NSE	Seen Above
Equity Bank	NSE	USE	3,702,777,020
Jubilee Holdings	NSE	USE	45,000,000
Kenya Commercial Bank Group	NSE	USE, DSE, and RSE.	2,217,777,777
National Media Group	NSE	USE, DSE, and RSE.	157,118,572

Market Report for the week ending 11th September 2015

STOCKS	Symbol	Price (UGX)	Previous Week (UGX)	Percentage Change	12-Month High	12-Month Low	Volume Traded (No. Shares)	Turnover (UGX)	DPS (UGX)	EPS (UGX)	P/E ratio
LOCAL LISTINGS											
British American Tobacco Uganda	BATU	8,700	8,700	0.00%	8,766	7,505	-	-	748	748.82	11.62
Bank of Baroda Uganda	BOBU	160	155	3.23%	161	110	2,008,900	311,387,000	2.50	14.76	10.84
Development Finance Company Uganda Ltd	DFCU	958	980	-2.24%	982	650	4,193	4,104,740	23.53	84.69	11.31
National Insurance Corporation	NIC	13	13	0.00%	25	12	10,000	130,000	1.00	1.10	11.82
New Vision Ltd	NVL	600	600	0.00%	610	540	1,736	1,041,600	35.00	46.00	13.04
Stanbic Bank Uganda Ltd	SBU	33	33	0.00%	35	31	19,501,110	643,536,630	1.66	2.64	12.50
Uganda Clays Ltd	UCL	14	14	0.00%	20	14	905,700	12,679,800	-	(5.75)	(2.43)
Umeme Ltd	UMEME	605	600	0.83%	692	445	3,090,578	1,854,646,800	28.9	43.00	14.07
CROSS LISTINGS		Price (Kshs)	Prev						DPS (Kshs)	EPS (Kshs)	P/E ratio
Centum Investments	CENT	1,758	1,737	1.21%	2,297	1,644	-	-	-	136.20	12.91
East African Breweries Ltd	EABL	10,376	9,600	8.08%	11,027	7,850	-	-	167	267.95	38.72
Equity Bank Ltd	EBL	1,576	1,449	8.76%	1,766	1,285	-	-	46	109.06	14.45
Jubilee Holdings Ltd	JHL	17,236	17,490	-1.45%	20,104	12,130	-	-	213	1,154.44	14.93
Kenya Airways	KA	202	197	2.54%	385	176	-	-	-	(68.36)	(2.95)
Kenya Commercial Bank	KCB	1,610	1,536	4.82%	2,090	1,492	-	-	61	126.99	12.68
Nation Media Group	NMG	5,571	5,655	-1.49%	9,366	5,571	-	-	304	407.09	13.68
Uchumi Supermarkets	UCHM	331	302	9.60%	410	221	-	-	9	41.01	8.07
REGIONAL LISTINGS		Price (Kshs)	Prev						DPS (Kshs)	EPS (Kshs)	P/E ratio
Safaricom	SAF	14.40	15.20	-5.26%	17.55	12.10			0.47	0.57	25.26
British American Investments	BTM	17.15	17.10	0.29%	37.00	14.35			0.25	1.40	12.25
Nairobi Securities Exchange	NSE	20.50	20.00	2.50%	26.25	18.50			0.38	2.04	10.05
		Price (Rwf)	Prev						DPS (Rwf)	EPS (Rwf)	P/E ratio
Bank Of Kigali	BOK	280	280	0.00%	370	274			11.06	22.13	12.65
Brailirwa	BLR	283	283	0.00%	446	283			15.00	30.06	9.41
Crystal Telecom	CTL	125	125	0.00%	144	112			10.36	6.10	20.49
Totals							25,522,217	2,827,526,570			

Volume: is the number of shares of the company traded on the stock market during a given period of time (a week in our case).

Turnover: is the volume multiplied by the weighted average price of the company (as of Friday). It gives you the total amount (in UGX) traded on a particular stock (for example Stanbic).

EPS (Earnings per Share) is a measure of the annual net profit per share outstanding. It's an indicator of the company profitability.

DPS: (Dividend per Share) is the total dividend paid out over an entire year (including interim dividends, but excluding special dividends) div outstanding ordinary shares.

P/E Ratio is a valuation ratio of the company's current share price compared to its earnings per share.

Average Market Capitalization: is the total Shilling value of all company's outstanding shares. Its calculated as company's shares outstan market price of it's share. It gives the company's size and market value.

Source : *Crested Capital Equity Research Sept 2015*

b) Types of Orders

There are two types of orders in the capital markets: market orders and orders contingent on price.

Market Orders Market orders are buy or sell orders that are to be executed immediately at current market prices. For instance, Becky (an investor) might call her broker and ask for the market price of UMEME Ltd., and the broker might report back that the best bid price is UGX 500 and the best ask price is UGX 520, meaning that Becky would need to pay UGX 520 to purchase a share, and could receive UGX 500 a share if she wished to sell some of her own holdings of UMEME Ltd. Note that the bid–ask spread in this case is UGX 20.

On the contrary, the best price quote may change before her order arrives, again causing execution at a price different from the one at the moment of the order.

Price-Contingent Orders: this is a scenario where investors also may place orders specifying prices at which they are willing to buy or sell a security. A limit buy order may instruct the broker to buy some number of shares if and when UMEME Ltd may be obtained *at or below* a stipulated price. Conversely, a limit sell instructs the broker to sell if and when the stock price rises above a specified limit; a collection of limit orders waiting to be executed is called a limit order book.

c) Securities' Markets Indexes

Stock Market Indexes

While the Dow is the best-known measure of the performance of the stock market, it is only one of several indexes used in the global financial markets to measure and analyze financial securities. The ever-increasing role of international trade and investments has made indexes of foreign financial markets part of the general news as well and also household vocabulary for the lovers of investments.

Dow Jones Averages

The Dow Jones Industrial Average (DJIA) of 30 large corporations has been computed since 1896. Its long history probably accounts for its pre-eminence in the public mind. Originally, the DJIA was calculated as the simple average of the stocks included in the index. Thus, one would add up the prices of the 30 stocks in the index and divide by 30; that is why it is called a price-weighted average. A percentage change in the Dow would then be the percentage change in the average price of the 30 shares. Since it corresponds to a portfolio that holds one share of each component stock, the investment in each company in that portfolio is proportional to the company's share price.

Standard & Poor's Indexes

The Standard & Poor's Composite 500 (S&P 500) stock index represents an improvement over the Dow Jones Averages since it is a more broadly based index of 500 firms; and it is a market-value-weighted index. It is computed by calculating the total market value of the 500 firms in the index and the total market value of those firms on the previous day of trading. A percentage increase in the total market value from one day to the next represents the increase in the index. The rate of return of the index equals the rate of return that would be earned by an investor holding a portfolio of all 500 firms in the index in proportion to their market values.

On the contrary, the sophistication in the global financial markets has occasioned the birth of many other indexes depending on the needs of various economies, and the construction has been championed by MSCI (Morgan Stanley Capital International. These can include: the Nikkei (Japan), FTSE (U.K.), DAX (Germany), Hang Seng (Hong Kong), and TSX (Canada).

Bond Market Indexes

There are basically two most well-known bond market indexes that measure the performance of various categories of bonds, and these are: the Merrill Lynch; the Lehman Brothers; and the Salomon Smith Barney (which currently is part of Citigroup).

d) EAC CAPITAL MARKETS

"Policy coordination enhances financial stability in the EAC region."

Background

The East African region has a relatively shallow capital market compared to some markets in Northern and Southern Africa. Kenya has by far, the largest and most developed bond market in the region, comprising about 67% of the total outstanding government bonds in issue.

In the recent years, corporate firms in Kenya have turned to the bond market to raise medium to long term debt following the moves by the Central Bank of Kenya (CBK) to maintain a stable interest rate policy. Currently, the Nairobi Securities Exchange (NSE) has over US$ 750 million dollars in listed corporate bond issues, most of which are tradable. Infrastructure bonds in Kenya have been taken up well by both local and foreign investors with the government lengthening the yield curve to 30 years in the March 2011 issue. This is the longest dated government bond in the region.

Regionally, there currently does not exist a common stock/bond exchange. However, over the recent years, the East

African partner states have made strides in formulating policy to integrate the markets. The East African Securities Exchange Association (EASEA) is there to help the Securities Exchanges of each member country in this integration.

In 2010, the East African Community (EAC) Monetary Policy Committee, which includes the EAC Central Banks has commenced work on the interlinking of the EAC payment systems. Besides, African Regional Economic Communities are beginning to establish regional and sub-regional capital markets. Among the ongoing efforts to integrate financial markets is the East African Common Market Protocol (EACMP) which was signed and ratified on July 1st 2010. Furthermore, the East African Securities Regulatory Authorities (EASRA), which is the regional umbrella body for capital Markets regulators, is drafting legislation that will allow for companies in Kenya, Uganda, Tanzania and Rwanda float bonds within the region.

The East African Community is a potential precursor to the establishment of the East African Federation, a proposed federation of its five members into a single state. In 2010, the EAC launched its own common market for goods, labor and capital within the region, with the goal of creating a common currency and eventually a full political federation. In 2013 a protocol was signed outlining their plans for launching a monetary union within 10 years.

Objectives of the Stock Market Development Committee (EASEA):

1. To establish within the Community of the cross listing of stocks, a rating system of listed companies and an index of trading performance to facilitate the negotiation and sale of shares within and external to the Community;

2. To ensure the unimpeded flow of capital within the Community by facilitating the removal of controls on the transfer of capital among the Partner States;

3. To prevent money laundering activities through the capital markets;

4. To ensure that the citizens of and persons resident in a Partner State are allowed to acquire stocks, shares and other securities or to invest in enterprises in the other Partner States; and

5. To encourage cross-border trade in financial instruments.

Regional institutions dealing in stock markets

East African Community

East African Securities Regulatory Authorities (EASRA)

East African Stock Exchanges Association (EASEA)

East African Development Bank (EADB)

Efficient Securities Markets Institutional Development (ESMID)

Types of stock markets in East Africa

Primary markets

This is market where new issue (securities) are sold, also called the Initial Public Offering (IPO). The primary market consists of the issuer and the first buyers of the issue. All subsequent trading takes place on the secondary market. Underwriting is the process by which the primary market functions, that is, how issues are sold to the primary buyers. The primary market can at times be more volatile than the secondary market because it is difficult to determine the underlying value of new issues. In any case, the primary market accounts for only a portion of trade on a given trading day.

Secondary markets

The secondary market, is also called aftermarket, is the financial market in which previously issued financial instruments such as stock, bonds, options, and futures are bought and sold. Private equity secondary market refers to the buying and selling of pre-existing investor commitments to private equity funds. Sellers of private equity investments sell not only the investments in the fund but also their remaining unfunded commitments to the funds

Functions of Securities exchanges (secondary markets).

- In this market, securities are sold by and transferred from one investor or speculator to another. It is therefore important that the secondary market be highly liquid (originally, the only way to create this liquidity was for investors and speculators to meet at a fixed place regularly; this is how stock exchanges originated). In general practice, the greater the number of investors that participate in a given market, and the greater the centralization of that market, the more liquid the market.

- Fundamentally, secondary markets mesh the investor's preference for liquidity i.e., the investor's desire not to tie up his or her money for a long period of time, in case the investor needs it to deal with unforeseen circumstances with the capital user's preference to be able to use the capital for an extended period of time.

- Accurate share price allocates scarce capital more efficiently when new projects are financed through a new primary market offering, but accuracy may also matter in the secondary market because price accuracy can reduce the agency costs of management, and make hostile takeover a less risky proposition.

Participants involved in stock market exchange in East Africa.

- Broker-dealer. A brokerage firm that buys and sells securities on its own account as a principal before selling the securities to customers
- Floor broker. An independent member of an exchange who is authorized to execute trades on the exchange floor on behalf of clients.
- Floor trader. A member of a stock exchange or commodities exchange for his or her own account.
- Investor. An individual who commits money to invest in products with expectation of financial return.
- Market maker. A dealer in securities or other assets who undertakes to buy or sell at specified prices at all times.
- Quantitative analyst. A person who analyzes a situation or event especially a financial market by means of complex mathematical and statistical modeling.
- Regulator. A body which regulates the activities of both the stock market and the market players so as to protect investors' interests.

Benefits of stock markets in East Africa

- In principle, the stock market is expected to accelerate economic growth by providing a boost to domestic savings and increasing the quantity and the quality of investment. The stock market is expected to encourage savings by providing individuals with an additional financial instrument that may better meet their risk preferences and liquidity needs. Better savings mobilization may increase the savings rate.

- Stock markets also provide an avenue for growing companies to raise capital at lower cost. In addition, companies in countries with developed stock markets are less dependent on bank financing, which can reduce the risk of a credit crunch. Stock markets therefore are able to positively influence economic growth through encouraging savings amongst individuals and providing avenues for firm financing.

- The stock market is supposed to ensure through the takeover mechanism that past investments are also most efficiently used. Theoretically, the threat of takeover is expected to provide management with an incentive to maximize firm value. The presumption is that, if management does not maximize firm value, another economic agent may take control of the firm, replace management and reap the gains from the more efficient firm. Thus, a free market in corporate control, by providing financial discipline, is expected to provide the best guarantee of efficiency in the use of assets. Similarly, the ability to effect changes in the management of listed companies is expected to ensure that managerial resources are used efficiently. Efficient stock markets may also reduce the costs of information. They may do so through the generation and dissemination of firm specific information that efficient stock prices reveal. Stock markets are efficient if prices incorporate all available information.

- Reducing the costs of acquiring information is expected to facilitate and improve the acquisition of information about investment opportunities and thereby improves resource allocation. Stock prices determined in exchanges and other publicly available information may help investor make better investment decisions and thereby ensure better allocation of funds among corporations and as a result a higher rate of economic growth.

- Stock market liquidity is expected to reduce the downside risk and costs of investing in projects that do not pay off for a long time. With a liquid market, the initial investors do not lose access to their savings for the duration of the investment project because they can easily, quickly, and cheaply, sell their stake in the company thus, more liquid stock markets could ease investment in long term, potentially more profitable projects, thereby improving the allocation of capital and enhancing prospects for long-term growth.

NB: It is important to point out, however, that, theory is confusing about the exact impacts of greater stock market liquidity on economic growth. By reducing the need for precautionary savings, increased stock market liquidity may have an adverse effect on the rate of economic growth.

Demerits of Stock Markets in East Africa.

There are serious limitations of the stock market that have led many analysts to question the importance of the system in promoting economic growth in African countries; and among others these are:

- Critics of the stock market argue that, stock market prices do not accurately reflect the underlying fundamentals when speculative bubbles emerge in the market. In such situations, prices on the stock market are not simply determined by discounting the expected future cash flows, which according to the efficient market hypothesis should reflect all currently available information about fundamentals. Under this condition, the stock market develops its own speculative growth dynamics, which may be guided by irrational behavior. This irrationality is expected to adversely affect the real sector of the economy as it is in danger of becoming the by-product of a casino.

- Besides, stock market liquidity may negatively influence corporate governance because very liquid stock markets may encourage investor myopia. Since investors can easily sell their shares, more liquid stock markets may weaken investors' commitment and incentive to exert corporate control. In other words, instant stock market liquidity may discourage investors from having long-term commitment with firms whose shares they own and therefore create potential corporate governance problem with serious implications for economy.

- Moreover the actual operation of the pricing and takeover mechanism in well functioning stock markets lead to short term and lower rates of long term investment. It also generates perverse incentives, rewarding managers for their success in financial engineering rather than creating new wealth through organic growth. This is because prices react very quickly to a variety of information influencing expectations on financial markets.

- Thus, prices on the stock market tend to be highly volatile and enable profits within short periods. Additionally, because the stock market undervalues long-term investment, managers are not encouraged to undertake long-term investments since their activities are judged by the performance of a company's financial assets, which may harm long run prospects of companies. Furthermore, empirical evidence shows that the takeover mechanism does not perform a disciplinary function and that competitive selection in the market for corporate control takes place much more on the basis of size rather than performance therefore, a large inefficient firm has a higher chance of survival than a small relatively efficient firm.

- Such problems are further magnified in developing countries especially East African economies with their weaker regulatory institutions and greater macroeconomic volatility. The higher degree of price volatility on stock markets in developing countries reduces the efficiency of the price signals in allocating investment resources.

Problems facing the East African stock markets (Frontier Markets)

- Macroeconomic Factors: macroeconomic risks include inflation risk, interest rate risk, low foreign exchange reserves and thin financial market which all together affect the performance of a stock market since macroeconomic policy has a great impact on the performance of the stock market.

- Corporate Governance: Coup d'états is quite famous in East African history. It appears that constitutional rule are present there and politicians are manipulating constitutions to either seek longer terms in office or perpetuate their stay. Thus, there is a lack of good corporate governance in the countries. In the absence of corporate governance, there is inappropriate policy taken by the government and regulatory frameworks. Moreover, there is no control of corruption, capacity building, and there is an ineffective, inefficient, no transparent and accountable system for mobilizing and allocating public as well as private resources.

- High unemployment: there is abundance of unskilled labor in the EAC region and this may lead to decline of the working class. The growth in demand for skilled labor does not match the decline of unskilled and semi-skilled jobs. The labour market is shifting towards more skilled workers, professionals and managers. There is looming unemployment in the region, which adversely affect household disposable incomes, and consequently frustrates the operations of investing in capital markets by many citizens.

- Trade Development: many East African economies are faced with a multiplicity of challenges that prevent them from participating in the global economy and reaping the benefits of increased globalization. East Africa is one of the most fragmented regions, with some countries being landlocked, the roots of the problem lie in chronic constraints to competitiveness including: poor infrastructure, small and fragmented markets, undeveloped financial markets, weak systems to facilitate trade, weaknesses in key institutions, and the lack of adequate human resources.

- Political Risk: political instability, institutional incapacity and social unrest restrain foreign capital inflows. These in turn lower investment appetites, and have a negative impact for economic opportunities and investment climate. Perceptions of political risk arising from particular events, such as those related to the recent elections in the EAC member states which generate market volatility and discourage investment. Some countries are seen as zones of high political risk, and significant risk premium are demanded by equity investors, lenders and insurers.

- Currency fluctuation risk: the global economic slowdown in world growth has affected East African exports of agricultural products, minerals and other resources. East African's dependence on natural resource exports has made many countries vulnerable to commodity price shocks that are outside their control. Sudden increases in export revenues or import costs cause currency instability and budget uncertainty; and, there is strong evidence that currency depreciation has negative effect on the performance of the East African stock markets.

Strategies for Boosting East African Capital markets

- They ought to develop well-functioning capital markets regulatory, compliance and risk-monitoring systems. Pragmatic evidence has shown that a well-functioning stock market, along with well-designed institutions and regulatory systems, fosters economic growth. Improvements in the regulatory and economic environments in some EAC countries have led to improvements in the liquidity and capitalization of their stock markets.

- Economies should enforce disclosure rules, accounting standards and enforceability of contracts so as to improve transparency and boost investor confidence.

- They should enhance the privatization of state-owned entities since privatization provides promise for private equity as well as helping with increasing the number of listed shares on exchanges if the IPO option is chosen.

- States should shift to automated systems across EAC markets: It is important for these markets to promptly adapt to automation and electronic systems. Automation not only minimizes inefficiencies associated with manual systems, it also reduces the costs of transacting, increases trading activity, liquidity in the stock markets and speeds up operations.

- Economies ought to demutualize their stock exchanges to improve governance as a result of separate ownership. Demutualization has become a global trend; in EAC region, demutualization can help deter undue government influence. In certain stock markets where demutualization occurred, there was a noted improvement in liquidity and foreign investment.

- Economies ought to amplify focus on pension reforms since often investor participation is directly or indirectly through pension plans, insurance policies, unit trust funds, etc. Reform for these collective investments vehicles will assist in increasing institutional demand for investments and improve the savings rates across the region and Kenya is a good example for this reality in contrast to the Ugandan pension system.

- The financial systems need to introduce measures that enable companies' growth from informal sectors into capital markets. This can be through the provision of incentives and assistance to grow the large number of small, medium and micro enterprises (SMMEs) to, at some stage, list on the stock exchanges or be considered for private equity investments.

- These economies ought to deliberately attract capital inflows and encourage foreign participation (FDIs) in these financial systems. Africa has been attracting positive attention driven particularly by improved regulatory, good economic fundamentals and empowering private initiative.

- Governments should develop comprehensive capital market databases to foster investment analysis and academic research. This will enable the capital markets to adopt best research practices that will lead to increased investor attention to the region.

- Capital Markets Authorities and other investments industry regulators should enhance education of the public regarding the benefits of investing in capital markets. This will serve to increase retail investing on stock markets and also assist in increasing the number of unlisted companies that look to stock and bond markets for growth.

vii) Why Firms desist from Listing

Companies listed on Uganda Securities' Exchange (USE) are way lower than those on Nairobi Stock Exchange (NSE), and even Dar es Salaam Stock Exchange (DSE); there are only 8 local firms that have floated on USE, and 8 cross-listings from NSE yet hundreds qualify for floatation. So, among other reasons, these are:

- Many firms have other cheaper sources of finance, which would have been the major reason for listing on stock exchange. Firms like Stanbic Bank are believed to have issued shares not basically to raise finance but to give Ugandans a chance to acquire ownership in the company.

- Listing can prove to be an expensive means of raising finance due to the high floatation costs, such as: underwriting & brokerage commissions; printing a prospectus; advertising, legal, audit & clerical fees.

- Some firms in Uganda have shunned away from going public due to fear of being exposed to corporation and other taxes, which they have either been avoiding or evading; thus it is logical to remain private.

- Many firms in Uganda are owned by families, who would not wish to lose their control due to these firms going public that can lead to dilution of their control by new shareholders.

- Going public is quite tedious a process since the firm as to: get permission from Capital Markets Authority (CMA); get permission from USE; organise to get an underwriter; prepare a prospectus; compile the firm's books of account for previous five years; etc.

- Many prospective firms fear the loss of secrecy to the public which is a requirement for listing on stock exchange; corporate details would be available to shareholders, and competitors who can use them to out-compete the firm.

- Many firms in Uganda are subsidiaries of multi-national companies which are already listed at home, and the original owners of the parent company may not be willing to sell their interest.

- Some firms in Uganda have certain core objectives which they can't compromise with in a bid for finance; such as cooperatives, which when listed, entails loss of members' interests for which they were formed to serve eg dairy cooperatives.

- Many firms may not have long-term interests in the country due to short-term needs of owners and nature of the market in question such as tour companies, construction firms.

- Most firms in Uganda can't maintain proper books of accounts, which is not only a requirement by CMA but also a security to the investing public that would question the performance of such firms.

- The nature of many businesses in Uganda may be in high risk areas such as agriculture that is affected by volatile weather conditions and prices. Such firms may not attract potential investors if they were to list their shares.

- Besides, the USE and CMA have not really created a favourable and enabling environment for many firms to go public: failure to boost the public's investment knowledge; failure to sensitize SMEs on financial opportunities in capital markets; inadequate professional activities in the capital markets industry; inadequate initiatives & funding in the area of investment research.

viii) Policy interventions & suggestions

- The State should facilitate the establishment of commodities exchanges since many Uganda is predominantly an agro-based economy yet farmers don't have access to markets. This would consequently boost the resource base of basically rural households that would also enable them to save/ invest their incomes on the stock market.

- The government should revise the conditions and costs required by the regulatory authorities to list securities since these would become disincentive to infant companies to issue securities in securities markets.

- Disclosure requirements of listed firms should be enforced so that information whether good or bad can be availed to all the companies and the general public that wishes to transact on the stock market.

- CMA ought to up its sensitization drives to all Ugandans about the advantages of saving inform of investing so that the financial system can raise the volumes required for financing by all corporations that have deficit budgets.

Chapter 12

DERIVATIVE MARKETS

DERIVATIVES

One of the most significant developments of financial markets in recent years has been the growth of futures, options, and related derivative market instruments. These instruments are sometimes called "Contingent claims" since their values are contingent on the value of other assets.

A derivative is a financial instrument (or more simply, an agreement between two people) that has a value determined by the price of something else. For example, a sack of beans is not a derivative; it is a commodity with a value determined by the price of beans. However, you could enter into an agreement with a friend that says: If the price of a sack of beans in one year is greater than UGX 300,000; you will pay the friend UGX 100,000. If the price of beans is less than UGX 300,000; the friend will pay you UGX 100,000. This is a derivative in the sense that you have an agreement with a value depending on the price of something else (in this case, beans).

Though many folks may argue that this is not a derivative but just a bet on the price of beans, derivatives can be thought of as bets on the price of something. Of course, we can't absolutely rule out the element of betting in the derivative operations because: let us presume your family grows beans and your friend's family buys them for their restaurant. The bet provides insurance: you earn UGX 100,000 if your family's sack of beans sells for a low price; this supplements your income. Your friend earns UGX 100,000 if the sack of beans his family buys is expensive; this offsets the high cost of a sack of beans.

Therefore, this bet hedges the two parties against unfavorable outcomes; and the contract has reduced risk for both parties. In fact, many investors use this kind of deal simply to speculate on the price of a sack of beans. On the contrary, the context in which this dealing is done determines everything; since this contract is neither insurance nor the contract itself, but how it is used, and who uses it, which determines whether or not it is risk-reducing.

a)   Uses of Derivatives

The following are some of the reasons why derivatives are becoming popular in their usage:

Risk management: Derivatives are a tool for companies and other users to reduce risks. The beans example above illustrates this in a simple way: The farmer/ seller of beans enters into a contract which makes a payment when the price of beans is low. This contract reduces the risk of loss for the farmer, who we therefore say is hedging: and this is not a complex transaction, just as many other derivatives are simple and familiar. As a matter of fact, every form of insurance is a derivative in the real sense. Automobile insurance is a bet on whether you will have an accident or not.

Speculation: Derivatives can serve as investment vehicles since derivatives can provide a way to make bets that are highly leveraged (that is, the potential gain or loss on the bet can be large relative to the initial cost of making the bet) and tailored to a specific view. For example, if you want to bet that a liter of Petrol will be between UGX 3500 and UGX 4500 one year from today, derivatives can be constructed to let you do that.

Reduced transaction costs: Sometimes derivatives provide a lower cost way to effect a particular financial transaction. For example, the manager of a unit trust fund may wish to sell stocks and buy bonds; and doing this entails paying fees to brokers and paying other transaction costs. But it is possible to trade derivatives instead and achieve the same economic effect as if stocks had actually been sold and replaced by bonds; hence, lower transaction costs than actually selling stocks and buying bonds.

Regulatory arbitrage: It is sometimes possible to dodge regulatory restrictions, taxes, and accounting rules by trading derivatives. Derivatives are often used, for example, to achieve the economic sale of stock (receive cash and eliminate the risk of holding the stock) while still maintaining physical possession of the stock. This transaction may allow the owner to defer taxes on the sale of the stock, or retain voting rights, without the risk of holding the stock.

b)   Perspectives on Derivatives

How a player thinks about derivatives depends on his position/ interest in the derivative markets, and so the following are the three distinct perspectives on derivatives:

The end-user perspective: These are the corporations, investment managers, and investors who enter into derivative contracts for the reasons listed in the previous section: to manage risk, speculate, reduce costs, or avoid a rule or regulation. End-users have a goal (such as, risk reduction) and care about how a derivative helps to meet that goal.

The market-maker perspective: These are intermediaries, traders who will buy derivatives from customers who wish to sell, and sell derivatives to customers who wish to buy. In order to make money, market-makers charge a spread. They buy at a low price and sell at a high price, just like shop/ market vendors who buy at the low wholesale price and sell at the higher retail price; and their inventory reflects customer demands rather than their own preferences. Market-makers typically hedge this risk and thus are deeply concerned about the mathematical details of pricing and hedging.

The economic observer: After a clinical analysis of the use of derivatives, the activities of the market-makers, the organization of the markets, the logic of the pricing models; then there is need to make sense of everything. This is the activity of the economic observer/ regulators who must often be guided in deciding whether and how to regulate a certain activity or market participant.

c)   What are the players in derivatives markets?

Derivatives markets are investments markets that are geared toward the buying and selling of a certain type of securities, or financial instruments. The following are the players or participants in derivatives markets;

Hedgers:

These are investors with a present or anticipated exposure to the underlying asset which is subject to price risks; and they use the derivatives markets primarily for price risk management of assets and portfolios. Hedger is a user of the market, who enters into futures contract to manage the risk of adverse price fluctuation in respect of his existing or future asset. Among hedgers are stockists, exporters, and producers: these have an underlying interest in commodities/ financial assets and use futures market to insure themselves against adverse price fluctuations

Speculators:

These are individuals who take a view on the future direction of the markets: whether prices would rise or fall in future and accordingly buy or sell futures and options to try and make a profit from the future price movements of the underlying asset. A trader, who trades or takes position without having exposure in the physical market, with the sole intention of earning profit is a speculator. Speculators are those who may not have an interest in the ready contracts but see an opportunity of price movement favorable to them. They are prepared to assume the risks, which the hedgers are trying to cover in the futures market; and they provide depth and liquidity to the market. They provide a useful economic function and are an integral part of the futures the market and their absence may at times lead to the collapse of markets

Arbitrageurs:

These take positions in financial markets to earn riskless profits. The arbitrageurs take short and long positions in the same or different contracts at the same time to create a position which can generate a riskless profit. Arbitrage refers to the simultaneous purchase and sale in two markets so that the selling price is higher than the buying price by more than the transaction cost, resulting in risk-less profit to the arbitrageur.

Day-traders:

Day traders take positions in futures or options contracts and liquidate them prior to the close of the same trading day.

Floor-traders:

A floor trader is an Exchange member or employee of a member, who executes trade by being personally present in the trading environment. The floor trader has no place in electronic trading systems.

Market makers:

A market maker is a trader, who simultaneously quotes both bid and offer price for a same commodity throughout the trading session. Some of the commodities have liquid market and some have either less liquid or illiquid markets. To bring the liquidity in the market of particular commodity, the exchange gives privileges to certain market players who are "market makers". As they normally belong to the class of speculators, they quote both rates for sale and purchase simultaneously

d) Instruments & Markets in Derivatives Industry

There are four types of derivatives contracts and markets: forwards, futures, options, and swaps. And they are discussed below with the help of some specific examples of these instruments.

1. Forwards contracts Market

A forward contract is an agreement to buy or sell a specified quantity of an asset at a specified fixed price with delivery at a specified date in the future. The value of the contract at inception is zero and typically does not require an initial cash outlay. The total change in the value of the forward contract is measured as the difference between the forward rate and the asset's spot rate at the forward date. An example of a forward contract is illustrated below;

Conveys UGX 100, 000 in 90 days

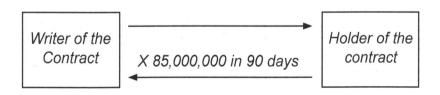

Shillings at the forward rate in 90 days.........UGX 85,000,000

Assumed spot rate in 90 days......................UGX 90,000,000

Gain in the value of the forward....................UGX 5,000,000

2. Futures contracts Market

Futures contract is a contract between two parties; to buy or sell an asset for the price agreed upon today with the delivery and payment occurring at a future point (the delivery date) because it is a function of an underlying asset. Like forward contracts futures are;

- Traded on an organized exchange

  The exchange clearing house becomes the intermediary between the buyer and the seller of the contract

- Contracts are standardized versus customized

- An initial deposit of funds is required to create a marked to market each day

- Represent current versus future monetary value therefore eliminating the need for discounting

- The party that writes the contract is said to be the short and the owner of the contract is said to be the long

An example of a futures contract is illustrated below;

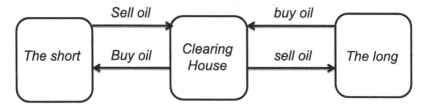

Futures price per barrel on day 1.................UGX 4, 000, 000

Futures price per barrel on day 2.................UGX 5, 000, 000

Gain in the value of the contract..................UGX 1, 000, 000

3. Options contracts Market:

Options contracts can be either standardised or customised. There are two types of option: call and put options.

Call option: these contracts give the purchaser the right to buy a specified quantity of a commodity or financial asset at a particular price (the exercise price) on or before a certain future date (the expiration date).

Put option: these are contracts that give the buyer the right to sell a specified quantity of an asset at a particular price on or before a certain future date, based on the American-style option. But for a European style option, the contract can only be exercised on the expiration date. In options transaction, the purchaser pays the seller an amount for the right to buy or sell called the option premium. An important difference between options contracts; and futures and forwards contracts is that options do not require the purchaser to buy or sell the underlying asset under all circumstances. An example of an option is illustrated below;

Assume the market price for Matooke is 35, 000 per bunch

Notional amount is 100 bunches

Option value is UGX 800, 000

Intrinsic value is the difference between the strike price and the market price (100 bunches × (UGX 30, 000 – UGX 35, 000)) = UGX 500, 000)

Time value is the value of the option less the intrinsic value (UGX 800,000 – UGX 500, 000 = UGX 300, 000

4. Swaps Market

Swaps are agreements between two counterparties to exchange a series of cash payments for a stated period of time. The periodic payments can be charged on fixed or floating interest rates, depending on contract terms. The calculation of these payments is based on an agreed-upon amount, called the notional principal amount or the notional. Swaps are a type of forward contract represented by a contractual obligation arranged by an intermediary that requires the exchange of cash flows between two parties. For example, a company with a loan payable with a fixed (variable) interest rate of interest expense for a variable (fixed) rate of interest. An example of a swap contract is illustrated below;

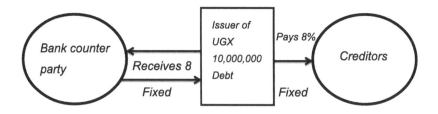

If variable rate is 7.5%, debtor;

Pays to creditors..UGX 800, 000

Pays to bank counterparty...............................UGX 750, 000

Receives from bank counterparty...................…....UGX 800, 000

Net interest expense.......................…...…...............UGX 750, 000

e) Underlying assets and derivative products

While forwards, futures, options and swaps can be viewed as the mechanics of derivation, the value of these contracts are based on the prices of the underlying assets. Below are assets that derive their values from the performance of five underlying asset classes: equity, fixed-income instrument, commodity, foreign currency and credit event.

1. Equity derivatives

Equity futures and options on broad equity indices are perhaps the most commonly cited equity derivatives securities. Index futures contract enable an investor to buy a stock index at a specified date for a certain price. It can be an extremely useful hedging tool. For example, an investor with a stock portfolio that broadly matches the composition of the Umeme Ltd share index, he will suffer losses should the Umeme Ltd index record a fall in market value in the near future. Since he means to hold the portfolio as a long term strategy, he is unwilling to liquidate the portfolio. Under such circumstances, he can protect his portfolio by selling Umeme Ltd index futures contracts so as to profit from any fall in price. Of course, if his expectations turned out to be wrong and the Umeme Ltd index rose instead, the loss on the hedge would have been compensated by the profit made on the portfolio. Other commonly traded equity derivatives are equity swaps.

2. Interest rate derivatives

Interest rate swap is one of the most popular interest rate derivatives in developed financial systems. It may involve a bank agreeing to make payments to a counterparty based on a floating rate in exchange for receiving fixed interest rate payments; thus providing an extremely useful tool for banks to manage interest rate risk. Given that banks' floating rate loans are usually tied closely to the market interest rates while their interest payments to depositors are adjusted less frequently, a decline in market interest rates would reduce their interest income but not their interest payments on deposits. By entering an interest rate swap contract and receiving fixed rate receipts from counterparty, banks would have hedged interest rate risk.

3. Commodity derivatives

Basically on Commodities exchanges, the earliest derivatives instruments have been associated with commodities, driven by the problems about: storage, delivery and price volatility. The resulting price volatility in the spot markets gave rise to demand of commodity traders for derivatives trading to hedge the associated price risks. This saw for example, the popularity of forward contracts on Brent and other grades of crude in the 1970s following the emergence of the Organisation of Petroleum Exporting Countries.

4. Foreign exchange derivatives

Essentially in the foreign exchange markets of the global financial system, the increasing financial and trade integration across countries have led to a strong rise in demand for protection against exchange rate movements over the past few decades. A very popular hedging tool is forward exchange contract: a binding obligation to buy or sell a certain amount of foreign currency at a pre-agreed rate of exchange on a certain future date.

For currencies of those economies with restrictions on capital account transactions, the profit or loss resulting from the forwards transaction can be settled in an international currency called non-deliverable forwards contract, and often traded offshore. Another type of foreign exchange derivatives are cross-currency swaps which involves two parties exchanging payments of principal (based on the spot rate at inception) and interest in different currencies.

5. Credit derivatives

A credit derivative is a contract in which a party (the credit protection seller) promises a payment to another (the credit protection buyer) contingent upon the occurrence of a credit event with respect to a particular entity (the reference entity). A credit event in general refers to an incident that affects the cash flows of a financial instrument (the reference obligation). The fastest growing type of credit derivatives over the past decade is credit default swap (CDS). In essence, it is an insurance policy that protects the buyer against the loss of principal on a bond in case of a default by the issuer. The buyer of CDS pays a periodic premium to the seller over the life of the contract. In the event of a credit incident, the buyer has a right to demand compensation from the seller.

Characteristics of derivatives markets in Frontier market economies

The following are some of the features of derivatives markets in these economies, and the reasons as to why they are not popular in EAC region:

- Undeveloped: Derivatives in frontier economies are characterized by lack of development. This is mainly because the markets are still in their initial stage and the infrastructures needed for these markets to operate are not fully in place. The capital markets are not fully equipped to handle the aspects involved in such instruments as futures and forwards.

- Unregulated: Since the derivatives markets in frontier economies are underdeveloped, the laws and regulations that must guide them are still being formulated to suit the African business environment, which is characterized by volatility. Laws regarding futures and forwards are not enforced and thus it makes it difficult to trade in such financial instruments due to high risks that are involved without the regulation.

- Informal markets: Frontier economies are characterized by a large number of informal markets, sometimes called black markets. These markets trade in goods and services without being regulated, taxed, and monitored. Due to these informal markets, trading in derivatives makes it a risky business.

- Highly complex: Derivatives instruments are highly complicated for many people in frontier economies who do not even have basic levels of financial literacy; and, are complex to understand due to their nature of uncertainty. This is mainly because of lack of education and information regarding the way the markets are organised.

- Few companies: Few corporations and basically large multinationals in frontier economies do trade in these financial instruments. Those companies that engage in such instruments are due to their exposure to the risks and opportunities of the global financial system.

- Low liquidity: Capital markets in these economies are characterized by low liquidity and high transaction costs. This is because the government has not put measures to protect their currency from the fluctuations hence the value of the derivatives keeps on changing as the value of the currency changes hence scaring many people from transacting in these markets leading to few participants who have a higher risk appetite.

In conclusion, derivatives are invented in response to some fundamental changes in the global financial system. If properly handled, they should help improve the resilience of the system and bring economic benefits to the users. In this context, they are expected to grow further with financial globalisation. However, past credit events exposed many weaknesses in the organisation of derivatives trading. The aim is to minimise the risks associated with such trades while enjoying the benefits they bring to the financial system. An important challenge is to design new rules and regulations to mitigate the risks and to promote transparency by improving the quality and quantity of statistics on derivatives markets.

Chapter 13

FOREIGN EXCHANGE MARKETS

Glance

In the early 1970s, Ugandan commodities (both goods and services) were less competitive with their EAC counterparts; this saw many Ugandan traders and consumers spend a lot on importation of commodities from economies like Kenya, including simple household commodities like agricultural products which were even domestically available. Record has it that not only was the economy doing well but the value of Uganda shilling was slightly lower than the US dollar, and of course, better than the EAC currencies, hence making domestic commodities more expensive than imported ones. By the 1990s and early 2000s, after a couple of financial crises in Uganda, the value of the Ugandan shilling had fallen significantly from its highs in the 1970s, Ugandan commodities were cheaper and domestic businesses more competitive regionally. This was evidenced by significant increases in the agricultural exports, influx of EAC and other foreign students in Ugandan education institutions, the growth in GDP, among other economic metrics

The foreign exchange market is one financial market that is characterized by high levels of volatility; and the exchange rates affect our daily life as households, the business sector, and the economy at large. This is because when the UGX (Uganda shilling) becomes more valuable relative to foreign currencies, foreign goods become cheaper for Ugandans and consequently Ugandan goods become more expensive for foreigners. On the contrary, when the UGX falls in value, foreign goods become more expensive for Ugandans and Ugandan goods become cheaper for foreigners. This has actually seen China in a situation of managing its Yuan so as to favourably compete in the global commodities markets but which is against the IMF policies of free market economy where the price mechanism should determine the foreign exchange rates amongst economies.

Uganda adopted a free-floating exchange rate regime in response to the macroeconomic instabilities in the early 1990s to ensure a consistence path towards economic development. This implies that the Bank of Uganda permitted the free market forces of demand and supply to determine the exchange rates. On the contrary, this has exposed the economy to great macroeconomic shocks (domestic and external) due to the high volatility in the exchange rates. The public, basically traders and consumers have always wondered why the government doesn't come to their rescue by intervening in the exchange market during hard times which has continually a thorn in the State's flesh and the Central bank has at times failed to have full control over the macroeconomic movements as compared to the free market forces.

Nonetheless, while addressing the business community on the 10th Private Sector Foundation Uganda International Trade Expo on why the Uganda Shilling is falling, Prof. Emmanuel Tumusiime-Mutebile made informative remarks. Uganda's exchange rate has faced repeated bouts of pressure since the first half of 2014; and on the trade weighted basis, the exchange rate has depreciated by around 23% since August 2014. The basic reason for this was that Uganda has suffered external shocks that have adversely affected her exports, tourism, and foreign direct investments yet actually the imports have remained quite strong. It is imperative note that depreciation of the exchange rate has implications for the Uganda's macroeconomics and the different sectors of the economy. Besides, given the flexible exchange rate regime, B.O.U doesn't attempt to control the level of exchange rate because it is neither feasible in a small open economy subject to external shocks nor desirable but restricts its intervention in the foreign exchange market to dampening volatility when the exchange rate becomes excessive. He adds that the exchange rate depreciation is a negative supply shock for the economy since it raises the cost of supplying goods and services in the economy; because many of these commodities are either directly imported or are produced locally but required imported inputs during their production. Thus, such shocks will inevitably raise inflation though it may take up to a year for the full effect of an exchange rate depreciation to be felt on the domestic prices.

From a theoretical perspective, any increase in demand for foreign currency or increase in supply of the local currency has in most cases been followed by escalation in the exchange rates.

Foreign Exchange Market

These are markets in which players are able to buy, sell, exchange and speculate on foreign currencies. Foreign exchange markets are made up of banks, commercial companies, central banks, investment management firms, hedge funds, and retail foreign currency brokers and investors. This market is considered to be the largest financial market in the world.

The Instruments of Foreign Exchange Markets

Forward: it is an agreement established between two parties wherein they purchase, or trade an asset at a pre-agreed upon price called a forward contract. Normally, there is no exchange of money until a pre-established future date has been arrived at. Forwards are normally performed as a hedging instrument used to either deter or alleviate risk in the investment activity.

Future: this is a forward transaction that contains standard contract sizes and maturity dates are. Futures are traded on exchanges that have been created for that purpose exclusively. Just like with commodity markets, a future in the foreign currencies market normally designates a contract length of 3 months in duration; and interest amounts are also included in a futures contract.

Option: these are derivative instruments wherein the owner has the right to, but is not necessarily obligated to exchange one currency for another at a pre-agreed upon rate and a specified date. When referring to options in any form, the foreign exchange market is the deepest and largest, as well as the most liquid market of any options in the world.

Spot: where futures contracts normally employ a 3-month timeframe, spot transactions encompass a 48-hour delivery transaction period. There are four characteristics that all spot transactions have in common, namely:

-   A direct exchange between two currencies

-   Involves only cash, never contracts

-   No interest is included in the agreed upon transaction

-   Shortest of all transaction timeframes

Swap: currency swaps are the most common type of forward transactions. A swap is a trade between two parties wherein they exchange currencies for a pre-determined length of time. The transaction then is reversed at a pre-agreed upon future date. Currency swaps can be negotiated to mature up to 30 years in the future, and involve the swapping of the principle amount. Interest rates are not "netted" since they are denominated in different currencies.

Players in the Foreign Exchange Market

There are many parties that trade on the foreign exchange market for completely various reasons than those in other financial markets. Therefore, it is very important to identify and understand the functions and motivations of these main players in the foreign exchange market.

Governments and Central Banks

The most influential participants involved in the forex market are the central banks and government bodies. In most countries, the central bank is an extension of the government and it conducts its policy in unison with the government objectives. However, some governments feel that a more independent central bank is more effective in balancing the goals of managing the country's macroeconomics and achieving a sound financial system that are critical towards economic growth. Central banks are often involved in maintaining foreign exchange reserves in order to meet certain economic goals.

Banks and Other Financial Institutions

Along with central banks and governments, other largest participants in foreign exchange transactions are banks for people, who need foreign currency for small-scale transactions. Banks also make currency transactions with each other on electronic brokering systems that are based on credit; and only banks that have credit relationships with each other can engage in transactions. The larger banks tend to have more credit relationships, which allow those banks to receive better foreign exchange prices yet the smaller the bank, the fewer credit relationships it has and the lower the priority it has on the pricing scale.

Hedgers

All financial agents, regardless of their size, are appreciably affected by the volatility of foreign currencies; whether a business is selling to an international client or buying from an international supplier; and foreign exchange risk is a big problem for many multinational corporations. Since the exchange rate can fluctuate in any direction over the course of a year, any company that transacts in the global financial system has no way of knowing whether it will end up paying more or less foreign currencies at the time of delivery. One choice that a business can make to reduce the uncertainty of foreign-exchange risk is to go into the spot market and make an immediate transaction for the foreign currency that they need.

In the world of business, hedgers are entities (individuals or businesses) wanting to reduce their risk of loss from price changes. Their risk naturally occurs because they are doing business with economic goods and/or financial instruments. In broad terms, there are two types of hedgers: short hedgers and long hedgers; i.e., hedgers who either want to protect against a price decline or a price rise, respectively. Because hedgers have one foot in the money markets, they tie future prices to present prices. Thus, as we move into the future, future prices become present prices (convergence).

Because the various FOREX markets tend to move parallel to one another, it is possible to hedge currency risk. While there are both long and short hedgers providing liquidity to one another, hedging is also facilitated by speculators who provide the bulk of liquidity that makes for ease of entry and exit for hedgers.

Speculators

Another class of participants in foreign exchange markets is speculators. Instead of hedging against changes in exchange rates to finance international transactions, speculators attempt to make money by taking advantage of fluctuating exchange-rate levels. Speculators assume risk in the pursuit of profits, and their risks are calculated to maximize profit potential. They might speculate that prices will rise, decline, go sideways or that price differentials will widen or narrow

Arbitrageurs

Arbitrageurs buy and sell the same currency at two different markets whenever there is price discrepancy. The principle of "law of one price" governs the arbitrage principle. Arbitrageurs ensure that market prices move to rational or normal levels. With the proliferation on internet, cross currency, cross currency arbitrage possibility has increased significantly.

SWIFT

In an interbank forex transaction, no real money changes hand. All transactions are done electronically through SWIFT. Banks undertaking forex transactions simply transfer bank deposits through SWIFT to settle a transaction. SWIFT is the Society for Worldwide Interbank Financial Telecommunication is a cooperative organization headquartered at Belgium. The Swift network connects around 8300 banks, financial institutions and companies operating 208 countries. Swift provides a standardized messaging service to these members. As and when two counterparties undertake a transaction, SWIFT transports the message to both financial parties in a standard form.

As the forex market is mainly an OTC market, SWIFT message provides some kind of legitimacy to the transactions.

SWIFT is solely a carrier of messages, and it does not hold funds nor does it manage accounts on behalf of customers, nor does it store financial information on an ongoing basis. As a data carrier, SWIFT transports messages between two financial institutions. This activity involves the secure exchange of proprietary data while ensuring its confidentiality and integrity. For every participating member, SWIFT assigns a unique code which is used to transport messages.

Big Multi-National Corporations

Big multinational companies earn their revenue and incur expenses in various currencies eg, Switzerland-based Nestle operates in 86 countries across the globe. To hedge their foreign exchange risk these multinational companies directly participate in the wholesale market.

Hedge & Mutual Funds

Hedge funds are also major player in this market since they collect huge sums from high net-worth individuals and undertake speculative trades in equity, debt, forex and derivatives market. Mutual funds with international equity portfolio are also major players in this market because they can't escape the volatility of foreign currencies, and their effects on the fund's risk/return profiles.

Chapter 14

MORTGAGE MARKETS

Mortgage: is a debt instrument, secured by the collateral of specified real estate property that the borrower is obliged to pay back with a predetermined set of payments. Mortgages are used by individuals and businesses to make large real estate purchases without paying the entire value of the purchase up front. Over a period of many years, the borrower repays the loan, plus interest, until he/she eventually owns the property.

Mortgage market: is a market for loans to people and organizations buying property or market for mortgages that have been bought by financial institutions and are then traded as asset-backed securities.

Classification of mortgage market

Primary mortgage market. The market where borrowers and mortgage originators come together to negotiate terms for mortgage transaction. Mortgage brokers, mortgage bankers, credit unions and banks are all part of the primary mortgage market. After being originated in the primary mortgage market, most mortgages are sold into the secondary mortgage market. Unknown to many borrowers is that their mortgages usually end up as part of a package of mortgages that comprise a mortgage-backed security (MBS), asset-backed security (ABS) or collateralized debt obligation (CDO).

Secondary mortgage market. The market where mortgage loans and servicing rights are bought and sold between mortgage originators, mortgage aggregators (securitizers) and investors. The secondary mortgage market is extremely large and liquid.

A large percentage of newly originated mortgages are sold by their originators into the secondary market, where they are packaged into mortgage-backed securities and sold to investors such as pension funds, insurance companies and hedge funds. The secondary mortgage market helps to make credit equally available to all borrowers across geographical locations.

Mortgage loan types

There are many types of mortgages used worldwide, but several factors broadly define the characteristics of the mortgage. All of these may be subject to local regulation and legal requirements.

- Interest: Interest may be fixed for the life of the loan or variable, and change at certain pre-defined periods; the interest rate can also be higher or lower.

- Term: Mortgage loans generally have a maximum term, that is, the number of years after which an amortizing loan will be repaid. Some mortgage loans may have no amortization, or require full repayment of any remaining balance at a certain date.

- Payment amount and frequency: The amount paid per period and the frequency of payments; in some cases, the amount paid per period may change or the borrower may have the option to increase or decrease the amount paid.

- Prepayment: Some types of mortgages may limit or restrict prepayment of all or a portion of the loan, or require payment of a penalty to the lender for prepayment.

The two basic types of amortized loans are the fixed rate mortgage (FRM) and adjustable-rate mortgage (ARM) (also known as a floating rate or variable rate mortgage). In some countries, such as the United States, fixed rate mortgages are the norm, but floating rate mortgages are relatively common. Combinations of fixed and floating rate mortgages are also common, whereby a mortgage loan will have a fixed rate for some period, for example the first five years, and vary after the end of that period.

1. Fixed Rate Mortgage. The interest rate remains fixed for the life (or term) of the loan. In case of an annuity repayment scheme, the periodic payment remains the same amount throughout the loan. In case of linear payback, the periodic payment will gradually decrease.

2. Adjustable Rate Mortgage. The interest rate is generally fixed for a period of time, after which it will periodically (for example, annually or monthly) adjust up or down to some market index. Adjustable rates transfer part of the interest rate risk from the lender to the borrower, and thus are widely used where fixed rate funding is difficult to obtain or prohibitively expensive. Since the risk is transferred to the borrower, the initial interest rate may be, for example, 0.5% to 2% lower than the average 30-year fixed rate; the size of the price differential will be related to debt market conditions, including the yield curve.

Balloon Mortgages

These last for a much shorter term and work a lot like a fixed-rate mortgage. The monthly payments are lower because of a large balloon payment at the end of the loan. The reason why the payments are lower is because it is primarily interest that is being paid monthly. Balloon mortgages are great for responsible borrowers with the intentions of selling the home before the due date of the balloon payment.

The charge to the borrower depends upon the credit risk in addition to the interest rate risk. The mortgage origination and underwriting process involves checking credit scores, debt-to-income, down payments, and assets. Jumbo mortgages and subprime lending are not supported by government guarantees and face higher interest rates. Other innovations described below can affect the rates as well.

3. Interest Only Mortgages : The borrower only pays the interest on the mortgage through monthly payments for a term that is fixed on an interest-only mortgage loan. The term is usually between 5 and 7 years. After the term is over, many refinance their homes, make a lump sum payment, or they begin paying off the principal of the loan. However, when paying the principal, payments significantly increase. If the borrower decides to use the interest-only option each month during the interest-only period, the payment will not include payments toward the principal. The loan balance will actually remain unchanged unless the borrower pays extra.

Players in the mortgage market

- Deposit Taking Microfinance-Institutions (DTMs)

- Private Equity Firms

- The Government

- Investors.

- The banking sector

Challenges to Developing the Mortgage Market in Uganda

Lack of Long-term Funds: Uganda's financial system still lacks sufficient long-term liabilities, owing to an undeveloped pension industry and limited life insurance funds.

The commercial banks, which play the dominant role, have mostly short-term deposits and are therefore inclined to provide loans only for periods not exceeding two years.

Infrastructure Provision and Costs: the Local Government Act (1997) empowers local authorities to control development and provide urban services. However, delivery of the vast bulk of infrastructural services (access roads, water, sewerage and electricity connections) has been pioneered by developers and individual builders, to make their housing estates more attractive to end buyers (See box 2 for more details). Infrastructural investments are estimated at between 15 and 25 percent of the price of the house depending on the location of the site on top of the existing infrastructure services.

Land Provision and Cost: Uganda's land tenure systems have presented a major hurdle to the supply of decent housing stock, especially in urban areas.

The Land Act provides that land is held under four tenures; mailo3, customary4, freehold and leasehold. However, terms set on how they are exercised (other than leasehold) do not adequately respond to changes in urbanization5. For example, in the case of the mailo tenure, the Act separates ownership of land (title holder) from occupancy or ownership of development by 'lawful' occupants.

Affordability: The lack of affordability is a combination of factors which includes the low levels of income (especially in rural areas), and the high and volatile level of inflation and relatively high margins charged by banks. Issues on the supply side also create a price barrier for many, where the cost of even the most basic new house is out of reach for the vast majority.

Risk Management: Deficiencies in a lender's ability to capture or understand risks mean that lenders have to charge a high 'risk premium'. This is due to the fact that credit bureaus do not yet offer comprehensive credit histories, there is a high level of informality, and the value of collateral is tempered by deficiencies in the foreclosure process, resale market and the valuation process.

Financing: This is ranked as the biggest obstacle but the facts suggest a relatively liquid banking sector with a low loan to deposit ratio. The issue is the availability of long term funds and the mismatch between short term deposits and the longer term mortgage loans. However, the current ratios suggest that banks could engage in further maturity transformation before hitting limits. Some of the large lenders however are constrained and certainly if current levels of growth continue, the rest of the sector will be also.

Economic growth: Periods of economic growth exhibit key characteristics that influence the mortgage market. Growth generates positive consumer and investor expectations of continued economic development. The added confidence in economic performance encourages consumer spending and business investment. Higher levels of spending and investment increase the demand on the money supply moving through the economy. Higher demand for money puts upward pressure on interest rates throughout the economy.

Inflation: this places upward pressure on prices resulting in the erosion of purchasing power for both consumers and investors. During periods of economic growth where the demand for money grows, competition for money increases, pushing interest rates continually higher. The result in the mortgage markets is that financing costs increase while home values decrease.

Economic Decline: periods of economic decline can have negative consequences for the mortgage market. When the economy shrinks, consumers and investors spend less money. The decrease in spending shrinks the demand for money.

With less competition for money, interest rates are pushed downward. For prospective home buyers, lower interest rates during periods of low economic growth can help decrease the long-term cost of home ownership.

Unemployment: this is one of the most significant developments in Uganda during periods of economic decline. Higher unemployment rates decrease the levels of consumer spending as incomes are reduced. For the mortgage market, lower incomes for potential homeowners and overall economic uncertainty helps decrease the demand for homes and mortgages.

Developing the Ugandan Mortgage Markets

The following measures seek to address the challenges and barriers which prevent the development of Uganda's mortgage market:

Expand the stock of mortgage-able properties: The supply of land for housing and having a functioning secondary market for housing sales are essential elements of an efficient mortgage system. This requires a more streamlined and cost efficient property registry system; and a unified and simplified mortgage law.

Provide Affordable Finance: the current cost of mortgage financing is prohibitive for the vast majority of the population. The urban population could consider taking out a mortgage loan which represents just 2 or 3 percent of the national population however, Mortgages are completely out of reach for the entire rural population but steps could be taken to improve affordability such as new products design

Improve Risk Management: As the market grows in size, some economies of scale will arise, but efficiency gains and lowering of the risk premium can also help to bring down the cost of loans. Thus, improvements such as: expanding coverage of the Credit Reference Bureau to have fuller credit histories, as well as to non-bank financial intermediaries; standardization of documentation; fortifying confidence in the sector by introducing prudential standards for loan underwriting

Development of a secondary mortgage market: there is need to develop a mortgage liquidity facility which would benefit the sector as a whole, while also pursuing the development of a mortgage covered bond framework for the larger lenders. This will target institutional investors, but it would be important to review investment rules of Pensions Funds and Insurance Companies.

Chapter 15

THE UGANDA COMMODITIES EXCHANGE

Introduction

A commodities exchange can be defined as an entity, usually an incorporated non-profit association that determines and enforces rules and procedures for the trading of commodities and related investments, such as commodity derivatives. Commodities exchange also refers to the physical center where trading takes place.

The exchange carries out its commodity derivatives transactions on the basis of an open and free market system, and it also facilitates the procurement system of standardized commodities by identifying warehouses. Ancient commodity markets began with the trading of agricultural products, such as: corn, cattle, wheat and pigs in the 19th century. Contemporary commodities markets trade many types of investment vehicles, and are often utilized by various investors from commodity producers to investment speculators. For example, a corn producer could purchase corn futures on a commodity exchange to lock in a price for a sale of a specified amount of corn at a future date, while at the same time a speculator could buy and sell corn futures with the hope of profiting from future changes in corn prices.

Background of the Uganda Commodities Market

The establishment of a Commodities exchange in Uganda dates back to 1995 when the Agricultural Committee of the Bank of Uganda recommended that as part of the risk management systems, the institution of a commodities exchange in the country should be investigated. This was followed up by a group comprising of Uganda Co-operative Alliance, Agribusiness Development Centre of the USAID funded IDEA project and VOCA whose final report was in October 1997 recommended the establishment of commodities exchange. This would primarily trade in agricultural commodities: maize, beans, rice, simsim, soya beans and wheat but later other commodities would come on board. The sole tangible outcome of the project was the company registration of the Ugandan Commodity Exchange UCE in December 1998, with four founding shareholders, such as: Ugandan Co-operative Alliance; Ugandan Coffee Trade Federation; National Farmers Association; and Commercial Farmers Association. Since then no further tangible progress or activities have taken place regarding the exchange.

The UCE envisions, "establishing a market that brings value to its members and the general trading public". Its mission is "to provide market information and services to buyers and sellers of commodities by establishing and operating a commodity exchange of the highest integrity available to Ugandans as well as regional and international buyers and sellers, based upon an open and free market system for the mutual benefit of the sellers and buyers; and to facilitate the procurement of and marketing of any commodity provided or desired by any consenting parties through the auspices of the exchange".

Current situation in Uganda; and Operations of UCE

In spite of being fully liberalized, the marketing of agricultural products continues to face problems particularly in the non-traditional export crop sector, where markets are poorly structured, and transaction costs are high. There is a paucity of market price information on these crops upon which producers can make appropriate marketing decisions and this coupled with an almost complete absence of inventory finance results in large fluctuations in price throughout the two annual marketing seasons.

The commercialization of agriculture in Uganda is a slow but ongoing process; commodities such as coffee and cotton are predominantly small holder produced for the export markets and as such are cash crops. The small holders producers for these commodities are integrated into the marketing chain and as such benefit from greater access to market information and financial instruments such as inventory credit from the processors and exporters of these commodities.

Regional buyers and sellers, as well as international producers and consumers participate in the commodity trading activities on this Commodities Exchange, and it carries out its commodities derivatives (futures and options) transactions on the basis of an open and free market system. The exchange is governed by Board of Directors but the day to day trading activities of the UCE are managed by professional managers. The key shareholders of Uganda Commodity Exchange are Uganda Farmers Federation, Uganda Cooperative Alliance, Commercial Farmers Association and Uganda Coffee Trade Federation. And the UCE is under the Ministry of Trade, Industry and Cooperatives, which currently serves as the regulator of this sub-sector.

Participants on the Uganda Commodities Exchange

Efficient commodities markets require a large number of market participants with diverse risk profiles; but ownership of the underlying commodity is not required for trading in commodity derivative (just like for all derivative markets).

The market participants simply need to deposit sufficient money with brokerage firms to cover the margin requirements;

and market participants can be broadly divided into hedgers, speculators, arbitrageurs, and regulators.

Hedgers: These are the commercial producers and consumers of the traded commodities, who participate in the market to manage their spot market price risk. Commodity prices are volatile and their participation in the futures market allows them to hedge or protect themselves against the risk of losses from fluctuating prices. As an example of a hedger, one might be a large maize farmer wanting to sell your product at the highest possible price. However, unpredictable weather may create risk, as well as excess supply that could drive prices down. One could take a short position in maize futures, and if prices fall, one could then buy back the futures at a lower price than had previously sold them (this is a risk management system). Of course, if prices rose, one would lose money on the futures transaction, but the idea is to use futures as a hedge.

Speculators: They are traders who speculate on the direction of the futures prices with the intention of making money. Thus, for the speculators, trading in commodity futures is an investment option. Most Speculators do not prefer to make or accept deliveries of the actual commodities; rather they liquidate their positions before the expiry date of the contract. A speculator, including individual investors and professionals such as hedge funds or managed futures traders, could take the opposite side of the hedger's futures transaction. That participant would bear the risk that prices are going to rise in hopes of generating a profit on the long futures position. Most likely, this type of speculator has no actual stake in the business, other than futures trading.

Arbitrageurs: These are traders who buy and sell to make money on price differentials across different markets. Arbitrage involves simultaneous sale and purchase of the same commodities in different markets; it keeps the prices in different markets in line with each other (normally such transactions are risk free).

Regulators:
Instruments Traded on the Commodities Exchanges

- Agricultural produce

- Mineral fuels, oils, distillation products, etc.

- Electrical, electronic equipment

- Machinery, nuclear reactors, boilers, etc

- Vehicles other than railway, tramway

- Plastics and articles thereof

- Optical, photo, technical, medical, etc. apparatus

- Pharmaceutical products

- Iron and steel

- Organic chemicals

- Pearls, precious stones, metals, coins, antiquity, etc

NB. Agricultural commodities are the major commodities traded in the Uganda commodities exchange and these include grains, food and fiber as well as livestock and meat, various regulatory bodies define agricultural products.

How to use the ware houses system

- Register your organization with the UCE.

- UCE will then give you a user name and password to use the system.

- You must be located within the hinterland of UCE licensed warehouses. Currently we have a ware house in Jinja, Masindi ,Mbarara, Tororo, Gulu and Kasese

Benefits of using the Ware House System (WRS)

- Proper storage facilities that are professionally run and secure.

- WRS exposes one to markets like World Food Program, larger grain traders and the regional markets.

- WRS exposes one to institutional buyers that you would have never met both domestically and regionally

- Access to finance through the banking system. Allows one to get 60% of the value of the commodity in order to defer its sale.

- It allows one better control over the sale of agricultural commodities.

Functions of Uganda Commodity Exchange

- On the UCE, commodity trading activities take place twice in every week, and the transaction dates are announced by the exchange in advance through its' website. The exchange itself determines its' commodity trading procedures.

- The exchange identifies and operates warehouses, which stores standardized commodities.

- UCE recruits brokers who engage in commodity trading of agricultural products. Commodity Traders benefit from the market knowledge and professional expertise of these commodity brokers.

- Along with UNBS (Uganda National Bureau of Standards), the UCE determines the Agricultural Commodity Standards for Uganda.

- The exchange works as a linkage between the regional and international buyers and sellers.

- Through the publications of this exchange, the commodity traders get informed about the trends in commodity prices.

Initiatives to Develop the Uganda Commodities Exchange.

Clear Objectives. The Uganda commodity exchange needs to make a clear plan with a well-defined scope. The exchange must have a detailed business plan, operating budget and strategy to engage productively with stakeholders basically the private sector.

Good Governance. Any commodity exchange must have a well-thought-out governance structure that emphasizes and responds to membership needs while maintaining an effective board and advisory structure that upholds business standards and meets performance targets. The board should include representatives from government, banking, storage/warehousing and the agricultural sector (e.g. traders, processors, input suppliers, etc.). The exchange employees must be committed to the exchange's mission and understand/promote the benefits of the exchange for all users and potential users.

Stakeholder Buy-In: The Uganda Commodity exchange leadership must meet with farmers, traders, processors, banks, the Central Bank, Ministry of Agriculture, Ministry of Finance, and development partners/relief agencies to generate support for the exchange. It is essential that each constituency understand the function of the exchange, their role in the process and the expected benefits so as to rally the requisite usage, trust, support and recognition from all stakeholders.

Economic and Legal Infrastructure: Uganda as a country needs to have legislation in place that consistently addresses agricultural, financial, trade and legal policies. However, legislation specific to a commodity exchange is not necessary for it to operate. Policies should allow for free market tendencies. Uganda also needs sound infrastructure – payment systems, brokerage services, storage, and transport. While legislation governing the functioning of the exchange can evolve over time, the rigidity it imposes up front can impede the development and limit the exchange's flexibility to address changing market needs.

Well-Designed Trading and Clearing Systems: The exchange must develop a system that is appropriate to the environment in which it is operating. This can include open outcry (shouting and the use of hand signals to transfer information), electronic or a combination of the two. Electronic systems allow for longer trading sessions, greater flexibility and greater freedom for members. An exchange must have graded products that meet quality standards, but it should not limit what grades and type of product can be traded.

Clear Rules, Consistent Enforcement: The UCE should have clear, consistently applied and balanced rules and regulations designed to protect the integrity of the exchange. The rules must govern all parties to the exchange: members (including their employees and clients), brokers, arbitrators, exchange employees, and other relevant parties. The rules should stipulate capital requirements for members, acceptable conduct of all parties, performance and sanctions for infractions. Trading rules need to include delivery guarantees or a means of alternative dispute resolution that ensures performance by all parties. The exchange must develop a transparent surveillance and monitoring system and act decisively when breaches in rules occur.

Accurate Contracts: The exchange should work with members and the industry to develop an agreed contract to facilitate trades and more detailed commodities-specific contracts that contain standard information on quality standards, analysis, delivery and weights, demurrage, force majeure and arbitration, among others.

Extensive, Continuous Education and Training: The Uganda commodities exchange must carry out training and certification of members and brokers to ensure the integrity of the exchange. The exchange should develop training and testing materials for this purpose and require certification of all parties trading through the exchange.

Relevant and Adaptable: An exchange serves the market; and therefore, it must constantly re-evaluate its performance, regulations, systems and membership to ensure that it is delivering value and maintaining its integrity. Exchanges must understand that they will make mistakes but the important lesson is to learn from those mistakes and be willing to adapt and change whenever necessary.

Large Volumes of Commodities Traded: To stay viable, the Uganda commodities exchange must attract large volumes of commodities across its trading floor. The commodity exchange planning phase must research trade volume potential. If the potential doesn't exist, neither should the exchange.

The Overall Economy and the Financial Markets

Below, I discuss the relationship between, and the impact of the overall Economy and the Financial Markets, as follows:

The overall economy may affect the future cash flows of the financial agents, eg, a strong economy implies that firms are working near capacity, profit margins are high and hence the expected future dividends are high (stock markets).

Business cycles may also influence the risks of the cash flows. A weak economy may increase the risk of stocks of firms with degree of financial leverage (interest costs) or a high degree of operational leverage (fixed operational costs). Besides, bonds of such corporations are more risky due to an increased probability of default (bond markets).

The general economic environment may affect the interest rate regimes, which forms the basis for the discount rates basically in the money markets.

Finally, the risk premiums charged by investors for accepting risk depend on the overall economy. Risk premiums habitually are high during a recession period, which reflects the subjective pain of losing Shillings to spend on consumption goods is higher during ruthless times than during friendly times; and on the other hand, the market risk premium is normally low during periods of economic expansion.

Despite these impacts on financial markets, it is difficult to beat the market using macroeconomic data; but it doesn't mean the macroeconomic analysis is useless for financial agents. For application eg portfolio selection, risk management and performance evaluation; it is imperative to to use good estimates for risk-return profiles of securities. These normally change during the business cycles; and this can be measured using the "Consumption-to-wealth ratio": the ratio of aggregate consumption to aggregate wealth. For example, during recession, investors expect a higher future market return and they increase the consumption-to-wealth ratio.

PART 4

FINANCIAL ASSETS

Chapter 16

Real assets Vs Financial assets

Real assets are those resources that are used by the company in its normal line of business to produce goods and services so as to generate profits. They are categorized into tangible and intangible assets. Tangible real assets are those that physically exist such as: land, equipments, machinery, buildings, plant, and furniture. On the contrary, intangible real assets are those that don't physically exist such as: goodwill, trademarks, brand names, technical know-how, technological collaborations, copyrights, etc.

Financial assets are claims/securities to the income generated by real assets or claims on income from the government; and these assets are a store of value to their owners. They include securities (stocks and bonds); derivative contracts; currencies; and alternative assets eg infrastructure, unit trust funds, hedge funds, private equity, commodities, and specialized real estate.

Financial securities can be classified as debt or equity: whereby debt securities are promises to repay borrowed funds while equity securities represent ownership positions in a firm. Publicly traded securities on exchanges or through securities dealers are subject to regulatory oversight nonetheless private securities are not traded in public markets and they are often illiquid and not subject to regulation.

Derivative contracts have values that depend on the values of other assets. Financial derivative contracts are based on equities, equity indexes, debt, debt indexes or other financial contracts and are traded on securities' exchanges. Physical derivative contracts derive their values from the values of physical assets e.g. gold, oil, coffee, wheat, among others and are traded on commodities exchanges.

1. Securities

These can be classified as fixed income or equity securities, and individual securities can be combined in pooled investment vehicles. Corporations and governments are the most common issuers of individual securities.

a) Fixed income securities

Debt securities are promises to repay borrowed money in the future: short-term generally have a maturity of less than one or two years; long-term are 5yrs-10yrs and intermediate term maturities fall in the middle of maturity ranges.

Bonds are long-term; notes are intermediate term; commercial papers refer to short-term debt issued by firms. Governments issue bills yet banks issue certificates of deposit (CDs). In repurchase agreements, the borrower sells a high-quality asset and has both the right and obligation to repurchase it (at a higher price) in the future; repurchase agreements can be for terms as short as one day in the interbank money markets.

Convertible debt: this is where an investor can exchange for a specified number of equity shares of the issuing firm with a debt instrument.

b) Equity securities

These represent ownership in firms; include common stock, preferred stock and warrants, among other as discussed later.

Warrants are similar to options in that they give the holder the right to buy a firm's equity shares (usually common stock) at a fixed exercise price prior to the warrant's expiration.

c) Pooled Investment Vehicles

These include unit trust funds, mutual funds, real estate investment trusts (REITs), depositories and hedge funds. The term refers to structures that combine the funds of many investors in a portfolio of investments, and investors' ownership interests are referred to as shares, units, depository receipts or limited partnership interests.

- Unit trust funds are collective investment vehicles in which investors can purchase shares either from the fund itself (open-end funds) or the secondary market (closed-end fund).

- Exchange-traded funds (ETF) and exchange-traded notes (ETN) trade like closed-end funds but have special provisions allowing conversion into individual portfolio securities or exchange portfolio shares for ETF shares that keep their market prices close to the value of their proportional interest in overall portfolio. These funds are sometimes referred to as depositories and their shares called depository receipts.

- Asset-backed securities represent claim to a portion of a pool of financial assets e.g. mortgages, car loans or credit card debt. The return of the asset is passed through to investors with different classes of claims (called tranches) having different levels of risk.

- Hedge funds are organized as limited partnerships with investors as limited partners and the fund manager as the general partner. Hedge funds utilize various strategies and purchase is usually restricted to investors of substantial wealth and investment knowledge. Hedge funds often use leverage and their managers are compensated based on the amount of assets under management as well as on their investment results.

2. Currencies

These are issued by the central bank and some are called reserve currencies, which are those held by governments and central banks worldwide. These include the dollar and euro; secondarily the British pound, Japanese Yen and Swiss franc. In spot currency markets, currencies are traded for immediate delivery.

3. Contracts

These are agreements between two parties that require some action in the future; for example exchanging an asset for cash. Financial contracts are often based on securities, currencies, commodities or security indexes (portfolios). They include futures, forwards, options, swaps and insurance contracts.

- Forward contract is an agreement to buy or sell an asset in the future at a price specified in the contract at its inception. An agreement to purchase 100 ounces of gold 90 days from now for $1000 per ounce is a forward contract. These are not traded on exchanges or in dealer markets

- Futures contracts are similar to forward contracts except that they are standardized as to amount the asset characteristics and delivery time and are traded on an exchange (in a secondary market) so that they are liquid investments.

- Swap contracts: two parties make payoffs that are equivalent to one asset being traded (swapped) for another. In simple interest rate swap, floating rate interest payments are exchanged for fixed rate payments over multiple settlement dates. A currency swap involves a loan in one currency for the loan of another currency for a period of time. An equity swap involves the exchange of the return on an equity index or portfolio for the interest payment on a debt instrument.

- An option contract gives its owner the right to buy or sell an asset at a specific exercise price at some specified time in future. A call option gives the option buyer the right (but not obligation) to buy an asset. Sellers or writers of call (put) options receive a payment called the option premium when they sell the options but incur the obligation to buy or sell the asset at a specified price if the option owner chooses to exercise it. Options on currencies, stock, stock indexes, futures, swaps and precious metals are traded on exchanges but also in the Over-the-Counter markets.

- An insurance contract pays a cash amount if a future event occurs. They are used to hedge against unfavourable, unexpected events; examples include life, liability and automobile insurance contracts. Insurance contracts can sometimes be traded to other parties and often have tax-advantaged pay outs.

- Credit default swaps are a form of insurance that makes a payment if an issuer defaults on its bonds. They can be used by bond investors to hedge default risk. They can also be used by parties that will experience losses if an issuer experiences financial distress and by others who are speculating that the issuer will experience more or less financial trouble than is currently expected.

Commodities

These trade in spot, forward and futures markets and include precious metals, industrial metals, agricultural products, energy products and credits for carbon reduction.

Futures and forwards allow both hedgers and speculators to participate in commodity markets without having to deliver or store the physical commodities. Rather than buying the physical assets that are highly illiquid and would require substantial due diligence before investing; and coupled high costs of managing them. Investors may choose to buy them indirectly through an investment such as Real Estate Investment Trust (REIT). Besides, an investor can also buy the stock of firms that have large ownership of real assets.

NB: Investment/capital budgeting decisions relate to decisions on what real assets the firm should invest in; while financing decision relate to how the cash for investment should be raised. Financial analysis in capital budgeting involves bringing together estimates and ideas from a variety of disciplines: marketing, technology, accounting, law, tax; in order to reveal the financial implications of different possible courses of action.

The following can be called financial assets available to the investors in such instruments; or can also be sources/types of finance available to the issuers such as corporations and government bodies:

Chapter 17

EQUITY FINANCE (assets)

This is the largest source of finance to any company, and forms the base on which other finances are raised. Among the features of this type of finance, these are:

- These shareholders are endowed with voting powers which empowers them to control policies and the kind of management that will achieve their interests in the firm.

- This finance can only be raised by limited companies according to the regulations in the country.

- This finance is permanent in the company which can only be refunded to its providers during liquidation of the firm.

- This finance positively affects the gearing level of the firm and it can't lead the firm into liquidation; on the contrary, it lowers down the firm's debt liability.

- This finance is the single largest source of capital to limited companies, on which other kinds of finance are raised.

- It is the only type of finance that grows with time as a result of retention called "growth in equity."

- Ordinary shares carry no nominal cost to the company since ordinary dividends are not a legal obligation to the firm.

- This finance carries a variable return meaning that in a good year, a shareholder might get higher dividends depending on the firm's profitability; unlike debt finance that has a fixed rate of return regardless of the level of profitability of the firm.

- Ordinary shareholders are the third-class claimants (residual claim) in the event of liquidation after all other finance providers have claimed their dues; this finance poses the highest risk in the company.

Equity finance is a function of the following sub-categories:

Ordinary Shares: these are share of ownership and also finance to the company that is provided by the real owners of the firm. Ordinary shareholders have full rights to vote at Annual General Meetings; they are entitled to dividends and surplus revenue in the event of liquidation. However, dividends are not a legal obligation and this ordinary shares carry the highest risk in the firm since they are paid after all classes of claimants have been settled.

Preferred Ordinary and deferred ordinary shares: the former rank for payment of an agreed rate of dividends before the latter receives anything. Mutual agreements may also permit the preferred holders to a share in the corporate profits after they have received their priority percentages.

Non-voting Shares: such shares are used to raise equity finance without losing control over the firm which most family-managed and private limited firms fear. Nonetheless, these share holders can't influence policies and the executive management of the firm the fact that they don't have voting rights to either vote out or in favor of any policy.

Retained Earnings: this finance arises out of undistributed profits over and above dividends paid to shareholders. It is normally a company policy to put aside (into a fund) a certain percentage of annual profits.

It is a cost free source of finance and the opportunity cost to the investors is just the money that ordinary shareholders who have taken home as additional dividends for their consumption expenditures. This finance constitutes "growth in equity", and many firms find the following advantages in retained earnings: acts as stabilizer for future dividends during unprofitable years; it is a cost free finance unlike fresh capital form financial markets; it serves to cover contingencies to the firm; it lowers the company's gearing level; it positively affect the company's share price on the stock exchange.

Capital Reserves: these are funds which can't be classified as normal trading profits arising out of the firm's ordinary trading activities. For instance, if Asante Capital Hub Ltd (a financial services firm) intended to sell its share to the public at UGX 200 per share; then maybe due to oversubscription of the IPO (Initial Public Offering) and the price mechanism, the share goes to UGX 250 above the par value, then the UGX 50 is a profit/ share premium to the firm. Lets hypothetically assume that the firm had offered 500, 000,000 shares; the share premium would be (500,000,000 shares × UGX 50 = UGX 25,000,000,000). And this UGX 25 Billion would be credited to the capital reserves to offset some expenses like those involved in the IPO.

Founders' Shares: with such finance/assets, dividends are paid only after all other categories of equity shares have received their rates of dividends. Much as they carry the highest returns in case of a good/profitable year, they have the highest risk in the firm, especially, in years of low/no profitability.

Golden Shares: (in newly privatized industries) these are held by the government following a privatization, and they give the State certain rights such as voting rights and veto rights on certain critical and strategic issues.

Share Warrants: these are entitlements to buy a stated number of shares at a specific price up to a certain date; and often attached to loan stocks (available in derivative markets).

Shares with multiple voting rights.

Islamic financing: this is an equity-based form of finance that works to obey Islamic law (Shariah law – not interest-based financing). Some bankers and finance companies are currently seeking to tap this market in Uganda by engaging in home-owning "partnerships" with the Muslim and some non-Muslim customer, since according to the Islamic faith; Shariah forbids paying or receiving interest.

Its primitive stage is traced back in the 15th Hijira Century (Islamic calendar) in the mid 1970s; but it was not until 1974 that the world's first development bank in compliance with the Sharia laws was established called "the Islamic Development Bank". The system emerged as an alternative financial system that neither gave nor took interest, thereby introducing a fair system of social justice and equality while fulfilling the financial needs of people and maintaining high standards of ethics, transparency, and a sense of responsibility.

It helps financial agents to build tangible and appreciating assets for themselves; founded on a solid economic base but also encouraging the spirit of entrepreneurship amongst its customers. It is based on a unique concept of profit and loss sharing by way of Sharia-compliant financing and investment tools. It is the first where financial agents are not just customers but partners with the financial institution; since both share risks, as well as profits of such partnership or ownership. This system offers a portfolio of innovative, Sharia-compliant financial models such as: Murabaha, Musharaka, Mudaraba, Istisna, Salam, and Ijara that are formalized and arranged uniquely between a customer and a financial institution.

Chapter 18
PREFERENCE SHARES (Quasi-equity)

This finance is contributed by quasi-owners or preference shareholders; it combines characteristics of both equity finance and debt finance. It is termed "preferred" due to the preferential treatment accorded to owners of such finance over other equity sub-categories such as: sharing in dividends; and sharing of assets in the event of liquidation.

Features of Preference Share capital are as follows:

- These shares are only sold by limited companies but not sole traders and partnerships.

- If these shares are not redeemed after their maximum redemption period (normally 7 years), then they turn into creditors who can actually sue the firm.

- These shares carry fixed dividends as return except the participative preference shares that are given more accommodation during dividend distribution.

- Holders of these shares are referred to as "second-class claimants" on the company assets during dissolution or liquidation ie before ordinary shareholders but after debt finance providers.

- Cumulative preference shareholders have a benefit of claiming their dividends in arrears in the event of a good year after non-profitable years.

- Convertible preference shares have an advantage of being convertible to ordinary shares which renders their holders real owners of the firm.

This kind of finance is classified into majorly four sub-categories:

Classification according to dividend payment: cumulative preference shares their dividends in arrears if a firm takes like five years without earning profits but on the sixth year it earns profits, then they would get dividends for the years they missed their dividends due to unprofitability of the firm. However, the non-cumulative preference shareholders are not treated in that way; if they miss dividends in any year, they can't claim it in arrears.

Classification according to convertibility: convertible preference shares can be converted into ordinary shares upon the approval/request of the firm, shareholder or both parties. Conversely, non-convertible preference shares can't be converted into ordinary shares.

Classification according to redemption: redeemable preference shares must be bought back from their holders normally at the minimum period of time (5 years) or at the maximum period of time (7 years) beyond which they will turn into company creditors. On the other hand, irredeemable preference shares are permanent finance to the company and they can only be redeemed in the event of liquidation or they can be transferred to other parties through the stock exchange infrastructure.

Classification according to participation: participative preference shares are entitled to more than their fixed rate of return during high profits seasons or high asset value along with the ordinary shareholders. In opposition, non-participative preference shares can't claim anything over and above their fixed claim of dividends.

Chapter 19

DEBT FINANCE (assets)

Debt finance has the following characteristics:

- It has a fixed rate of return: interest on debt instruments is fixed regardless of the level of the firm's profitability.

- Debt instruments don't carry voting rights, which cripple their holders' ability to influence policies and choice of management for the company.

- Interest on debt finance is a tax-allowable expense to companies.

- Interest on debt securities is a legal obligation on the part of the firm to pay, and failure to pay may lead to either receivership or liquidation at extreme cases.

- Debt finance is always refundable except for irredeemable debentures.

- Debt finance is usually given on conditions and restrictions basically bank loans.

- Debt securities carry a first claim on profits and company assets before any other provider of finance (first-class claimants).

- Debt finance negatively affects the firm's gearing level.

- Most types of debt finance are secured against the firm's assets.

Long-term Debt

i) Debentures: these are secured loan stocks or corporate bonds issued by financial sound corporate bodies to raise finance for their operations. It is a legal document showing the right to receive interest and a capital repayment; they are often negotiable. The following are the types of Debentures:

Fixed-charge Debentures: (also called mortgage debentures) these have fixed assets nominated as security for this debt finance.

Floating-charge Debentures: for these debentures, all the present and future assets of the firm are held as security for the loan stock.

Zero Coupon: with these debentures, no interest is paid, but there is a large difference between initial payment for the bond and its redemption value.

Among the merits of using Debenture financing, these are:

- The use of debenture doesn't entail dilution of the company's control since they don't carry voting rights as do ordinary shares.

- Interest on debenture is tax-allowable expense, and as such it lowers down the firm's tax liability.

- They are not expensive to raise as they entail less formalities in comparison to equity capital raising.

- They are used without preconditions and restrictions, hence making them flexible to use in flexible company financing initiatives.

- If they are redeemable, both interest and principal are reduced in real monetary terms due to the effect of inflation on the value of money.

Irredeemable debentures can form permanent finance o the company which can be invested in long-term ventures like and fixed assets.

ii) Unsecured Loan Stock: it is a legal document showing the right to receive interest and capital repayment. Such loan stocks are positioned low down in pecking order for payment in the event of liquidation. Coupon/ interest payment is higher than debentures due to also higher risk involved in their transactions.

iii) Floating-rate Notes (FRN): it is a bond on which the rate of interest is linked to short-term interest rates basically in the Interbank money markets.

iv) Convertible Unsecured Loan Stock: these are loan stocks which can be converted into equity capital at the option of either the holder, the firm or both parties. These have lower interest rates than debentures, and are normally cheaper to the firm. Interest is a tax deductible expense and they are often self-liquidating.

v) Bank Loan: this can either be term lending at fixed rate or floating rates. This type of debt finance has administrative fees; it is usually secured; and guarantees by directors. Covenants are usually required, that is, target interest cover ratios or limits on further borrowing.

vi) Syndicated Lending: this is a situation where a group of banks provide a large loan to either a retail borrower or an institutional borrower that would otherwise have been hard for a single bank to offer such a debt facility.

Medium-term Debt

i) Bank Loans: these are the same as the details above for bank loans except the period is one to seven years (1 – 7 years).

ii) Medium-term Notes (MTNs): this is a promise to pay a certain amount of money on a specific date. This type of debt finance is unsecured and its maturity is 9 months to 20 years, and normally sold in financial markets. This can either be fixed, floating or zero interest rates debt facility.

iii) Floating rate Notes (FRNs): these are promissory notes with a floating interest rate traded basically in the Interbank markets; but mostly used in the Euromarkets.

iv) Leasing: this is whereby an equipment owner conveys the right to use the equipment in return for rental payments over an agreed period of time. This saves firms from up-front lump-sum payments that would be quite huge for smaller firms; and this kind of finance is available when other sources have been exhausted. Besides, it has tax advantages to the firm since leasing expenses are tax deductible costs; and it can classified into:

Finance (capital) lease: this covers the whole useful life of an asset, and the finance house receives back the full capital investment plus interest over the lease period.

Operating lease: this only covers a proportion of the useful life of the asset such as machinery, vehicles, concrete mixer, etc.

v) Hire Purchase: this happens when a hire purchase company buys an asset which is used by the hirer; who after a series of payments becomes the owner of such an asset. This type of debt finance is so convenient and it is normally available when other sources of finance are either expensive or not quite available. This kind of finance is more expensive than bank loans, and a firm needs a guarantor since it doesn't call for collateral securities to raise it. The hirer must honor all the terms of the agreement ie if it fails to pay any installment before it clears 2/3 then the hiree may repossess the asset.

Below are the circumstances under which it is an ideal type of finance:

- If the asset is so expensive that there is hardly a single source of financing eg purchase of aircrafts.
- If the asset will meet the company's future expansion programs despite current financial constraints.

- If the firm is highly geared and can't afford borrow so as to finance the asset's purchase.

- Under conditions of restrictive credit control by the Central bank and the only option is purchase through hire purchase.

- If the firm doesn't have enough real assets to cover a loan as collateral security.

- If the asset is not very sensitive to technology that it would become obsolete soon.

Short-term Debt

i) Trade Credit: this is the most popular type of debt finance available basically to small business units in Uganda due its lower conditions for its access as a source of finance. It is all about delaying payments for goods received; as a source of finance, it is so convenient and informal though not necessarily free. The only (opportunity) cost it has is the loss of the discount that the trader would have received as a result of cash/ spot payment.

Below are some of the reasons why Trade credit is popular in Uganda:

- It is a cheap source of finance because the only cost involved is the discount lost.

- This type of finance is rarely misused and many firms are willing to give it due to lower risks in its misuse.

- Many a firms in Uganda lack collateral securities which are a necessity to raise other debt finance from financial institutions.

- This finance doesn't require a firm to be so financially sound so as to be eligible to acquire it unlike other finance sources.

- This finance hardly affects the gearing level of the firm and such it can't lead the firm into liquidation.

- Due the credit control measures of the Central bank, the only resort for firms is the trade credit which is not at all affected by the monetary policies of the Central bank.

- It is quite flexible in that it may be the only way how firms can get their commodities sold and this boosts the firm's sales' volumes.

- Most businesses in Uganda are not known to financial institutions, which makes trade credit the most sought after kind of finance due to its lower qualification criteria for this finance.

ii) Overdraft: this is a facility that commercial banks offer to its known clients of drawing a lot more funds than the balance they had on their accounts. Such finance is easy to arrange, flexible, unsecured, and repayable on demand. Its challenge is the it is way too expensive and it can a only be used as working capital but can't be used for the purchase of fixed capital requirements of a firm.

iii) Factoring: this is the outright purchase of the firm's debtors, normally the Factor Company pays the firm 80% of the value of its outstanding. And in confidential invoice factoring, the customer is unaware that the debts have been sold; so, he continues sending payments to the firm but not the factor.

In Uganda, there is only one major factoring company called Oscar Associates. It basically deals with debtors of financial institutions; it begun its operation in the 1990s during the collapse of a couple of banking institutions, and it was approved by the Bank of Uganda. The sector is not regulated because:

- There are very few players, which makes regulation not practical.

- Apparently, no fraudulent transaction has taken place on the part of the player.

- The sector is not popular; and very few people know about the existence of such financial services. Although, from 2007, B.O.U came up with a policy that would govern any new factoring firm to register with B.O.U.

Here are some of the key necessities for establishing a factoring business:

- One should have good background knowledge in legal issues: contractual knowledge and its application.

- One should have basic knowledge in accounting.

- There is need for wide sources of finance since there are many clients but very few players in the sector.

- Thorough background in liquidation of assets, discounting techniques and principles are all required.

- There is need to network with a couple of law firms for risk management and legal interpretation (litigation).

iv) Invoice Discounting: this type of finance is closer to factoring though for it, it has stages such as: (1) the firm sends its invoices to the finance house, and the firm guarantees that its invoices will be paid. (2) the finance house pays up to 80% of invoice amount to the firm. (3) three months later, the firm collects debt from customer and pays financial house. The costs are normally variable depending on the financial requirements of the firm and the financial capacity of the finance house.

v) Deferred tax payments: this arises as a result of intervals between earnings of profits by the firm and its payment of tax liability that produces cash availability.

vi) Commercial Paper: this is a legal document expressing loan terms with a maturity that ranges from 1 week to 2 years.

vii) Bills of exchange: it is an unconditional order in writing addressed by one person to another signed by the person giving it, requiring the person to whom it is addressed to pay on demand at a fixed or determinable future date a certain sum of money to the bearer; most of these mature between 90 – 120 days. An accommodation type of bill of exchange is that type where two parties X and Z are such that X has no finance and is not known to banks but Z is known to banks as a client. The two enter into an agreement whereby X draws a bill on Z, and Z accepts it and thereafter X can either discount the same bill or endorse it to another party to get finance which X will have to refund later to Z

viii) Bank Bills (Acceptance credit): this is type of finance whereby a bank promises to pay out the amount of a bill of exchange at a future date, which empowers the firm to sell the bill. On maturity, the bank pays the bill holder and later the firm pays the bank.

ix) Revolving Underwriting Facility (RUF): this is a kind of finance whereby a bank underwrites the borrower's access to funds at a specified rate in the money markets throughout an agreed period of time.

Chapter 20

Others: HYBRID TYPES OF FINANCE (assets)

i) **Mezzanine finance:** (closer to preference shares and convertible loans) this is a fusion type of finance that is characterized by high-yielding loans, usually with equity warrants attached to this finance. They are low security finance that implies high risk; and are useful for corporate restructuring, buyouts and leveraged takeovers. They are normally sold in the primary financial markets; and these include among others junk bonds.

ii) **Venture Capital:** this is a type of financing for new businesses or management buyouts (as already discussed under "Private Equity investments"). Financial institutions are the major suppliers of such finance and normally looking for exit route between 5 years to 10 years; due to high failure rates, high returns are required.

iii) **Sale and leaseback:** this is a situation whereby firm A, due to its financial requirements, decides to sell its property so as to raise the requisite finance and then after agrees with the party that has bought it to lease the same property to firm A for its continuous production processes

iv) **Mortgaging:** this is a type of finance which is available to firms with freehold and leasehold real assets such as land and buildings. It works as an arrangement where the mortgagee agrees to give a specific sum of money to the mortgagor on the strength of the real asset acting as collateral security for the finance. This finance is good for firms due to its long-term orientation towards financing which serves for the acquisition of fixed assets that are so critical for long-term growth and sustainability of the firm.

v) Eurobonds: these are international bonds sold outside the jurisdiction of the country of the currency in which the issue is denominated. Some of the characteristics of Eurobonds: there is no formal regulatory framework; interest is paid before tax; normally cheaper than domestic bonds; and they give borrowers access to international investors. Eurobonds are commonly issued by governments, corporations, and international organizations; and since the 1950s, it has been possible to arrange with investment banks for debt facilities to be issued to investors without it being affected by the legal or tax jurisdiction of any country. The market for this type of debt is called the *Euro-market*, though incidentally it is not confined to Europe. In fact, Eurobond issues can be made in almost any currency including the "euro" but most Eurobond issues are denominated in dollars. Among the types of Eurobonds, these are:

Straight Eurobonds: these are bonds with fixed rate of return and fixed redemption.

Subordinated issues: these are bonds where the bondholder's right to payments (principal and interest) is subordinate to the right of creditors.

Assed-backed issues: these are bonds where the credit of the securities depends on segregated assets.

Convertible bonds. These can be exchanged for shares, at a predetermined price.

In the East Africa Community, most countries have not issued Eurobonds. It's only Kenya that issued USD 2 Billion sovereign bond basically for infrastructural development that was oversubscribed by investors in June 2014.Uganda has disregarded plans to issue a Eurobond due to claims that it can borrow money more cheaply from Asia's economic power houses, according to Keith Muhakanizi (P.S Ministry of Finance

& Secretary to the Treasury). Finally, Rwanda plans to issue a $350 million Eurobond soon as it seeks to seal budgetary gaps following suspension of donor aid by several countries.

vi) Securitization: this is a kind of finance whereby a package of financial claims such as the right to receive payments from 500 mortgage holders for 20 years is sold as a derivative instrument. Among the assets that can be securitized include: mortgages, commercial papers, car loans, credit card receivables, etc.

vii) Export finance: this entails documentary Letters of Credit (LCs) whereby the trader's bank undertakes to pay at maturity on a bill of exchange. This means that the exporter's bank discounts the bills of exchange so that international trade can be facilitated.

viii) Forfeiting: this type of finance involves the bank purchasing a couple of sales invoices or promissory notes from an exporting firm; and normally the importer's bank guarantees the invoices.

ix) Project finance: this kind of finance is a medium-term borrowing for a particular purpose and the bank's security is the project itself. There are high risk/return profiles for lenders; and many Islamic banks are into such transactions eg the Arab Investment Bank , and Afri-exim Bank (Egypt). This kind of funding has been so instrumental in boosting infrastructural projects basically in the emerging economies and frontier-market economies that have high growth potential but resource-constrained.

x) Bull dog Bond: this is, for instance, a UGX-denominated bond that is issued by an overseas borrower in the traditional Uganda bond market, and its trading occurs on the stock exchange, unlike the Euro-bond whose trading occurs through investment banks.

PART 5

AGENTS / PLAYERS OF THE FINANCIAL SYSTEM

Financial Agents in the Financial System

In a synopsis, there are three major financial agents (players) in the financial system:

Firms as net borrowers: they raise capital now to pay for investments in plant and equipment. The income generated by those real assets provides the returns to investors who purchase the securities issued by the firm. They receive their incomes from remuneration of capital, transfers from the government and the rest of the world plus net capital transfers from households; and they pay corporate tax to the government which is a proportion of their incomes.

Households as net savers: they purchase the securities issued by firms that need to raise funds, thus providing them with finance for their operations. They receive their incomes from primary factor payments, transfers from the government, and also from the rest of the world but they pay income tax that is proportional to their incomes

Governments can be borrowers or lenders, depending on the relationship between tax revenue and government expenditures. Since most economies globally run budget deficits, meaning that their tax receipts are been less than its expenditures. The government, therefore, has had to borrow funds to cover its budget deficit. Issuance of Treasury bills, notes, and bonds is the major way that the government borrows funds from the public. In contrast, in the latter part of the 1990s, the government enjoyed a budget surplus and was able to retire some outstanding debt. In the real financial world, government revenue is composed of direct taxes from households and firms, indirect taxes on domestic activities, domestic value added tax, tariff revenue on imports, factor income to the government, and transfers from the rest of the world.

Corporations and governments do not sell or even most of their securities directly to individuals. For example, about half of all stock is held by large financial institutions such as pension funds, mutual funds, insurance companies, and banks. These financial institutions stand between the security issuer (the firm) and the ultimate owner of the security (the households).

In the financial environment, we classify majorly three agents due to their demands on the financial system, and how they can be addressed: the household sector; the corporate/business sector; and the government sector. The corporate sector has been made to comprise of also the not-for-profit agencies and the hybrid organizations such as the unincorporated or family-run businesses for simplification purposes.

FLOW OF FUNDS & FINANCIAL AGENTS LINKAGES

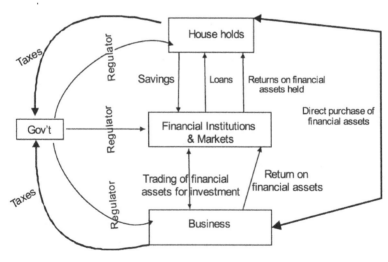

Chapter 21

BUSINESS SECTOR (Corporate Finance)

A household is, among all other financial agents, an imperative factor in the operation of any business venture since he furnishes his resources to the running of a business. These resources can be in form of: human (both mental and physical capacities); financial (monetary and otherwise); physical (land, machinery and buildings); among other resources for the production processes. Hence, it is upon his discretion to invest these resources in any line of business which will definitely affect the form of business organization he needs to set up so as to realize his business objectives. This critical investment decision has significant implications for growth and development of the chosen form of business, basically in: the way it can raise capital, enjoyment of benefits like profits and decision-making; but also on liability in form of debts and law suits; among other consequences that come with a particular ownership form.

Business financial decisions are concerned with the need to raise finances for investment in real assets such as plant, equipment and technology. But also invest surplus funds in either financial and/or other real assets. There are two major ways that are available for businesses to raise funds: equity financing by taking on new shareholders through issuing stock/shares of ownership in the firm; or debt financing through borrowing from banks and directly from households by issuing bonds.

i) Forms of Business Organisations in Uganda

a) Sole Proprietorship

This is a form of business owned and run by one person. The sole trading business has no legal requirements before it is established. With little capital or skill, a household can start a sole trading business. This form of business is the oldest and commonest type in Uganda today. Many factors have made people to start a sole proprietorship on their own; these factors include inheritance of business from a relative, desire to be independent, desire to build a fortune, unemployment and exploitation of ideas. It is basically run on family grounds and members of a family manage such business for profit. This type of business was necessitated by the fact that there was surplus of production over and above the need of a certain household; and this surplus had to be sold to those with deficiencies/ shortages. It begun initially as a barter system, then the monetization of societies transformed the whole setting; whereby money was later used as a medium of exchange. Such business undertakings are usually short-term and they can live as long as the owner still lives; and so, legally there is no difference between the business and the owner. Hence, the owner has full liability; and his sources of finance remain the traditional ones: owner's savings, loans from relatives and friends, trade credit, and may be short-term loans from financial institutions.

Advantages

- It is easy to start with minimum cost and no legal formalities.

- All profits belong to the entrepreneur.

- Sole trading does not pay tax like statutory companies. They only pay personal income tax.

- The business can be liquidated easily if the need arises just as it was started.

- Decision can be taken quickly since the owner need not consult anybody.

- The owner enjoys top secrets and privacy in the matters of his business affair.

- The sole trader can give his personal attention and touch to his customers due to the small size of the business.

- He can supervise all the employees more closely and try to motivate them to work more efficiently.

- This type of business is highly adaptable and flexible form of business due to changes in: customer preferences, seasons, social changes, and regulatory environment in the society.

Disadvantages

- Unlimited liability of the owner, all loses are the responsibilities of the owner and if he fails to bear the losses his property may be forfeited.

- The business lacks originality in that the owner may not be able to get expert ideas that may be required in running a modern business.

- There is no continuity in the business as it may die with the owner.

- Insufficiency of capital is one of the major drawbacks to this form of business.

- The success of the business depends upon the judgment and managerial capacities of its owner: with rational judgment, it will thrive.

- Due to its being confined to only traditional sources of finance, the profitability levels will be rather low.

Conditions Favorable For Establishing a Sole Proprietorship Business

- When capital is small and there is a desire to go into business

- When there is a need to start the business quickly and urgently in order to exploit an advantage.

- When the skill of the owner is an important consideration in the operation of the enterprise

- Where the business is operating in a high risk area and thus needs prompt decision-making to counter any possible catastrophes.

- In situations where the customers need special attention due to the nature of services rendered such as: medical, legal and consultancy services.

b) Partnership

When two or more persons come together to conduct a business enterprise, a partnership is said to exist. These people come together with the sole aim of sharing profits and losses arising from the partnership. It is formed to boost capital base of a business and benefits from the contributions of the owners. The nature of partnership is such that the partners are co-owners of the business. Partnership can operate under different degrees of formality ranging from an informal oral understanding to a formal written state.

Formation of Partnership

Common law provisions and other statutes guide formation of partnership in Uganda, and this could be in the following ways:

- Oral agreement

- Simply by the actions of the persons concerned: if they are acting as if they were partners

- By a simple written agreement

- By a deed: an agreement under seal, signed by persons who have committed to become partners.

On the contrary, if partners wish to run their business under a certain name registered by the Registrar; they must furnish the Registrar with the following particulars:

Some provisions in the partnership agreement include the following:

- The business name
- The general nature of the business
- The principle place or location of the business
- The Christian and surnames, and any former name of each partner with their usual residence
- The nationality of each partner
- Any other occupation of each partner
- The date of commencement of their business

Forms of Partnership

i) General Partner (Active Partners): Unless otherwise stated, all partners are regarded as general partners. Such partners have unlimited liability and may personally bear the responsibility of the debt of the business, especially in cases where others could not meet up with their liabilities.

ii) Special Partners: These are partners whose liabilities are limited by the agreement. Such partners do not normally involve themselves in the management of the business.

iii) Sleeping or Dormant Partners: These partners are not known by the public to be actively involved in the business. They are silent partners and do not involved themselves in the daily management of the business.

Features of a Partnership Business

- Business is formed by a minimum of two members and a maximum of twenty members.
- Partners have unlimited liability status: in the event of dissolution of the business, personal assets of partners can be attached if the business fails to clear its creditors' claims.

- Each partner is treated as part and parcel of the business except for limited partners.

- Each partner may act as an agent of the business.

- Ownership of any one partner can't be transferred without the consent of other partners.

- Admission or dismissal of any partner must have the consent of others.

- Books of account of a partnership business are not audited.

- The death or bankruptcy of any one partner leads to dissolution of the business.

Conditions Favorable for the Operation of Partnership

- When a moderate amount of capital is required and where diversified managerial talents could be got from partners.

- Professionals who specialized in different areas could find an opportunity in partnership agreement for better performance and efficiency such as: legal and auditing professions

- When risk is relatively low and could be borne by the partner.

- Where there are clear boundaries of a business and each partner can be identified to a specific area such as engineering field.

- In case the would-be partners have a common bond that they are not willing to sacrifice by inviting other parties such as relatives, family members, professionals, and parties with long association.

Advantages of Partnership

- Partners could have diversified skills, which could be put to the business advantage.

- The business has the opportunity of securing more capital in that there is more than one owner.

- The operation of the business is relatively free from government control.

- It is easy to form and organize in that there are no complicated legal requirements to meet before starting.

- Decision-making process is done by unanimous position of all partners, which can lead to rational decision-making. This would lead to efficiency, high profitability and sound business policies.

Disadvantages

- Inability to transfer ownership in partnership business poses a drawback to this form of enterprise.

- The partners are jointly and separately liable for business debt. This means that if a partner is unable to meet the claims resulting from the liquidation of the partnership, the remaining partners must take over the unsatisfied claims, drawing on their personal assets if necessary.

- It may be difficult to find compatible partners who could work together peacefully, especially in a situation where people do not trust each other.

- Uncertainty of the lifespan of the business. If a partner withdraws or dies, the withdrawal or death of the partner dissolves the partnership.

- There is a like-hood that partners may not pool their talents equally and this may lead to indifference amongst partners during the general running of the partnership business and frustration on the part of the others.

- Some active partners may use the partnership assets to achieve their personal gains at the expense of the interests of the dormant partners.

- There may be lack of mutual trust amongst partners: each viewing the other with suspicion; this may create friction among partners and consequently lead to dissolution.

c)   Joint Stock Companies (Limited Liability)

These are advanced forms of partnership where a group of people pool their resources together and contribute to the capital base of such corporations through the purchase of shares of such firms. They are governed by an Act of Parliament called the Uganda Companies' Act (Cap. ....); which lays down their formation and general conduct.

For formation, the promoters of a company will have to register it with the Registrar of Companies under the Ministry of Trade, Investments and Co-operatives so as to become a legal entity, and it will be issued with a Certificate of Incorporation after the submission of the following documents:

-   The Memorandum of Association, which contains: the objectives of the company; the authorized share capital; and the types of accounts the company should maintain.

-   The Articles of Association, which entails: the issue of share capital; borrowing powers of company's directors; appointment, remuneration and powers of company's auditors; meetings and their schedules; voting powers of shareholders; appointment and remuneration of company directors; but also dividend policy to shareholders.

-   The company's registered office

-   A list of members who have been appointed directors; their names, qualification, age, occupation, and share holding in a company.

The limited liability companies are usually divided into two basic types in Uganda; and these are:

a)   Private limited liability companies whose shares are not quoted on the stock exchange market that is, the public do not subscribe to their shares but sell their share privately to interested members of the pubic, which is called private placement.

Such companies are very many in Uganda, and they basically run on family grounds with no intentions of going public so as to safeguard their secrets and control.

b) Public limited companies are those whose shares are quoted on the stock exchange and subscribed to by the public through the sale of ordinary (common stock) or preference shares. These companies normally raise large sums of money from the public after being granted permission from: the Capital markets Authority (CMA) which is under the Ministry of Finance; and also approval from the Uganda Securities Exchange (USE) which manages the stock exchange infrastructure. The USE would consequently appoint/ propose a financial services firm called investment/wholesale/merchant bank or an underwriter to advise that company on how to go about the issuing of financial securities (underwriting process).

Advantages of Limited Liability Companies

- The company enjoys continuity in that the company is expected to exist forever unless it is dissolution by the law.

- Liabilities of owners are limited to the amount of capital contributed. This means that in event of liquidation, if creditors' claims exceed the value from company's assets then shareholders' assets will not be attached.

- It is easier to raise additional capital on identity of the company either by issuing shares or borrowing.

- Shares can easily be transferred.

- Shares of such companies can be used as collateral security for loans, as long as the company is financially sound.

- It gives wide scope to different investment.

Disadvantages of Limited Liability Companies

- Limited liability companies suffer too much control from government.

- There are great difficulties in starting the company because of the legal requirements.

- They suffer from double taxation for example, companies pay tax on profit, dividend, properties, etc.

- The growth of bureaucracy can bring slow decision-making.

- Possibility of impersonal relationship between management of the company and its workers.

- The requirement to publish audited accounts and shareholders access to corporate books leads to loss of privacy/secrecy on the part of the company, and competitors can use such information to out-compete the company.

d)   Co-operative Societies

This is a form of enterprise which fosters cooperation among its members with the view to enhancing mutual and self-help; promote economic interest and welfare of the participating members. A cooperative society derives its strength from the interest and patronage of its members who provide nearly all its finance, own, manage and control its operations.

They are usually guided by statutes and sponsored by government especially because of their aim, which is to make life better for people in terms standard of living.

Types of Co-Operative Society in Uganda

i) Producers' Co-operatives: This form of co-operative society involves co-operation in production area to facilitate greater output, economies of scale, better pricing and improved marketing of product to minimized members' exploitation eg Bugisu Cooperative Union, Busoga Cooperative Union, etc.

ii) Consumers' Co-operatives: This co-operative society is based on consumer ownership and control. Consumers' co-operative society involves co-operation in retail distributive trades. The society purchases consumer goods in bulk and at wholesale prices and sell to its members. Their objective is to eliminate intermediaries in the distribution of goods thereby enabling members to buy at lower cost. These are so common in Uganda due to: poor policies on consumer protection; individualism/ self-centeredness; and lack of knowledge on the advantages of economies of collective strategies among many Ugandan consumers.

iii) Saving and Credit Co-operatives: These co-operatives societies are formed with the aim of promoting culture of long-term perspective towards life among members; members save money in the association based on their ability. The major objective of the saving and credit or saving co-operatives is to discourage the habit of living from hand to mouth and encourage the habit of saving among members. Funds pooled together through savings are given as loan to members at lower interest rates than those of money markets.

Members of these co-operatives are often drawn from the low-income people.

Advantages of Co-Operative Societies

- They facilitate easy access to some external sources of finance ie these funds serve to leverage other funds.

- Members enjoy economies of both scale and collective strategies.

- They serve as useful agents of economic development in that through the societies, incomes of members are raised and more businesses are established by obtaining capital from the cooperatives.

- The saving and credit societies have encouraged saving habit among people.

- Co-operative societies enjoy less tax burden from government since they act as agent of development for the government.

Disadvantages of Co-Operative Societies

- Co-operatives suffer from the lack of adequate finance which put severe limitations on their development and expansion in the range of activities they can offer to the society.

- Many of these organizations soon or later turn in political grounds for political parties and personal egos, which compound their poor management skills set.

- Co-operative societies are mostly run by inexperienced managers who are not well equipped with modern managerial techniques.

e)   Public Corporation (parastatals)

Public Corporation is a business organization whose ownership is vested in the government who also owns the capital as a trustee for the people. The corporation has its own legal existence and; it is usually organized along a business line but normally a not-for-profit organization. There are many such corporations in Uganda, though their number significantly reduced during the 1990s as a result of the World Bank's Structural Adjustment Programmes (SAPs) that was commonly known as privatization. For each corporation, there is an Act of the Parliament that determines the scope of its activities and the broad policies that governs its operations; outlines the format of the organization; and formulates the financial structure and other basic features. It is worth noting that the management and control of a parastatal is vested in a Board of Directors whose members are appointed by a Commissioner/Minister of the Central Government. In many economies, regardless of their economic systems, parastatals are undertaken in areas of public utility such as electricity, telecommunication, water, oil and gas, steel development, television authority, etc. And so among the surviving parastatals in Uganda, there are: Bank of Uganda, National Water and Sewerage Corporation, Uganda Printing Publication Corporation

Justification for Government Ownership of Parastatals

- Some corporations provide services that cannot be left in the hands of private individuals. Examples are the services Bank of Uganda, National Water and Sewerage Corporation, Uganda Printing Publication Corporation......, among other parastatals that provide strategic and sensitive services.

- The capital requirement for some projects is so enormous that an individual may not be able to afford it.

- The desire for rapid economic development may necessitate the government to provide (through ownership), long-term capital projects such as infrastructures and basic services which require huge sums for their investments and which cannot, therefore, be profitably attractive to/and undertaken through private investment.

- Government's ownership in business is necessary because, provision of certain goods and services by private enterprises may not be adequate in a way that can promote social justice.

ii)   Goals / objectives of business organisations

Promoters of business organisations initiate them for a variety of objectives/ goals, depending on the nature of the business, its prospective clientele, and long-term vision. Some of these objectives overlap each (achievement of one will, by default, embed that of some other objective) while others are absolutely conflicting with each other (achieving one will entail a hindrance to the achievement of some other objective), as my reader will later make a critical analysis of them all. These objectives can be broadly classified into financial objectives & non-financial objectives, as discussed below:

a)   Financial Objectives;

-   Profit maximization: many a firms are established to gain as much profits as humanly possible so as to give a return to their owners; offer attractive salaries and benefits to employees; but also to use these profits to contribute to social causes.

-   Wealth maximization: some firms aim at maximizing the net-worth of both the business but also of the shareholders through avenues such as retaining and consequently re-investing their profits in viable long-term ventures and capital formation.

b)   Non-Financial Objectives

-   Welfare maximisation of employees: some firms appreciate the value of human resources, and so they strive to boost their welfare since it significantly correlate with high corporate productivity through sales and profits. This can be done through giving reasonable and commensurate salaries; transport and medical facilities; but also assurance of terminal benefits, and recreation facilities for relaxation and managing work-related stress.

-   Welfare of the Society: businesses have a social responsibility to community were they operate and earn profits. This can be through ethical practices such as; maintaining good relations with communities, avoiding harmful production processes, and also companies contributing to social causes eg MTN Marathon that raises funds for provision of clean water to remote rural areas.

-   Fair dealing with Suppliers: a business can aim at having a good dealing with its suppliers of goods and services through meeting its obligations in due time; avoiding double dealings in procurement process.

- Customers' Interests: organisations ought to be mindful of their customers and seek to retain them by; providing quality products, ensuring the provision of value for money transactions, avoiding ill-treatment of the customers.

- Duty to the Government: in modern mixed economies where governments no longer lead production, their role is basically regulatory and provision of public goods & services. Given that fact, businesses should pay corporation taxes & other taxes; they should operate within the government's development plans; but also operate within a legal system that control their production processes.

- Some firms seek for growth and diversification in the industry.

- Other firms aim at improving productivity and becoming market leaders in the industry.

- Companies seek to survive autonomously from their mother companies.

- Some firms seek to maintain a competitive labour force.

iii)   Finance Functions in the Corporate Sector

Finance functions in a corporate body are greatly intertwined with other business operations such as production, marketing, strategic management, and others. They require skilful planning, control and execution of the company operations since these functions affect the size, profitability, growth, value of the firm and its risk management systems. Thus, the following are the major finance functions/decisions in a given firm:

Investment Decision (long-term asset-mix)

Corporate investment decisions greatly entail capital expenditure analysis, and so these are referred to as capital budgeting decisions: decisions of allocation of capital to long-term assets that would yield benefits in the future. Investment decisions are a function of: evaluating the prospective profitability of new investments; and, measuring/comparing the cut-off rate against the prospective returns of new investments. This further entails aspects of risk management due to uncertainty, and also replacement decisions of less productive real assets of the firm.

Financing Decisions (capital mix)

Corporate financial managers should be skilled enough to make rational decisions on when, from where, and how to acquire finances to meet the business' investment needs. This leads to an important element in corporate finance "capital structure": the appropriate mix of debt and equity long-term financing of the firm. They must endeavor to obtain the best financing mix called the optimum capital structure which is achieved when the market value of the company's shares is maximized. Despite its challenges, on the contrary, debt financing is so critical in corporate financing in variety of ways.

Dividend Decision (profit allocation)

This decision is quite imperative to firms, and so corporate financial managers ought to prudently decide whether the business will distribute all its profits; retain some profits; distribute a certain percentage of profits and then retain the remain portion. The fraction of profits distributed as dividends is called the dividend-payout ratio, while the retained fraction of profits is called the retention ratio. An optimum dividend policy is one which maximizes the market value of the firm's shares since a dividend policy should be determined in terms of its effect on the shareholders' value.

Liquidity Decision (short-term asset-mix)

Liquidity is so critical in corporate financial management due to its contribution either to corporate liquidation or survival in operations. And it is significantly affected by investment decision in current assets; these must be managed efficiently so as to safeguard the firm against liquidity risks. In corporate finance, profitability management and liquidity risk management normally clash basically in context of investment in current assets due to need to keep enough funds for recurrent operations of the firm yet some idle current assets don't earn profits to the firm. Thus, the profitability-liquidity trade-off advocates for sound techniques of current assets management by the finance department through estimating the firm's currents financial requirements so as to make available such funds when need arises.

iv)   Investment Options available for Corporate Treasuries

As already emphasized, corporate treasurer have a wide array of investment avenues available to them not only to safeguard the corporate funds or provide for the liquidity requirements of the firm but also create more value (returns) for the firms from any funds that are not currently in use. These have been thoroughly discussed in "Financial Assets", but among others, these are:

-   Deposits at banks (current accounts): these are instantly withdrawn, highly liquid but low returns.

-   Time deposit at a bank: a notice is required to withdraw the funds; interest rate is slightly higher than for current account but still close to the rate of inflation which actually almost washes away the supposed return.

- Certificate of deposit (CDs) offered by banks

- Treasury bills: these are sold by the government for its liquidity requirements but also monetary policy instruments. These are tradable in the secondary market.

- Bank bills: also called acceptance credit (as discussed in earlier)

- Local Authority deposits: this is an avenue of lending to local governments/ authorities through instruments like municipal bonds, infrastructural bonds, etc. Kampala Capital City Authority (KCCA) has shown interest in issuing an infrastructural bond so as to boost its infrastructural development projects.

- Discount market deposits: these are deposits normally repayable at call (on demand) or made for a very short-term basically in Interbank money markets.

- Government treasuries: this is the purchase of Uganda government notes and bonds in the secondary market.

- Corporate bonds: this entails the purchase of bonds/ debentures issued by firms but in the secondary market.

- Eurobonds and Bull-dog bonds: this is about lending on an international bond market.

- Commercial papers: these are unsecured promissory notes usually 60 days or less to maturity.

- Shares: as already discussed for public limited companies.

- Derivatives: such as futures, swaps, options, etc. Unfortunately, the derivative industry in the whole East African Community has not had any trial or activity for a variety of reasons.

chapter 22

HOUSEHOLD SECTOR / Investors
(Personal finance)

These make decisions regarding activities such as: work; job training; retirement planning; savings Vs consumption. Most households are interested in a wide array of assets that are attractive; these can vary considerably depending on: one's economic situation; the tax liability and its management; coupled with the risk elements in the available assets and their hedging possibilities. These financial decisions are aimed at boosting the net-worth of each household through prudent investment, and are the driving forces behind financial innovation, so as to accommodate all investor categories, their tax management and risk and return profiles.

i) Personal Asset-Building

Investment research has shown that a person's age and level of responsibility affects the kind of investments he makes at each stage in life. Nonetheless, the most critical investment decision for most households concerns education in early life and interestingly this constitutes a perpetual investment in human capital development. It is imperative to note that any investment in human training is golden and life-long. In labor economics, we believe that human beings working in an organization are its most important assets (actually for me, I normally refer to them as "human assets", when discussing about personal and community asset-building). On the contrary, for them to be called human resources but not laborers they must be educated, trained, skilful and productive otherwise it could be amassing a population of people with no value to add to an organization or an economy.

This is because the major asset most people have during their early working years (after their education or training) is the earning power derived from their skills. At this point in the life cycle, the most important financial decision (asset) concerns insurance against the possibility of disability or sudden death before retirement.

Secondly, the first economic asset many people crave to acquire is their own house. In Uganda, for instance, it is an element of pride and prestige to live in owner-occupier property since this is viewed as a hedge against two types of risk: increase in rent payables annually; and the risk availability of that property for one to always occupy it since soon or later the landlord may give you a quit notice. The more interesting economics of owning one's own house is that landed property (land and building) are the only real assets, in theory and practice, that appreciate in value as time passes-by and as the locality where the house is located develops and gets more densely populated.

Towards old-age, as a household accumulates savings to provide for consumption during retirement, the composition of personal assets shift from human assets to financial assets. At this point, portfolio choices become progressively more important with shorter investment horizons unlike during middle age, when most households will be willing to take on a meaningful amount of portfolio risk in order to increase their returns.

Risk and Return Profiles

In the investment world, all investors would like to preserve their principal capital and make sure that it is always safe and free from any risk, and whenever they invest, to maximize the rate of returns on their investments (net of tax and inflation).

Unfortunately, these two objectives are always in conflict since, in Finance, we believe that: the higher the risk in an investment, the higher the anticipated returns (risk-return trade-off) so as to compensate for the probability of a loss. However, practical investment results have shown that, in the great majority of cases, less risky investments earn more income than high-risk investment, and there lies the dilemma of risk-return assumptions in investment. In practice therefore, increased investment risk does not always guarantee a higher return on investment.

ii) Investment Policies

In the investment world, three terms are so critical yet somewhat confusing in the field of portfolio management, though they ought to be handled by different people so as to maximize the risk/return profiles of the investors, and these are: investment management, investment policy, and investment strategy. In effect, *investment management* refers to the actual practice of selecting financial assets and placing them in a portfolio (collection of assets); while an *investment policy* (IPS) is a statement outlining the expectations of the portfolio manager and the constraints under which the manager must operate to achieve investment targets. On the contrary, an *investment strategy* is a series of short-term activities that are consistent with established investment policy and that will contribute positively toward obtaining the portfolio objective.

In the pursuit of making the most profits out the investments, there are some constraints, risks and huddles that must be scaled before getting to the ecstasy of investment profits. To be a successful investor, one should put sound policies and plans in place to ensure that he/she is not taking undue risks or making disastrous investment decisions.

Investment objectives	Investment Constraints	Investment Policies
Return Requirements Risk Tolerance	Liquidity needs Investment horizon Regulations on investments Taxes (tax liability) Unique needs of investors	Asset Allocations Diversification possibilities Risk positioning Tax positioning Income generation

Asset allocation refers to the allocation of the portfolio across major asset categories such as: Money market assets (cash equivalents), fixed-income securities, equities (both listed and private equity), real estates, real properties (precious metals and other commodities), and derivative assets. Only after the broad asset classes to be held in the portfolio are determined can one sensibly choose then specific securities to purchase. Investors who have relatively high degree of risk tolerance will choose asset allocation more concentrated in higher-risk investment classes, such as equity, to obtain higher expected rates of return. More conservative investors will choose asset allocation with a greater weight in bonds and cash equivalents

Retail Vs Institutional investors

Whereas households need not concern themselves with organizational efficiency, institutional investors with large amounts to invest must structure asset allocation activities to decentralize some of the decision making. A common feature of large organizations is the investment committee that includes top administrators, senior portfolio managers, and senior security analysts. The committee determines investment policies and verifies that portfolio managers and security analysts are operating within the bounds of specified policies. A key responsibility of the investment committee is to translate the objectives and constraints of the organization into an "asset universe", which is an approved list of assets for each of the organization's portfolios.

iii) Investment Decision-making

But by and large, investment decisions for any financial agent are sub-divided into: investment objectives; investment constraints; and investment policies. And below is a tabular representation of these three investment basics from a portfolio management perspective:

NB: Investment horizon refers to the final time to fund or the planned liquidation date of the investment. And regulations refer to universal investment laws like the prudent man's rule (all investments evaluated from a portfolio perspective); whereby an investment professional is held accountable for the IPS (investment policy statement) even in courts of laws; among other local laws that govern/ affect investments in a given financial system. The prudent investor rule requires a fiduciary to "cautiously" invest clients' assets as if they were his own, based on the knowledge the fiduciary has at the time and considering only the needs of the beneficiaries.

The prudent expert rule requires that the fiduciary manage the portfolio with the care, skill, prudence, and diligence, under the circumstances then prevailing, that a prudent investor would use. It extends the prudent investor rule beyond prudence by suggesting a higher level of expertise.

Investment objectives are basically centered on the risk/return profiles (trade-off), and so both investors and their investment managers ought to know the factors that govern each investor categories. Below are some of the established investor categories:

- Retail (household) investors and personal trusts
- Unit trust funds and other CIVs
- Pension funds & Retirement benefits schemes
- Endowment funds & Foundations
- Life Insurance companies
- Banking institutions

- Non-Life Insurance companies

Below is an analysis of the underlying determinants of the investment objectives & constraints vis-à-vis the investor categories:

Investor Category	Return Requirement	Risk Tolerance	Liquidity	Horizon	Regulation	Taxes
Retail investors & personal trusts	Life-cycle needs such as education, caring for their children, retirement needs etc.	Life-cycle risk profiles: younger investors are more risk tolerant in contrast to older folks.	variable	Life-cycle	None	Variable
Unit trust funds & CIVs	Variable (depending on underlying composition)	Variable (depending on underlying composition)	High	Variable	CMA & URBRA laws	Yes
Pension funds & Retirement Benefit funds	Dependent on presumed Actuarial rates	Dependent on proximity of pay-outs.	Variable due to age.	Long	URBRA laws	None
Endowment funds & Foundations	Based on current institutional income needs and asset growth.	Generally conservative.	Low	Long	Few/ none	None
Life Insurance companies	Above periodical money market rates so as to meet expenses & actuarial rates.	Relatively conservative.	Low	Long	Composite	Yes
Banking institutions	Based on the Interest spread.	Slightly below Average	High	Normally short	Changing	Yes
Non-life Insurance firms	No benchmarks	Relatively conservative.	Relatively high		Few	Yes

Source : Researcher's Data

iv) Asset Allocation Strategies

Besides, in investment management, one of the key policies that ought to be prudently designed is the asset allocation policy since some investment gurus have established that asset allocation decisions explain about 90% of the variability of returns over time (Ibbotson and Kaplan, 2000). And globally, various asset allocation systems have been developed from 1952 when Harry Markowitz established his seminal work on Modern Portfolio Theory (MPT) that introduced the science of the risk-efficient portfolio. So, among them are:

- Single asset allocation.
- Static asset allocation guided by the MPT.
- Strategic asset allocation guided by the CAPM (capital asset pricing model).
- Tactical asset allocation that was championed by Wells Fargo in the late 1970s after the market declines at that time.
- Risk-focused asset allocation (CAPM Tangent Added theory) introduced by Mellon Capital in 1989.
- Pine Bridge CML Approach introduced by Pine Bridge Investments research team in 2000.
- Risk-focused & Risk parity in the wake of the 2008 Global financial crisis.

Generally, designing asset allocation policies requires a four stages process:

- Specifying asset classes to be included in the portfolio, such as: money market instruments; fixed-income securities; stocks; real estate; commodities, etc. institutional investors are basically interested in the first four unlike retail investors.
- Specifying capital markets expectations using historical data and economic analysis.
- Deriving the efficient portfolio frontier: the portfolio achieving maximum expected returns for any given level of risk.
- Finding the optimal asset mix: one that best meets investors' risk/ return objectives while satisfying the constraints they face.

Chapter 23

GOVERNMENT SECTOR (Public Finance)

i) Its role as financial agent

Government also need finance for their expenditures due to their deficit budgets. Unlike corporations, governments can't issue equity securities and so they are confined to borrowing as a means of raising funds since normally tax revenues are not sufficient to cover expenditures. On the contrary, they can also print more money, though this source if excessively used has inflationary implications that can adversely affect the financial system soundness of a country. States are advantaged in the debt market due to their taxing power that makes them credit worthy and so they can borrow at low rates and for long-term.

ii) Public finance & its Constituents

Public finance is the science that studies avenues through which government sources for revenue and how it spends the funds. It refers to the total amount of money a government receives from a variety of both domestic and foreign sources in a given period for its expenditure, and this includes: public revenue; public expenditure; public debts; financial administration; fiscal policy management.

-   Public Revenue: this is the total income acquired by the government through its taxation and non-taxation measures. Among the taxation sources are: the direct taxes (income tax, property tax, corporate tax, land tax, among other taxes); while the indirect or expenditure taxes (sales tax, excise and custom duties, sumptuary tax, octroi tax, and value added tax). On the other hand, the non-taxation avenues are: collection of fees, market dues, road tolls and rates; acquisition of gifts and grants; borrowing internally and externally; sale of licences; government investments; deficit financing).

- Public Expenditure: this is the total amount of money which the government and its institutions spend on provision of public services and development projects such as infrastructure, health, education. This can be classified into: consumption expenditure on daily administrative activities like paying civil servants, and maintaining law and order; capital expenditure on medium and long-term State projects for economic development like establishing industries and infrastructures; and transfer payments such as grants, donations, bursaries, subsidies, pensions, and re-distribution of wealth.

- Public Debt: this is total amount of resources borrowed directly or indirectly by local governments and parastatals; from both internal and external sources. This can further be categorized into: reproductive debt which is invested in productive activities like infrastructure; dead weight debt whose returns can't cover the debt like financing wars and State functions; funded debt whose repayment period is not specified; floating debt whose repayment period is fixed and usually short term.

- Financial Administration: this is the process involving preparation of the budget and auditing of all government ministries, departments, and entities.

- Fiscal Policy Management: it is the use of taxation, borrowing and government expenditure to finance State activities and to bring about economic stability for proper growth and development.

iii) Need for public finance

- The State, as a financial agent, performs a wide array of functions which must be financed; thus, below is the rationale for public finance:

- Public revenue is used by the State to carry out investments that are aimed at efficiently allocating resources for national benefit.

- In mixed economic systems where resource are largely owned by individuals, public finance is used as a tool to direct private investments in a variety of ways: taxation to stimulate/discourage production in certain sectors and regions; public expenditure on infrastructure to attract private investors in a certain region.

- It helps government in provision of public services like road construction, establishing schools and universities, security, and communication facilities.

- Public finance is rather critical in undertaking risky and expensive ventures that can't be undertaken by private sector such hydro electricity power generation.

- It is used to give relief to vulnerable groups and also in overcoming catastrophes such as the Bududa landslide victims, Kasese floods victims, but also the poor, displaced and war victims in Nakivale, Rwamwanja and other refugee settlement camps.

- Public finance through the prudential management of Bank of Uganda serves to ensure economic stability through the use of fiscal and monetary policies so as to achieve macroeconomic stability and financial system soundness.

- It can be used as an instrument for the government to fight poverty through government expenditure on infrastructure that provides incomes to citizens who subsequently better their livelihood.

- The State uses public finance mechanisms to foster equitable distribution of incomes and also regional balances basically through the instrument of taxation and government spending.

- It can be used as a tool for public debt management through taxation and other revenue sources that help the economy in debt servicing.

iv) Objectives of Fiscal policy

- The Government aims at accelerating private-sector led economic growth.

- Maintain macro-economic stability, including low inflation close to the medium term target of 5% per annum, and a stable exchange rate.

- Improve domestic revenue mobilization and optimize a mix of financing sources such as PPPs, equity financing, less concessional external loans and other debt market financing instruments to implement critical priority infrastructure investments.

- Improve expenditure efficiency through public finance management reforms to ensure effectiveness of scarce resources.

- Support increased production and productivity as well as skills training to create jobs.

- Fiscal policy serves to regulate economic activities through government expenditures and taxation patterns that either boost or trim aggregate demand according to the need of the economy.

- Government uses taxation (which of part of fiscal policy) to protect the health of her citizens through over taxing demerit commodities (goods & services) such as toxic drugs, gambling, among others.

- The State uses fiscal policy to promote economic development by either direct investments using government expenditure or through the provision of tax incentives to private investors.

- The government aims at equitable distribution of income through the progressive taxation device that renders high-income earners' tax liability to be higher than low income earners, and consequently redistribute those tax funds to low income earners through service provision.

To accelerate economic growth, increase per capita income to middle income country status, and reduce poverty faster; priority will be given to improving domestic resource mobilization, expenditure efficiency and diversifying sources of financing, including exploring new financing options available on the global financial markets like Eurobonds, Bull-dog bonds, etc; and this will be an integral part of the fiscal strategy in this decade.

v) The National Budget

This is a statement/account outlining anticipated government revenue and expenditure together with measures to boost economic development in the forth coming financial year. This outline unearths the following fundamentals: economic, social and political objectives to be achieved; revenue expected and its sources; nature and allocation of expenditures; summary of economic performance; contribution of different sectors to GDP; among others.

Public Resource Mobilization

The government uses both domestic and external avenues to mobilize resources for its annual budget. Domestic tax revenue is the most crucial source of resources for funding the national budget; this is under the docket of the Directorate of Economic Affairs (Ministry of Finance) that is tasked with shaping the tax policy. This has far reaching implications across the government system, and this compounded by the dwindling donor aid, due to a variety of reasons, and has rendered the collection of adequate taxes more instrumental than ever before.

The total revenue collections for FY2013/14, registered a drop in nominal growth from an average of 19.4% in the previous consecutive three fiscal years to 12.4% that amounted to UGX 8,031.03 Billion. This decline is a function of: lower than projected GDP growth; lower performance in telecommunication and banking sectors; government not meeting tax obligations on behalf of some companies with tax holidays; tax avoidance by some telecommunication firms; volatile exchange rate; and also a number of policy measures aimed at increasing taxes but not approved by Parliament. Total direct taxes amounted to UGX 2,624.45 Billion against the projected UGX 2,873.57 despite a nominal year on year growth of 7.8% in that fiscal year.

Below is a comparative analysis of performance of selected direct taxes.

SECTOR	FY2012/13	FY2013/14	% CHANGE
Banking Sector	80.32	31.73	-60.50
Telecom Sector	115.02	91.06	-20.82
Beer Sector	33.2	4.32	-47.75
Cigarette Sector	9.1	7.86	-13.58
Withholding Tax Growth (Billions)			
Government Payment	53.25	59.06	10.92
Management & Professional fees	33.11	36.10	9.05
Dividends	46.73	29.20	-37.51
General Supplies	195.38	236.71	21.15
Foreign Transactions	64.70	45.30	-29.99
Total	**393.17**	**406.37**	**3.36**
Treasury Bills & Bond Payments (Billions)			
Tax on bank interest	67.66	68.66	1.48
Treasury bills/ bond	153.94	178.44	15.92
Total	**221.59**	**247.10**	**11.51**

Source: URA Databases, MoFPED

The underperformance of the banking sector was largely due to higher provisioning for bad debts which are deductible for tax purposes and hence reduce the taxable income of banks. This saw at least three financially strong banks (Stanbic bank, Citi bank, and Diamond Trust bank payment decline by UGX 10.12 Billion. Besides, regarding the withholding tax, poor performance basically stems from lower profits among the main tax payers and a decline in offshore loans from parent companies by 30% (UGX 19.40 Billion) which led to lower dividends especially in the banking and insurance sectors.

a) Types of National Budget

There are basically three types of national budget, these are:

Balanced Budget: this is a budget whose expected annual revenue is equal to the estimated expenditure in a given fiscal year.

Deficit Budget: this is a budget whose estimated annual expenditure is greater than the estimated annual revenue. This is characteristic of most LDCs which run deficit budgets that necessitate supplementary funds through: internal and external borrowing; using foreign exchange reserves; issuing more money; seeking for grants; among other avenues.

Surplus Budget: this is a budget whose estimated revenue is greater than the estimated expenditure in a given fiscal year. This kind of budget is aimed at: reducing money circulation in the financial system; raising more revenue for debt financing; encouraging hard work and strengthen the private sector; increasing national foreign reserves.

b) Functions of National Budget

- A national budget serves to regulate and allocate resources through the exploitation of certain resources and subsidizing some activities but also discouraging some production processes.

- It is used as an instrument of social and economic policy to mobilise citizens towards designed economic targets.

- It serves to foster appropriate monetary and fiscal policies to influence money supply, government expenditure and economic development that is desirable in a given fiscal year.

- It is used in bringing about regional balances by allocating more resources and subsidies to the less developed regions and sectors in an economy.

- A national budget is used as a mechanism to stabilize the balance of payments through boosting domestic production and exportation, and equally discouraging unnecessary importation.

- It is used to reduce income inequalities in the country through highly taxing the wealthy so as to subsidize the poor and provide equal income opportunities.

c) Rationale for Drawing a Deficit Budget in Uganda

- Deficit budgets are used as an avenue for stimulating aggregate demand in an economy, and consequently stimulate domestic investments.

- It serves to reduce unemployment through government's expansionary fiscal policy in a way of huge government expenditure in infrastructure and public service.

- It serves to reduce income inequality and regional imbalances through both taxation and government expenditures.

- Deficit budgets can be used as remedy to low government revenue in LDCs which is so crucial to public financing.

- There are circumstances when government borrowing can be a cheaper and quicker source of financing for its projects than revenue from other avenues like taxation.

d) Effect of Budget Deficit on Macro economic Stability

The national debt is the amount of money that the government owes those from whom it has borrowed, and this varies from year to year depending on the macroeconomic objectives of the economic and its needs for financial system soundness. In a year when government spending is less than tax collections, the difference is the government surplus. The national debt shrinks by the amount of the surplus. In a year when government spending is greater than tax collections, the difference is the government deficit. The national debt grows by the amount of deficit.

A government spending more than it collects in taxes (including the inflation tax) must borrow the difference in order to finance its spending. A government borrows through the facility of the Open Market Operations: sale of treasury securities to its citizens and foreigners, which are promises that the government will repay the principal it borrows with interest. These accumulated promises to pay make up the national debt. The government budget deficit is equal to purchases minus net taxes while the fiscal policy measures purchases and taxes. The government's budget balance is a measure of the fiscal policy but the budget deficit is not the right measure of the government's actual deficit (or surplus)

Economists are interested in the deficit for two reasons.

- The deficit is a convenient and often handy, though sometimes treacherous, measure of fiscal policy's role in stabilization policy. It is an index of how government spending and tax plans affect the position of the IS curve.

- The deficit is closely connected with national savings and investment: rising deficit tends to depress capital formation, and it lowers the economy's long-run steady-state growth path; besides reducing the steady-state GDP per worker. High national debt means that taxes in the future will be higher to pay with high interest charges. Such high tax liabilities are likely to further discourage economic activity and economic welfare of the citizens

The Budget Deficit and Stabilization Policy

An increase in government purchases increases aggregate demand, which shifts the IS curve out to the right, increasing the level of real GPD for each possible value of the interest rate. A decrease in government tax collection also increases aggregate demand, and shifts the IS curve out, as demonstrated in the following Curve.

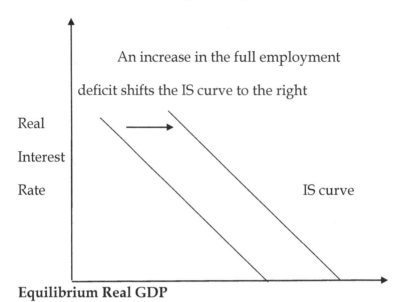

An increase in the full employment deficit shifts the IS curve to the right

Real

Interest

Rate

IS curve

Equilibrium Real GDP

The cyclically-adjusted budget deficit is a good measure of the impact of the government's taxing and spending on aggregate demand. When the cyclically or full employment adjusted budget deficit rises, the IS curve shifts right as government policy becomes more stimulative. When the cyclically-adjusted budget deficit falls, the IS curve shifts left as government policy becomes more contractionary.

However, Uganda's production capacity is low where most of the purchases are from abroad (imports), the increase in government purchases does not stimulate local production and demand to bring about an outward shift in real GDP. In this case, increase in government purchases has led to increase in resource outflow leading to slow economic growth and subjecting the economy to persistent high real interest rate as a result of the crowd-out effects.

In addition, most of government purchases are not productive investments, coupled with increase in capital expenditures such as Universal Primary Education, buying Fire arms and choppers to promote domestic security, interstate highway system, and improvement in the national parks. All these bring about benefits only in the future; it is hard to see any long-run dividing line between government investment and government consumption expenditures that would be sustainable from a political point of view. Thus, critics regard capital budgeting as simply too difficult to implement in a helpful way, nonetheless, supporters point out that not doing capital budgeting at all is, in a sense, worse than even the least helpful implementation.

Deficits: Short –Run Consequences

In the short run, a deficit produced by a tax cut stimulates consumer spending yet a deficit produced by an increase in government spending increases government purchases. Either way, it shifts the IS curve out to the right: Any given interest rate is associated with a higher equilibrium value of production and employment. If the monetary policy is unchanged to bring about a change in the LM curve, then output and employment rise in response to the tax cut. If the Central Bank does not want inflation to rise, it will respond to the rightward expansionary shift in the IS curve by tightening monetary policy and raising interest rates, neutralizing the expansionary effect of the deficit. J. Delong, the American Economist indicated that the decision making and policy implementation cycle for monetary policy is significantly shorter than the decision-making and policy implementation cycle for the discretionary monetary policy and it's the role of the central Bank to keep legislative actions to change the deficit from affecting the level of production and unemployment. The central Bank should try its best to guide the economy along the narrow path without excess unemployment and without accelerating inflation.

Effects of Budget Deficit on the Open-Economy

Such an increase in the government budget deficit also leads to an increase in the trade deficit. The outward shift in the IS curve pushes up interest rates: higher interest rates cause appreciation of the domestic currency and depreciation in the foreign currency which causes imports to rise and exports to fall. It is implicitly assumed that the composition of aggregate demand has no effect on the productivity of industry. Business sector is implicitly assumed to be equally happy and productive whether they are producing consumption goods, or capital goods for household use, or goods and services that the government will purchase, or commodities for the export market.

As large deficits that increase interest rates raise the value of the exchange rate, export industries that are highly productive shrink as exports shrink. This presumably reduces total productivity, though; nobody has a reliable and concrete estimate of how large these effects might be to the economy/ financial system.

The Effect of Budget Deficit on Economic Growth

High full employment deficits lead to low investment; on the IS -LM equilibrium, a deficit whether from more government purchases or lower taxes, shifts the IS curve to the right. In any run long enough for the full-employment flexible-price model, large full-employment deficits lead to lower aggregate savings, higher real interest rates, and lower investments. In a flexible-price context analysis, the analysis of persistent deficits is straight forward; and such deficits reduce national savings. Flow-of-funds equilibrium thus requires higher real interest rates and lower levels of investment spending.

Illustration: High Full-Employment Deficits Reduce Investments

Flexible Price Flow-of-Funds Diagram   Sticky-Price IS Curve

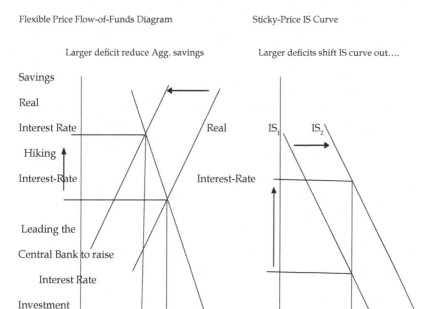

Larger deficit reduce Agg. savings   Larger deficits shift IS curve out....

And Reducing Investment

Even in a sticky-price context, it may be that higher deficits reduce investment. The central Bank can change the monetary policy to neutralize the effect of higher deficit on real GDP. The central Bank chooses its baseline monetary policy in order to try to strike the optimum balance between the risk of the higher-than-necessary unemployment and the risk of rising inflation. The central Bank does not want this balance disturbed by shifts in the IS curve, so it is highly likely to use monetary policy to offset the effect of the deficit- driven shift in the IS curve on the level of real GDP and employment.

A higher deficit means a higher debt, which means that the government owes more in the way of interest payment to bondholders. Even if the level of deficit is kept constant, the rise in interest rates will require tax increases and these tax increases will discourage entrepreneurship and economic activity. In addition to the reduction in output per worker resulting from the lower capital-output ratio, there will be an additional reduction in output per worker: the increased taxes needed to finance the interest owed on the national debt will have negative supply-side effects on production.

vi) Forms of Public Expenditure

There are majorly three forms of public expenditure, as discussed below:

Operational/Recurrent Expenditure: this is the total amount of resources spent by governments on funding its administrative or daily activities such as enforcing law and order, paying civil servants, financing foreign trips, etc.

Capital/Development Expenditure: this is money spent by governments on medium and long-term state projects which significantly contribute to economic development such as: establishment of industries, transport and communication infrastructure; but also social systems like schools and hospitals.

Transfer Payments: these are funds that States spend on non-profitable initiatives such as: giving grants, donations, bursaries, pension payments, scholarships, etc.

Roles of public expenditure

Public expenditure can be financed through either taxation financing, debt financing or both as already discussed earlier on. And below is the contribution of public expenditure to the financial system:

- It serves to boost economic development through huge expenditure in sectors like agriculture that can stimulate the private sector activities which are normally limited and resource constrained.

- It stimulates the economy's purchasing power and attraction of investors when governments spend on recurrent activities and transfer payments (President's hand-outs – Kibaasa) that boost aggregate demand in the country.

- Public expenditure is used to invest in projects that the private sector can't afford to invest in due to huge capital requirements such as electricity, oil refinery, and others.

- States use public expenditure to invest in non-profitable and public ventures that are so critical for economic development such as social and economic infrastructure.

- It serves to foster regional balance since governments expenditures ensures equal regional distribution of the national cake (resources) in form of investment and enabling atmosphere so as to facilitate balance economic growth.

- This also serves to maintain governments in power through the provision of services and delivering their mandate especially through good administration, health care provision and investment in internal and external security.

vii) PUBLIC DEBT

a) Classification of Public Debt

Public debt can be specifically classified according to the following criterion:

Debt Sources: whereby there are internal debts – funds borrowed by the government within the economy through the sale of government/treasury securities like bills, notes and bonds to the public while external debts are funds borrowed by the State from outside the economy such as: international aid, high net-worth individuals, other governments through securities like Eurobonds.

Debt Utilisation: some debts are reproductive debts – funds borrowed and invested in productive activities like infrastructure and parastatals; while dead weight debts are funds borrowed for financing activities that can't be used to repay debts like financing wars, State functions, etc.

Debt Repayment: a funded debt is one whose repayment schedule is not specified and such debts are secured; while an unfunded debt is debt whose repayment schedule is fixed and on short run basis like sale of treasury securities.

GOVERNMENT DEBT LIABILITY

The total public debt stock (debt outstanding & disbursed) has grown from a total of USD 7 Billion by end March 2014 of FY 2013/14 to USD 7.28 Billion by end February 2015 of FY 2014/15. Of which external debt contributes a whole 57% of the total debt and domestic debt is 43%; but this excludes loans approved by Parliament but had not been contracted by March 2015.

Below is the Total Public Debt by source category as at February 2015 (USD Billion)

Total Public Debt	FY 2013/14 (March 2014)	FY 2014/15 (Feb. 2015)		
	USD Bn	USD Bn	% of GDP	Share of Total Debt
External Debt Outstanding & Disbursed	4.18	4.18	15%	57%
Bilateral	1.15	0.59	2%	8%
Multilateral	5.50	3.59	13%	49%
Domestic Debt	2.82	3.10	11%	43%
Treasury Bills	1.07	1.01	3%	14%
Treasury Bonds	1.75	2.09	8%	29%
Total Public Debt	7.00	7.28	26%	100%

Source: MoFPED, BOU

Public Debt Stock Trends (2003/04 to 2013/14)

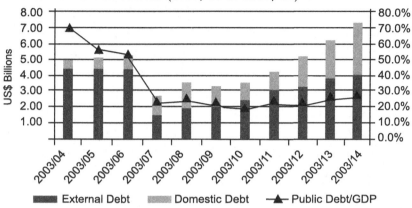

Debt Catagory by source

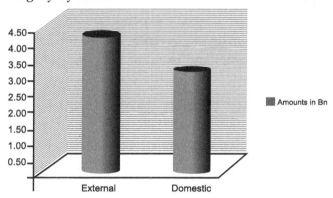

Below is the Stock of Domestic Debt as at end February 2015

MATURITY	STOCK (UGX)	STOCK (USD)	% of TOTAL STOCK
TREASURY BILLS			
91 Days	69,071,327,632	23,824,435.7	0.80%
182 Days	250,577,353,539	86,430,422.93	2.80%
364 Days	2,612,382,445,105	90,076,319.89	29.00%
Sub-total	2,932,031,126,276	1,011,331,178.57	32.60%
TREASURY BONDS			
2 Years	1,603,668,259,355	553,145,460.60	17.80%
3 Years	1,147,373,799,305	395,758,041.69	12.70%
5 Years	1,869,578,077,050	644,864,436.51	20.80%
10 Years	1,091,031,667,429	367,324,255.27	12.10%
15 Years	356,726,001,613	123,043,577.76	4.00%
Sub-total	6,068,377,804,752	2,093,135,922.83	67.40%
GRAND TOTAL	9,000,408,931,028	3,104,467,101.40	100.00%

Source: MoFPED

The total stock of outstanding government domestic debt, at cost, as of end February 2015 was UGX 9,000,408 Billion (USD 3.10 Billion) compared to the stock of UGX 7,213.5 Billion (USD 2,823.9 Million) as of end June 2014; which represents a 90% increase in the stock of domestic debt. Treasury bills amounted UGX 2,293.03 Billion (USD 1.09 Billion) while Treasury bonds amounted UGX 4,482.96 Billion (USD 2.36 Billion). The ratio of Bonds to Bills improved from the previous year when it was 61:39 at the end of March 2014 to 70:30 which is consistent with the ratio in the Public Debt Management Framework (2013).

b)   Rationale For Public Debt

Although some governments have enough capacity to levy taxes so as to cover their budgetary expenditure, there are concrete reasons as to why many a governments opt for debt financing in the form of internal and external borrowing. Among other bases, these are:

- Economic stability: borrowing, basically domestic debt through issuing treasury instruments (bills, notes, and bonds), helps to regulate the circulation of money. Consequently, this can reduce on inflation rates, but also direct both investments in target sectors and aggregate demand.

- Lessening the tax burden: public debt can serve to reduce on the effects of high taxation such as: deflationary situation whereby households' disposable incomes are way below the aggregate supply of commodities in the market due to high tax liabilities. Besides, taxation may discourage people from working hard (progressive tax system).

- Generating more government revenues: in reality, most frontier market economies like Uganda are characterized by high prevalence of tax evasion, corruption, tax avoidance, high informal sectors, and low taxable capacities. These render governments automatically to opt for debt financing due to the unproductiveness of taxation.

- Remedy for recession: economies that are facing economic depression normally borrow in a bid to boost aggregate demand, domestic investments and production for economic revitalization.

- Fixing the balance of payment position: LDCs are characterized by high operational expenditures, and this can only be financed through external borrowing.

- Public debt financing is sought for basically as the last resort in case of emergencies and disasters like famine, epidemics (Ebola, typhoid), wars that befall countries and many LDCs are not prepared enough to handle such eventualities. Hence, economies resort to foreign aid.

- Due to high debt burden in Frontier economies, at times they go into the debt market so as to clear/pay old loans that are chocking their economies.

- Political capital: many governments go in for borrowing like dead weight debt so as to render their regimes popular through the provision gifts (unstructured hand-outs) to people in a bid to mobilise support for the government.

- Debt financing can serve to redistribute incomes among the residents of a country in a bid to fight poverty.

c) Managing Public Debt

Public debt management are systems, mechanisms and policies through which the central bank contracts debts on behalf of the government, and services/clears both internal and external debts guided by the macroeconomic policies of an economy. This is primarily a function of the central bank since it is the custodian of the financial system and should ensure macroeconomic stability. Managing public debt entails the following roles:

- Determining when to contract the debt

- Determining the volumes of funds required

- Determining the source of debt (domestic or foreign)

- Determining the nature of the debt (treasury securities, euro-bond, bull dog bond, etc)

- Determining the means to service the debt (taxation, foreign exchange reserves, another loan, etc)

- Determining the mode of servicing the debt

d)   Methods of Public Debt Management

Public debt management, as already discussed, is a function of the country's central bank; and to achieve this macroeconomic goal, there is need separate between domestic debt management and external debt management so as to facilitate the process.

Managing Domestic Debt can be through the following methods:

- The State can seek for grants and donations from foreign sources to help clear internal loans to the government.

- The government can resort to a tax system that levies extra taxes on wealthy individuals and financially strong corporations

- Governments can opt for surplus budgets in a bid to mobilize additional resources for servicing domestic debts.

- Some economies use the avenue of privatisation of State parastatals so as to raise finances to clear domestic loans.

- There is also the opportunity of obtaining fresh debts from the public through the issuance of more government securities in a bid to either service or clear outstanding debts.

- In economic systems where the State still engages in production, accumulated profits from government parastatals can be used to service domestic debts.

- There is yet another monetary policy instrument that a State can exploit; that is running national rotaries like Jadah in the 1990s so as to extract excess liquidity from the public for macroeconomic equilibrium (domestic debt management).

On the contrary, systems of external debt management are as follows:

- The State might resolve to borrow further in the international financial markets so as to service and/or clear her foreign debts; through issuing Eurobonds, Bull dog bonds, and also from the IMF and World Bank.

- The government may use its foreign exchange reserves to service/ clear outstanding debts since they are actually used to manage the external economy vulnerabilities such as B.O.P alignment and debt servicing.

- There is also the option of seeking for foreign grants so as to service the country's outstanding debts.

- The economy can deliberately pursue policies that promote production for exports and also import substitution so as to better her B.O.P position and scale down on the debt liability.

- Besides, the government can use a wide array of mechanisms such as: debt rescheduling, barter negotiations, debt repudiation and debt cancelling in a bid to service/clear her outstanding debts.

- The State can also deliberately increase tariffs on international trade so as to mobilise funds for debt servicing/ clearing.

e)   IFMS (Financial Administration)

The Integrated Financial Management System (IFMS) was adopted and implemented by the Ugandan government since 2003 with a view to improve efficiency in budget preparation, execution and financial reporting. Its design was based on a centralized architecture which enables central processing and storage of financial transactions done in the data centre of the Ministry of Finance in Kampala, connecting all Ministries, agencies and Local governments (MALGs) over a Wide Area

Network (WAN) and accessing it through a web browser. Since its inception, it has been extended across all 22 ministries and 25 central government agencies; implemented close to 10 local governments, which has enabled government: to address many of the fiduciary issues faced before; greater expenditure control and discipline in budget management due to oversight ad enforcement of internal controls. Besides, there has been a reduction in taken time to process payments; improvement in account reconciliation; and more accurate & reliable financial reporting. Upon full implementation, the following transactions should be covered: all government transactions like revenue receipts, debt, expenditures (including transactions financed by donor or other agencies); and all government units (ministries, agencies, sub-national units, and projects). This will enhance implementation of common control regime and comprehensive fiscal reporting since the IFMS interfaces with URA, Bank of Uganda, and the integrated personnel & payroll system (IPPS) in the Ministry of Public Service.

Key IFMS COMPONENTS

IFMS Component	Role
Public Sector Budgeting	Enables vote holders to prepare & submit budgets electronically. Consolidation of transactions on the system
General Ledger	Enables electronic & automated posting of transactions on system.
Payables	Receiving & processing supplier invoices are linked electronically & validated in real time.
Purchasing	Links purchase orders to the online cash limits thus enhancing commitment controls.
Cash Management	Enables cash forecasting & bank reconciliation to be done online in real time. An interface with BoU is in place to facilitate automated reconciliation.
Revenue/ Receipting	Links Treasury with URA in respect of tax returns. Invoicing & collections of non-tax revenues can be managed online.

Chapter 24

PUBLIC PRIVATE PARTNERSHIPS (PPPS)

Public Private Partnerships (PPPs) are a form of financing that usually involves the use of private resources to provide a public good, especially infrastructure. They are a critical tool for fiscal control and management of public debt since budgetary commitments in respect of infrastructure and provision of services provided under the PPP arrangements are known in advance. In Uganda, the government prepared the Public Private Partnership Bill 2012 to establish the requisite legal framework for the operation of PPPs in Uganda and later it assented by the president into a law years later. These projects often require guarantees or allocate some risks to the State: retaining risks and issuing guarantees create contingent liabilities, which increases as the stock of PPPs increase. In response to this, the government has developed a tool which will carry out an assessment of the level of exposure of risk and contingent liability. By 2013/14, explicit contingent liability arising from PPPs stood at 0.23% of GDP over the medium-term. Governments, world over, believe that employing these PPP projects can procure the following to a given financial system:

- Mobilization of the private sector resources and development.

- Better utilization and allocation of public funds.

- More efficient development and delivery of the requisite public infrastructure.

- Achievement of value for money from public resources.

- Ensure good quality public services.

- Efficiency through healthy competition

The State has currently committed to explicit contingent liabilities through seven on-going PPPs though in FY 2014/15 no contingent liability was called upon from the existing PPP projects. Therefore, the summed estimated contingent liabilities on Government that may arise from these on-going PPP projects for FY 2015/16 fiscal year stand at UGX 123.6 Billion, equivalent to 0.15% of GDP. And below is the status of the PPP programs since 2003 and an analysis of the progress of on-going projects:

- Kalangala Infrastructure Services Project: it is a 20 year multi-sectoral project undertaking by Kalangala Infrastructure Services Ltd since 2009 under the Build, Own and Operate (BOT) modality. So far, among the deliverables: the ferry is operational and solar power and water supplies are readily available; the road component is 70% complete and Resettlement Action Plan (RAP) is substantially complete.

- Umeme Electricity Distribution Project: in 2004, Umeme Ltd was awarded a concession to distribute and supply electricity for a period of 20 years. Thus far, power outage has significantly reduced; connection to power grid increased; and power losses reduced from 38% initially to 24% currently.

- Kampala Serena Hotel Project: it is a 30 year concession contract signed between Tourism Promotion Services Ltd and Nile Hotel International Ltd on January 15, 2004. Despite the volatility of the tourism sector, the project has transformed Nile Hotel Ltd into a 5 Star Hotel and rebranded to Kampala Serena Hotel.

- Eskom Electricity Generation Project: it is a 20 year concession agreement between Eskom Uganda Ltd and Uganda Electricity Generation Company Ltd, which took effect in April 2003. Currently, the project supplies over 67% of Uganda's electricity energy.

- Kenya-Uganda Railway Project: in 2006, Kenya and Uganda signed a 25 year Kenya-Uganda Railway concession to improve transport conditions through restoration of railway operations. The railway comprises a total track length of 2,350 Km, of which 1920 Km is in Kenya and 430 Km in Uganda.

- Kilembe Mineral Project: it ia s 25 year concession arrangement between Kilembe Mines Ltd and Tibet Hima Automobile Industry Company Ltd executed in 2013 to further explore and develop minerals; hence creating jobs and preserving the natural environment.

- Bujagali Hydroelectric Project: it is a 30 year Build, Operate and Transfer (BOT) contract signed in 2005 between Bujagali Energy Ltd and Uganda Electricity Generation Company Ltd for the development of a 250MW hydroelectric plant, at an estimated construction cost of USD 902 million. The project was commissioned on 15th June 2012 and is currently operational.

The Public Investment Outlook & Vision 2040

In this decade, the government has progressively continued to promote the private sector as the engine of economic growth; and attracting increased investment both foreign and domestic is a key priority in the government's strategy to accelerate employment, productivity and socio-economic transformation of the country as envisaged in the Vision 2040. In the FY 2012/13, the Government conducted an Investor Survey to monitor the different government policies and interventions aimed at improving the business environment. The study revealed that macroeconomic issues continue to be a key concern of business: high inflation and exchange rate volatility have significantly and negatively affected business operations in almost 70% of the interviewed enterprises. Besides, many businesses operate below their capacity, and so there was a huge need to accelerate infrastructure development as well as skills provision for the domestic workforce so as to attract increased investment and also unleash Uganda's growth potential.

The survey targeted all domestic and foreign projects licensed by Uganda Investment Authority (UIA) from 1991 to 2010: it showed that of all the projects, 53.5% were owned by foreign investors, 42.2% by local investors while 4.3% were jointly owned by local and foreign investors. Foreign-owned projects attracted actual investment of USD 1, 493.1 Million; domestic-owned projects USD 1,283.7 Million; and joint venture projects USD 66.6 Million. Besides, the choice of Uganda as an investment destination was influenced by a number of both macroeconomic and political factors such as domestic and regional markets, and affordable labour.

Furthermore, in the fourth quarter of FY 2013/14, Uganda's actual investment grew by 8% to USD 46.8 Million with the foreign direct investments (FDI) astronomically surging by 92.51% to USD 1.721 Billion from USD 894 Million in 2011. This has been witnessed in basically the oil & energy as well as the manufacturing sectors but also the multinational corporations, and the recent USD 8 Billion project to expand Uganda's railway network to standard gauge by two Chinese firms. This strong increase in FDI reflect international investors' confidence in Uganda's long-term growth prospects, and will continue to underscore the country's economic development. Besides, more investment inflows are expected from trade summits like China-Africa, Euro-Africa, Turkey-Africa, Japan-Africa, US-Africa and Hong Kong-Africa. On the other hand, financial outflows have also reached unprecedented levels with developing economies being the net losers: more money flows out of African countries than actually into them rendering the hypothesis that multinationals' influx is just an onslaught to exploit the natural resources more valid now than ever before. The Global Financial Integrity (GFI) estimates that, for each USD 1 developing economies receive in foreign aid, USD 10 in illicit money flows abroad; facilitated by secrecy in the global financial system. The outflow is equivalent to the Africa's current GDP, and its about four times Africa's current external debt according to African Development Bank (AfDB) estimates.

On domestic investments, more private investment will require a larger share of credit channelled to production in the economy. Since the end FY 2006/07, credit to the private sector has expanded by more than 130% in constant terms though this has not yet translated into similarly high growth; and this weak link between private-sector-credit and growth implies that credit is predominantly channelled to consumption rather production with just 21. 4% channelled to productive sectors like agriculture and manufacturing.

Interest rates in advanced economies have been exceptionally low in response to low inflation and very low growth, and many central banks have been stimulating their economies through unconventional monetary policies code-named monetary easing. As those economies recover, central banks will have to reabsorb large amounts of liquidity, if not, this may lead to quickly accelerating inflation in those economies forcing their central banks to aggressively raise interest rates. For Uganda, this is of particular concern, as more than 40% of credit to the private sector is denominated in foreign currency.

PART 6
FINANCIAL INTERMEDIATION & SERVICES
Chapter 25
Financial Intermediation

Households want desirable investments for their savings, but their small financial assets makes direct investment pretty hard. These investors seeking to lend money to businesses in need of huge capital investments don't have any medium/ link to the willing and desirable borrower. Besides, such a small holder would not be able to diversify across a wide variety of borrowers as a risk management system. Thus, it is at this stage that *financial intermediaries* come into the investment picture, basically to act as a "conduit" that links lenders (those with surplus funds) to borrowers (those with deficit budgets). These include: banks, investment companies, insurance companies, and credit unions, who issue their own securities to raise funds to purchase the securities of other corporations. They are institutions that serve to connect the financial agents (households, business, and government) so that: households can invest their surplus incomes; businesses can finance production; and government can carry out its mandate to its citizens.

1.ELEMENTS OF A FINANCIAL SECTOR

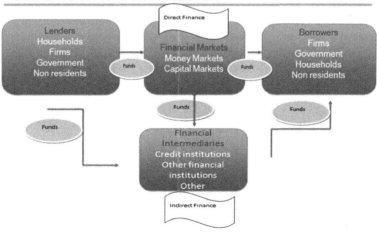

Despite the fact that many households can invest directly in securities of business firms and government agencies, many households prefer investing indirectly through the financial system facility of financial intermediaries who do financial transactions on their part. Thus, financial intermediation is the process by which individual savings are accumulated and mobilized by financial services firms, and in turn lent out or invested in a productive and prudent manner. It is the process of indirect financing using financial intermediaries as the primary route for moving funds from net lenders to net borrowers. And research has proved that financial intermediaries are a far more important source of financing for corporations than securities markets.

Financial intermediaries stand between buyers and sellers, facilitating the exchange of assets, capital and risk. Their services allow for greater efficiency and are vital to a well-functioning economy; and below are a tabular representation of some of the financial intermediaries in a financial system.

TYPES OF FINANCIAL INTERMEDIARIES

Type of Intermediary	Source of Funds (Primary Liability)	Uses of Funds (Primary Assets)
1. Depository Institutions		
Commercial Banks.	Deposits	Business & household loans; mortgages; treasury securities; municipal bonds.
Credit Institutions & MDIs (credit & savings assoc.)	Deposits	Mortgages.
Savings Banks.	Deposits & individual savings.	Mortgages.
Credit Unions.	Deposits.	Household loans.
2.Finance Firms		
Finance companies.	Commercial paper; stocks; bonds; other financial intermediaries.	Household & business loans.
Mortgage banking firms.	Stocks; deposits; other financial intermediaries.	Real estate; real property; mortgage.
Factoring companies.	Stocks; commercial paper.	Company & bank debtors; bills of exchange; invoices; real estate.

Type of Intermediary	Source of Funds (Primary Liability)	Uses of Funds (Primary Assets)
3. Securities Firms Investment companies (unit trust funds). Securitizers & Wholesale/ merchant banks. Brokerage firms.	Unit trusts/ shares; individual savings. Stocks; bonds; other intermediaries. Stocks; bonds; other financial intermediaries.	Stocks; bonds; real estate; real property; money market instruments. Stocks; bonds; other debt facilities. Stocks; bonds; other equity & debt instruments.
4. Contractual Saving firms Retirement benefit schemes; pension funds; government retirement funds. Life & Health Insurance firms. Property & Liability Insurance firms.	Employers & employees contributions. Premium paid on policies. Premium paid on policies.	Mortgages; corporate & treasury bonds; stocks; real property. Treasury & corporate bonds; mortgages; stocks; money market instruments. Treasury securities; municipal bonds; corporate bonds & stocks.
5. Other Intermediaries. Alternative Trading Systems (ATS). Arbitrageurs. Clearing houses. Custodians.		

Depository Institutions

Depository institutions are financial intermediaries that accept deposits or savings from individuals and institutions and then lend these pooled savings to all financial agents (households, businesses, and government). These institutions include commercial banks and the thrift institutions such as: credit institutions; Micro-finance Deposit Taking Institutions (MDIs); savings banks; etc, these accumulate individual savings and provide credit for asset-building such as machinery, automobiles, houses, education, among others.

These funds can further be invested by these depository institutions in a wide array of investment avenues such as: business and household loans; mortgages; treasury securities (treasury bills, notes, and bonds); and municipal bonds for profitability purposes.

Contractual Savings Firms

These firms collect premiums and contributions from their clients so as to provide them with retirement benefits and coverage against major losses in life. Among these are: insurance companies that provide financial protection to households and businesses for life, health, property and liability uncertainties. This is done through the payment of premiums by the insurance policy holders which are invested in treasury securities, corporate bonds and stocks, and money market instruments until the insured claims must be paid. On the other hand, retirement and pension funds are mobilized as contributions from employees and/or their employers periodically and proceeds are invested on behalf of the employees. Schemes such as Occupational (private) benefits scheme, National Social Security Fund (NSSF), government/ public service retirement funds are actively involved in financial intermediation by investing their contributors' funds in basically long-term financial assets such as: mortgages; corporate & government bonds; stocks; real property; etc.

In the developed and developing economies the pension sector (contractual saving) has drastically grown, since people are progressively realizing that they cannot rely on their children to care for them in their retirement. In rural settings, families tend to stay together on the farm; and property passes from generation to generation with an implicit understanding that the younger generations will care for the older ones. Contrarily, when families become more dispersed and move off farms, both the opportunity for and the expectation of extensive financial support of the older generations from the younger one significantly declines.

Types of Pension Plans

There are a variety of pension plans globally depending on factors such as the economic system of a country, level of economic development and civilisation, among others. The following are some of the popular types well known:

- Defined-benefit plan: is a pension plan whose retirement promise is framed according to benefits to be paid to participants. Benefits are often calculated by a formula related to years of service, rate of pay over some specified time period, or a combination of both such as the government pension system.

- Cash balance plan: is a hybrid defined-benefit plan that maintains individual account records for plan participants showing their current value of accrued benefit. The difference with traditional defined-benefit plans is that an account, rather than an actual fund, is maintained for each individual.

- Profit sharing plan: is a defined-contribution plan whose contributions are established somewhat by the profitability of the plan sponsor.

- Defined-contribution plan: is a pension plan whose retirement promise is framed according to the contributions made to the plan by the plan sponsor. The liability to the sponsor is only the contribution, not the benefit ultimately received by the participants eg NSSF.

Pension Plan Funding

Among the pension plan funding world over, there are:

- Funded status: is the relationship between the present value of the pension plan assets and the present value of the pension plan liabilities.

- Fully funded: means the present value of the pension plan assets is greater than or equal to the present value of the pension liabilities. When the present value of plan assets becomes much greater than the present value of plan liabilities, sponsors can at least temporarily stop making contributions to the plan's asset base.

- Surplus: is the difference between the present value of pension plan assets and the present value of pension plan liabilities.

- Underfunded: means the present value of pension plan assets is less than the present value of the pension plan liabilities. Underfunded plans may require the sponsors to make special contributions to the plan in addition to the usual, regular contributions.

Securities Firms

These firms accept and invest individual savings; but also facilitate the transfer of securities among investors. They mobilize funds by selling unit trusts/shares, stock; individual savings; issuing bonds; and using finances from other financial intermediaries, which they prudently invest in a diversified portfolio of corporate and government bonds, stocks, real estate and property, and money market instruments

Unit Trust funds allow shareholders to pool their resources so that they can take advantage of lower transaction costs when buying large blocks of stocks or bonds. Thus, allowing them to hold more diversified portfolios than they otherwise would afford; shareholders can redeem their shares at any time. On the other hand, wholesale/merchant banks despite their name, are not banks but financial intermediaries that help corporations issue securities through: advising on which type of securities to issue (stocks or bonds); then helping sell (underwrite) the securities by purchasing them from the corporation at a predetermined price and reselling them in the market. Besides, brokerage firms assist households who want to purchase new securities issues or who want to sell previously purchased securities.

Much as, wholesale banking and brokerage activities are often combined in the same firm in the contemporary financial world; wholesale banking is fundamentally a merchandising role (new issue) yet brokerage services are about marketing existing or seasoned financial assets.

Securitizers, however, are intermediaries that pool large amounts of securities or assets and then sell interests in the pool to other investors; the returns from the pool (net of the securitizers' fees) are passed through to the investors. By securitizing assets, these intermediaries create a diversified pool of assets with more predictable cash flows than the individual assets in the pool. This creates liquidity in the assets, and economies of scale in the management costs of large pools of assets, and potential benefits from the investment manager's selection of assets.. assets that are often securitized include: mortgages, car loans, credit card receivables, bank loans, and equipment leases.

Finance Firms

These firms provide finance, basically loans, directly to households and businesses, but also help borrowers obtain mortgage loans on real property. This could be through financing installment purchases of durable assets like cars, homes, machinery but also provision of small loans to those financial agents. Some of these firms are actively engaged in the outright purchase of company and banks' debtors at an agreed discount with the client, which is termed as factoring/ debt factoring.

Among the finance firms, there are: finance companies; mortgage banking firms; factoring companies; among others that mobilize their funds through issuing commercial papers, stocks, bonds, but also make use of funds from other financial intermediaries. They then invest such finances in a diversified portfolio of assets that include: household and business loans; purchase of real estates, real property and mortgages; purchases/ discounting of corporate debtors, bills of exchange, and invoices.

Other Intermediaries

Alternative Trading Systems (ATS)

These systems serve the same trading function as organized securities exchanges but have no regulatory function; they are also called Electronic Communication Networks (ECNs). There is one such system that is currently becoming popular in Uganda, it was developed by two students (at that time) and it deals in trading of foreign currencies and some equities/ stocks that are also traded on the Uganda Securities Exchange; it is called FX Trades.

Arbitrageurs

These intermediaries buy financial assets in one market and resell it in another market at a higher price. By so doing, they provide liquidity to participants in the markets where the asset is purchased and transferring the asset to the market where it is sold. Arbitrageurs try to exploit pricing differentials for similar assets, for example, a dealer who sells a call option will often also buy the stock because the call and stock prices are highly correlated. These intermediaries use complex models for valuation of related securities and for risk management reasons.

Clearing Houses

These act as intermediaries between buyers and sellers in the financial markets, and they provide the following services:

- Escrow services of transferring cash and assets to respective parties.
- Guarantees of contract completion (surety bonds)
- Assurance that margin traders have adequate capital (surety bond)

Through these activities, clearing houses limit counterparty risk: the risk that the other party to a transaction will not fulfill its obligations.

Custodians

These intermediaries improve market integrity by holding clients' securities and preventing their loss due to fraud or other events that affect the broker or investment manager.

Intermediaries Economies of Scale & Uniqueness

They are able to invest in financial assets of corporations at lower rate of return due to the following economies of scale:

- Efficiencies in gathering information on riskiness of purchasing a certain security: this is because individuals don't have easy access to such data sources (financial soundness) and/or expert analysis in that way.

- Risk spreading: intermediaries are able to spread funds in a wide portfolio of financial assets, thereby reducing the overall risk, which retail investors can't easily do.

- Transaction costs minimization: there is reduction in search, agreement and monitoring costs that would be incurred by retail investors in direct transaction. The reduced information costs, convenience and passed-on benefits from the economies of operating on large scale mean that retail investors are motivated to use the intermediation of such institutions.

- Liquidity & price risk: they provide financial claims to households with superior liquidity attributes and lower price risk.

- Maturity intermediation: intermediaries can better bear the risk of mismatching the maturities of their assets and liabilities.

- Transmission of monetary supply: depository institutions are the conduits through which monetary policy tools by the Central banks impact the rest of the financial system and the economy.

- Credit allocation: intermediaries are often viewed as the major, and sometimes only, source of financing for particular sectors of the economy such as agriculture, SMEs, and residential real estate.

- Payment services: the efficiency with which depository institutions provide payment services like checks, directly benefits the financial system.

- Denominational intermediation: intermediaries like unit trust funds allow small investors to overcome constraints and costs which are not borne by large institutional investors, and so they facilitate the pooling of small savers funds so as to help them enjoy economies of collective strategies.

- Intergenerational wealth transfers: intermediaries like insurance firms and pension funds provide savers the ability to transfer their wealth from one generation to the next one (children/beneficiaries).

Role of Financial Intermediaries in the financial system:

- To channel household savings to the business sector: this is the most crucial role of financial intermediaries, also referred to as the "social function". This is done by banks, unit trust funds and other intermediaries pooling the resources of many small investors, and then lends considerable sums to large borrowers like business organisations.

- To lend to many borrowers, whereby intermediaries achieve significant diversification, by giving loans that might be too risky from an individual point of view.

- Intermediaries build expertise through the volume of business they do and can use economies of scale and scope to manage credit risk.

- They lower the transaction costs of both investors and users of finance through their expertise in financial intermediation. Hence, facilitating an efficient, cheap and reliable way of allocating and transferring funds from one party to another.

The Advantages of Intermediaries

Financial professionals help channel savings from individuals into investments; an important service since individuals want opportunities to grow their savings, and it stimulates economic growth and development. Financial intermediaries can help manage investment risk with their specialized knowledge and experience. Below are the advantages of using financial intermediation in a financial system:

Risk management advantage: Intermediaries help to manage investment risk by providing professional advice on investment opportunities. However, the advice they give may increase overall risk because of the nature of the investments, the potential rewards also increase. They also provide expertise and the technology to carry out investment transactions easily and quickly, and while intermediaries often steer their clients to certain investments that may be managed by their company, they are obligated to act in the client's best interest rather than their own or that of their employer.

Fiduciary duties: They have a legal duty: to act in the best interest of the individual investor client; to disclose material information about their business that could affect the client; and they must refrain from activities that cause conflicts of interest with clients. Any self-dealing activities that involve clients are violations of fiduciary duties legally owed to clients. For example, an adviser should not unload unwanted securities on unsuspecting clients, or push a stock because of a higher commission even though it does not fit the client's portfolio.

Liquidity management: They help their clients sell their investments when the client needs or wants to sell. They make a market for the client by finding willing buyers, and this usually happens immediately using the stock exchange infrastructure.

Professional information: Financial intermediaries have a team of professionals that provides research and analysis on various investment opportunities. Such information is usually made available at no additional cost to the individual investor. In fact, providing this type information free is a marketing strategy used by financial intermediaries to attract clients. The better the information, the more competitive the financial intermediary will be when attracting clients.

Highly regulated trading environment: The Capital Markets Authority (CMA), the Uganda Securities Exchange (USE), and other regulators of the financial system regulate financial intermediaries. Although the stock exchanges are not government agencies, they have established rules that must be followed. If a financial intermediary does not follow these rules, no trading on the particular exchange involved will be allowed. There are licensing requirements that must be complied with and violations of laws, rules and regulations can result in severe fines, sanctions and even criminal charges. Individual investors can register complaints with any of the regulators that will be investigated since the role of the government is to protect its people and their assets.

Chapter 26

FINANCIAL DISINTERMEDIATION

Mugume et al (2009) argue that while the banking system has gradually become more sophisticated and complex over the last two decades, the Ugandan financial sector is still shallow compared to other countries in East Africa. This low level of financial intermediation indicates that although the Ugandan banking system accesses more resources through deposits, the resources are only partly extended to the private sector. Besides, World Bank (2007) complements that Uganda is thus intermediation constrained rather than savings constrained.

Financial Disintermediation can be referred to as the investing of funds that would normally have been placed in a bank or other financial institutions directly into financial assets issued by the ultimate users of the funds. Investors and borrowers transact business directly and thereby bypass financial intermediaries.

Besides, disintermediation can also be defined as the elimination of intermediaries between the first class providers of capital (basically the household sector and other collective investment vehicles) and the ultimate users of capital; withdrawal of funds from financial intermediaries such as banks, savings and credit institutions, and life insurance companies in order to invest directly with ultimate users.

While there has been a general trend toward bank disintermediation and a greater role for financial markets in many countries, the pace has differed and there are still important differences across financial systems. Therefore, differences in financial structures do affect how households and firms behave over the economic cycle.

In financial systems characterized by a greater degree of arm's length transactions (liberal economies), households seem to be able to smooth consumption more effectively in the face of unanticipated changes in their income, although they may be more sensitive to changes in asset prices. On the other hand, financial systems that rely less on arm's length transactions, firms appear to be better able to smooth investment during business cycle downturns, as they are better positioned to access external financing based on their long-term relationships with financial intermediaries.

However, when faced with more fundamental changes in the environment that require a real-location of resources across sectors, financial systems with a greater degree of arm's length transactions appear to be better placed to shift resources to take advantage of new growth opportunities. Evidence has shown that cross-border portfolio investors appear to allocate a greater proportion of their holdings in countries where the arm's length (laissez-faire/ non-interference/liberal) content of the financial system is higher, which may contribute to the financing of current account deficits.

Disintermediation can then be referred to as the removal of intermediaries from a process, supply chain or market. The disintermediation of capital markets is particularly important in an investment context, and it has become increasingly important in financial markets, largely as a result of the increasing use of securities to raise capital from capital markets, rather than from banks.

Banks usually act as financial intermediaries for debt, borrowing from depositors and lending to borrowers. By selling securities such as bonds, instead of borrowing, a borrower can borrow directly from investors, by-passing the banks. The greater use of a wider range of financial instruments such as asset-backed securities and convertibles (in addition to the bonds and debentures) has encouraged this. High levels of disintermediation reduce the amount of business available for commercial banks. It also increases the size of capital markets and generates more business for investment banks (advising on the issue of securities) and, indirectly, for other investment businesses (brokers, fund managers, stock exchanges etc.).

Borrowers can hope to borrow at lower cost as a result of disintermediation. Investors lose the safety of bank deposits but then they also should get better rates of return. Investors take on some extra risk which can be controlled through the usual mechanisms of diversification and the selection of appropriate investments. At the same time disintermediation eliminates the banks' interest margin and this benefit is shared by investors, borrowers and financial market intermediaries.

Financial disintermediation is gaining momentum in the modern economy: the advent of the Internet as well as the development of electronic exchanges has facilitated an efficient and effective way of buying and selling financial instruments. These phenomena also have contributed to less prominent roles for financial intermediaries in the economy. For examples, individual investors no longer need to call brokers before placing trades. They can log into a secure Web portal and make traces quickly, seamlessly and anonymously.

Causes of Financial Disintermediation:

During my interview with the Bank of Uganda – Director of Financial markets on the growth of the Asset/fund management sector, he commissioned me to equally do a research that establishes why some key players in the financial system deliberately dis-intermediate the financial system. And below are some of the causes/ reasons:

Money market funds : this is due to competition for bank deposits from investment banks, many investors have chosen to invest in unit trust funds other than deposit their money with banks.

Junk Bonds (downgraded bonds): currently, bond market competes with commercial banks for corporate borrowing yet before 1980s, only investment grade bonds were issued whose requirements are very strict. Therefore, only well-established companies had access to the bond market; and small, medium, lesser known, younger firms could not issue bonds, they had to go to a bank for a commercial loan which is no longer the case.

Commercial paper: this is an alternative form of disintermediation to short-term bank credit that was made possible by information revolution, and it is easier to assess credit risk. Pension funds and money market funds provide the supply of credit for commercial paper, and these two assets grew together. Money market funds started getting lots of funds to invest; commercial paper provided the ideal short term money market instrument features of liquidity, low riskiness, and short-term asset.

Securitization: this is disintermediation (financial innovation) resulting from information technology's capacity to lower transaction cost, and transforming illiquid financial assets into standardized, liquid, marketable securities. This is about banks and mortgage companies packaging mortgage loans in large bundles/portfolios, and selling ownership interests in the portfolios as securities in specific amounts. Securitization also developed in other areas such as: car loans, credit cards, computer leases, etc.

Regulatory flaws: some players in the financial markets make use of loopholes in the legal framework that governs the financial system so as to profit from such weaknesses and thus dis-intermediate the financial flows which render some institutions irrelevant in the process.

Large informal financial system: this is characterized by a diversity of institutions which are not monitored and regulated such as SACCOs, money-lenders, ROSCAs, Women groups, NGOs, CBOs. These have financial transactions that total to hundreds of Billions weekly but the regulators of the financial system have apparently failed to integrate them into the formal system. These organizations use such funds in ways they feel will protect their value, hence, aiding the disintermediation in the financial system.

Uganda's banking system is characterized not only by low levels of intermediation but also by high interest rates, wide intermediation spreads, and substantial bank profitability. High lending interest rates, whether caused by inefficiency or lack of competition, do more than add to borrowers' costs.

High interest spread and limited depth and breadth of the financial systems are closely related to each other. Countries with higher interest rate spread have lower levels of credit to the private sector as share of GDP and deposits in the financial system as share of GDP

If high interest spreads and margins and limited depth and breadth of financial services are the result of underlying deficiencies and impediments in the financial systems, then in order to increase access to financial services and reduce spreads and margins, these underlying causes have to be addressed.

Chapter 27

KEY CHALLENGES AND RISKS OF THE FINANCIAL SYSTEM

"Monitoring risks to the stability of the financial system from majorly the real estate sector is a critical element of policy formulation."

Among the challenges of the financial system, these are:

- Volatile and reversible capital inflows that characterize bank consolidation exercise.

- Major weaknesses in the business environment.

- Failure in corporate governance in banks and financial institutions.

- Inadequate disclosure and transparency in financial reporting.

- Engagement in/of multiple financial activities that increase the complexity of their operations.

- Uneven supervision and enforcement.

- Inadequate risk management frameworks for identifying, measuring and controlling risk associated with the activities of deposit money banks.

- Lack of investor and consumer sophistication (protection).

- The Ugandan population is significantly under-banked, with only ....million accounts.

- Uganda has a bank dominated financial system whereby 3 top foreign banks accounted for 44% of banks' total assets as by 2013.

- There is wide gap between the formal financial system and the informal financial system which has led to excessive levels of liquidity amongst the household sector while the financial markets are struggling with liquidity problems.

- The levels of domestic savings are so low; and Uganda ranks high among Sub-Saharan Africa economies with the lowest savings to GDP ratio.

- Poor households in rural settings are largely excluded from the formal financial system; leaving them to the mercies of informal financial institutions which are weak and not regulated. This doesn't only increase the risk to poor households' savings but also threatens the domestic financial system.

- The financial system is characterized by limited financial instruments such as treasury securities, corporate bonds, commercial papers, a few stocks/equities. This limits the choices of the would-be investors in financial assets since securities like derivative instruments, hybrid assets, and a wide array of actually more debt and equity assets would attract more to such investments.

- The banking system is characterized by very low returns on savings due to high liquidity in banks and also the effect of donor-funded wholesale funds for on-lending.

- Shallow capital markets in Uganda also constrain domestic resource mobilisation on the part of both the corporate and the government sectors which forces them to look for external sources of financing.

- There is also the problem of lack of information and confidence about contracts due to huge loopholes in the legal framework but also the absence of commitment to enforce legal and formal business processes.

- There is a poor savings culture which is propagated by low levels of financial literacy, limited access to safe and sound institutions, and scepticism about the domestic financial system (due to local currency volatility, alarming levels of corruption, desperation, among others).

- Uganda's financial outflow is over 13% of the total government revenue, approximately UGX 2.2 Trillion majorly through: tax evasion, bribes, trade mis-invoicing from fraudulent over-and under-invoicing of trade transactions from anonymous companies, and subsidiary companies overstating commercial loan interest payment to parent companies. The latest UGX 24 Billion fraud between Ministry of Roads & Transport and a non-existent American construction firm EUTAW for constructing a 74 Km Mukono-Katosi road.

Among the key risks to the financial system, these are:

Slowdown in the economy: this is basically caused by high non-performing loans (NPLs) for banks, unemployment and inflation.

Prices of assets: Securities, real estate prices could fall or change abruptly, creating uncertainty on the financial markets, with the result that investors may lose money.

Concentration risks by banks: Banks could grant large loans to a specific industry and then find that they are vulnerable to any downturn in that industry. .

Concentration risk for investors: Investors could make large-scale investments in stock or bond markets and then become vulnerable to falling prices in those markets.

Principal /agent problem: agents taking on excessive risk taking or some not taking enough risk which both jeopardizes the value of investors.

The following are the regulatory remedies to such risks and challenges:

Prudential regulation: these are rules that financial institutions have to comply with in order to ensure effective risk management and the safety of depositors' funds), accompanied by the disclosure of information so as to promote market discipline. These are embedded in the operations of Bank of Uganda, Insurance Regulatory Authority, etc.

Governments should prioritize mobilization for revenues; in this, much as there should be flexibility across countries, taxes ought to be simple, broad-based, and administered effectively; coupled to transparency in extractive industries.

Furthermore, these resources should be efficiently and effectively used in pursuit of development and supported by strong public financial management.

Prudential supervision: ensuring that financial institutions follow these rules as stipulated by Bank of Uganda.

A deliberate introduction and embracing of the Islamic financial system (banking, markets and insurance).

An efficient and independent central banking system that will implement sound macroeconomic policies such as containing inflation, boom-bust cycles, and public debt; and that will maintain health fiscal positions and adequate foreign exchange reserves for external-economy vulnerability management.

Financial engineering for both governments and corporations as a tool for both resource mobilization, and developing/ deepening the domestic financial markets (financial assets diversification)

Seeking for international partnerships/cooperation since all financial systems are interdependent on each other through a global financial system. This would usher in responsible policymaking that promotes global economic and financial resilience.

Besides, financial literacy and inclusion are the real lever to developing any financial system world over.

Monitoring and assessment activities, which identify

vulnerabilities and risks in the financial system as a whole. This is the responsibility of all regulators of the financial system such as: Capital Markets Authority, Uganda Retirement Benefits Regulatory Authority, Insurance Regulatory Authority, etc.

The private sector is an essential partner for development: developing the financial system by protecting creditor rights can expand access to basic financial services for households and small enterprises. This calls for carefully designed tax and trade regimes that can help attract foreign investment that are known for vital development payoffs.

Greater transparency in financial transactions contracts and thorough due diligence is key to improving and managing financial inflows and outflows in the financial system.

The tax body ought to double crackdown on tax evaders (both domestic and foreign firms); and further train its officers to better detect international mis-invoicing and other trade transactions malpractices.

The State needs to ensure proper central and public registries of meaningful beneficial ownership information for all companies formed in the country to combat the abuse of anonymous companies like EUTAW.

Commercial banks ought to know the true identity of the final beneficiary of any account opened in their financial institutions to avoid paying off anonymous companies.

Besides, Uganda needs to subscribe to international codes of practice like the Extractive Industry Transparency Initiative (EITI) to stamp out malpractices in the exploitation of natural resources.

APPENDIX 1: Updates from the URBRA (2015)

Table of Licensed Parties by URBRA as at end September 2015

PARTIES	LICENSED INSTITUTIONS
Schemes	58
Fund Managers	6
Fund Administrators	11
Custodians (Banks)	5
Corporate Trustees	4
Individual Trustees	484
TOTAL	568

Source: URBRA (2015)

Licensed Service Providers by Uganda Retirement Benefits Regulatory Authority (URBRA) as by September 2015:

FUND ADMINISTRATORS

1. Alexander Forbes Financial Services Uganda Limited

2. Liaison Financial Services Limited

3. AON Uganda Limited

4. Insurance Company of East Africa Limited

5. Liberty Life Assurance Uganda Limited

6. Padrepio Insurance Brokers Limited

7. Sanlam Life Insurance Uganda Limited

8. UAP Life Assurance Uganda Limited

9. Octagon Uganda Limited

10. The Jubilee Insurance Company of Uganda Limited

11. National Insurance Corporation Limited

FUND MANAGERS

1. PineBridge Investments East Africa Limited

2. Genesis Kenya Investment Management Limited

3. African Alliance Uganda Limited

4. ICEA Asset Management Limited

5. StanLib Uganda Limited

6. UAP Financial Services Limited

CUSTODIANS (Banks)

1. Housing Finance Bank

2. Stanbic Bank Uganda

3. Standard Chartered Bank Uganda Limited

4. KCB Bank Uganda Limited

5. Bank of Africa Uganda

CORPORATE TRUSTEES.

1. KCB Bank Limited

2. National Insurance Corporation Limited

3. Crane Bank Limited

4. Vivo Energy Uganda Limited

BIBLIOGRAPHY & REFERENCES

Abuka. C.A. and Egesa, K., (2010), *Services Sector Development in Uganda: An Analysis of the Financial Sector Services.*

Adelegan, O. Janet, and Bozena Radzewicz-Bak, (2009), *What Determines Bond Market Development in Sub-Saharan Africa?* IMF Working Paper 09/213 (Washington: International Monetary Fund).

Adjasi, K. Charles and Nicholas Biekpe, (2006), *Stock Market Development and Economic Growth: The Case of Selected African Countries.* African Development Review, Vol.18 (1) pp. 144-161

African Alliance Securities (2013), *Uganda Banking Sector Overview.* African Alliance Uganda Publications.

African Securities Exchanges Association, (2009), *African Securities Exchanges Association Yearbook 2009*

African Development Bank -AfDB, (2010), *Financial Sector Integration in Three Regions of Africa* (Tunis: African Development Bank Group).

Arnold, Glen (1998) *Corporate Financial Management.* Financial Times- Prentice Hall

Bank of Uganda Annual Report 2010/ 2011

Bank of Uganda Annual Report 2012/ 2013

Bank of Uganda; Annual Supervision Report; December 2010; Issue No. 1

Beck, T. and Hesse, H., (2006), *Bank Efficiency, Ownership and Market Structure: Why Interests Spread so High in Uganda?* World Bank Working paper series WPS4027. The World Bank: Washington, D.C.

Bodie, Z. Kane, A. and Marcus, A. J (2009), *Investments.* 8th Ed: McGraw-Hill

Byarugaba, Richard (September 2015) *Expected Synergies and Relationship Between NSSF and FSD/MOFPED for the Development of the Financial Sector.* Paper Presented to Officials of Ministry of Finance (Uganda)

Clapp, Jennifer (2012), *Position Limits for Agricultural Commodity Derivatives: Getting Tougher or Tough to Get?*

CMA Kenya Quarterly Statistical Bulletin Dec 2009.

Crested Capital Research Uganda (2015) *Stock Market Report for Week Ending 11th September 2015.* Uganda Securities Exchange

Eakins, S.G. & Mishkin, F.S. (2012), *Financial Markets and Institutions.* 7th Ed: Prentice Hall

Erongot, Paul Jembrace (2014) *Banking in Relation to Financial and Economic Growth in Uganda.*

Esch. L, Keiffer, R. and Lopez. T (2005), *Asset and Risk Management: Risk Oriented Finance.* Edition de Boeck Universite

Financial Sector Briefing Note 1, Quarter 1 of FY 2011/12: Macroeconomic Department; Directorate of Economic Affairs

Government of Uganda (2004), *Financial Institutions Act, 2004.* Uganda Printers and Publishing Corporation: Entebbe, Uganda

Government of Uganda (2003), *Micro Finance Deposit-Taking Institutions Act, 2003.* Uganda Printing and Publishing Corporation: Entebbe, Uganda. May.

Government of Uganda (1966), *Bank of Uganda Act, 1966.* Uganda Printers and Publishing Corporation: Entebbe, Uganda.

Haim, Levy., and Thierry, Post, (2005) *Investments.* Pearson Education Ltd

Honohan, Patrick. 2004. *"Financial Development, Growth, and Poverty: How Close Are the Links."* In *Financial Development and Economic Growth: Explaining the Links,* ed. Charles Goodhart, 1–37. London: Palgrave

Honohan P., and Beck T., 2007, *Making Finance Work for Africa,* The World Bank.

Ibbotson, R. and Kaplan, P.D. (2000), *Does Asset Allocation Policy Explain 40, 90, or 100 Per Cent of Performance?* Financial Analysts Journal 56 (1), pp. 26-33.

IMF Emerging Markets Database 2008-2009.

IRAU (January 2015) *List of Licensed Insurance Companies in Uganda (IRAU)*

Jackson, W.E., 1992, *The Price-Concentration Relationship in Banking: A Comment,* The Review of Economics and Statistics, Vol. 74: pp. 373-376.

Jin-Yong, C. and Banga, A. (2014, February) *Why financial inclusion is the lever that can move the world.* The East African

Kalema, William and Duncan Kayiira, (2008), *Access to Housing Finance in Africa: Exploring the Issues.* No.4 Uganda. FinMark Trust.

Kalungi, Robert (21 April 2010), *A primer on financial derivatives.* Business journal

Kaplan (2011), CFA Level 3 Book 2 Notes: CFA Institute

Ketley, R., Kramer, J., Hanouch, M., & Christo, W, (2009), *Expanding Housing Finance in Uganda: Task 2, Study to Examine the Use of Retail Funds for Mortgage Lending.* Genesis –Analytics for the Urban Institute, FIRST Initiative in Uganda, April 2009.

Magali, Azema-Barac (2010) *Be Dynamic in Your Asset Allocation.* PineBridge Investments Research- New York

Marvin, Powell (July 2015) *Bitcoin: Economics, Technology, and Governance.* CFA Digest, Vol. 45, No. 7: CFA Institute

MoFPED (2015) *Annual Economic Performance Report 2013/14.* Directorate of Economic Affairs – MoFPED January 2015.

MoFPED (2015) *Report on Public Debt, Guarantees, Other Financial Liabilities and Grants for Financial Year 2014/15.* Presented by Hon. Minister of Finance, Matia Kasaija, to Parliament on 1st April 2015.

Mugabe, David (2015, August) *Mobile Money Transactions Over 19 Million.* The New Vision

Mugerwa, Paul (2014) *Bugema University Endowment Fund: Project Proposal cum Business Plan*

Mugerwa, Paul (2015) *ESG (environmental, social & governance) Issues and the Strategic Asset Allocation of Institutional Investors: A case of Uganda, a Non-Signatory Country to UN PRI* (To be Published by United Nations' Principles of Responsible Investing)

Mugerwa, Paul (2014) *Corporate Governance Practices and Financial Performance of Listed Firms on Uganda Securities Exchange.* This article was submitted to Journal of Computing & Business Admin. (Bugema University)

Mugerwa, Paul (2013) *Capital Markets Monitoring Systems and Financial Performance of Formerly State-Owned Listed Companies in Uganda.* This article was peer reviewed & scheduled for presentation in the 25th International Business Research Conference in Cape Town, South Africa 14th January, 2014, and later to be published in their Business Journal.

Mugerwa, Paul (2015) *Sovereign Asset Preservation and the Strategic Asset Allocation by Central Banks of Frontier Economies: A case of Bank of Uganda.* To be presented in Bugema University International Conference in September 2015.

Mugerwa, Paul (2015) *Foundations of Risk Management and the Insurance Device: An Overview of Corporate and Personal Risks, Policies and Systems; & Insurance device in Frontier Economies* (Unpublished)

Mugerwa, Paul (2014) *Sovereign Assets and External-Economy Vulnerability Management by Central Banks in Sub-Saharan Africa: A Case for Bank of Uganda's Risk Management.* Unpublished.

Mugerwa, Paul (2014) *A 2013 Report & Analysis on the Ugandan Banking Sector; & Overview of the East African Community's Economic Fundamentals.* Unpublished.

Mugerwa, Paul (2013) *Appraising the Investment Philosophy of Central Banks in Developing Economies for National Wealth Creation: A Case for Bank of Uganda. Unpublished.*

Mugerwa, Paul (2014) *Pension Funds' Investment Strategies and Clients' Value Creation in Emerging Economies: A Case for NSSF-Uganda.* Unpublished

Mugume, A. (2008), *Market Structure and Performance in Uganda's Banking System.* Makerere University Printery

Mugume, A. Apaa, J. & Ojwiya, C. (2009), *Interest Spreads in Uganda: Bank Specific Characteristics or Policy Changes?* The Bank of Uganda Staff Papers Journal

Ojiambo, Benon (2015, August) *Kasekende Calls for a Broader Banking Sector.* The New Vision

Oketch, Martin Luther (23 April 2015) *Banking Sector Records Improved Performance.* Daily Monitor (Kampala)

Olagunju, Y. A. (2008). *Entrepreneurship and Small Scale Business Enterprises Development in Nigeria:* Ibadan. University Press.

Paul Mandl and Adrian Mukheb (2012), *Commodity Market Information and Risk Management: The Case for a Commodity Exchange and Warehouse Receipt System for Uganda*

Peggy Nooman, *William Safire*, Times, 12 October 2009

Sanya, S (2015, July), *Capital Markets Supplements.* The New Vision Ltd

Saunder, A. and Cornett, M. M. (2014) *Financial Institutions Management: A Risk Management Approach.* 8th Ed. Mc Graw-Hill Education

Sejjaaka Samuel (2011), *Challenges to the Growth of Capital Markets in Underdeveloped Economies: The Case for Uganda.* ICBE-RF Research Report No 02/11

Semakula, L. & Muwanga, R. (2012) *Uganda: Implementing an Integrated Financial Management System & the Automation of the Budget Process.* Budget Strengthening Initiative. Overseas Development Institute

Sembuya, D. and Lutwama, J (2012), *Capital Markets Investors' Survey Report 2012.* Publication of CMA-Uganda

Sembuya, D. and Lutwama, J (2011), *2010 Capital Markets Players' Survey.* Publication of CMA-Uganda

Sinha, R, Pratap and Bhuniya, Ashis (2011), *Risk Transfer Through Commodity Derivatives: A Study of Soya bean Oil.* Social Science Research Network (SSRN).

Solomon, Ezra. (1969) *The Theory of Financial Management.* Columbia University Press: p.3

Stephen, Odoki (2014) *The Uganda's Financial Outflow Conundrum.* In Bank of Uganda Official Internal Newletter. Vol.1 Issue No.8 November 2014

Strong, A. Robert (2009), *Portfolio Construction, Management and Protection.* 5th Ed: South Western University

UIA Report (2012) *The Investor Survey 2012.* Uganda Investment Authority Publications

William D. Coleman (2003). *Governing Global Finance: Financial Derivatives, Liberal States, and Transformative Capacity .* GHC Working Paper 01/2.

World Bank (2007), *Uganda Moving Beyond Recovery: Investment and Behavior Change for Growth.* Country Economic Memorandum Vol. II. Report Number 39221-UG.

www.123HelpMe.com/financial-disintermediation (viewed on 03-February 2015)

www.imf.org/external/np/facts/banking

www.ehow.com/info_8310903_financial-disintermediation.html

Printed in the United States
By Bookmasters